MEASURING LEADERSHIP DEVELOPMENT

MEASURING LEADERSHIP DEVELOPMENT

Quantify Your Program's Impact and ROI on Organizational Performance

Jack Phillips, Ph.D.
Patricia Pulliam Phillips, Ph.D.
and Rebecca L. Ray, Ph.D.

New York Chicago San Francisco Lisbon London
Madrid Mexico City Milan New Delhi
San Juan Seoul Singapore
Sydney Toronto

The *McGraw·Hill* Companies

1 2 3 4 5 6 7 8 9 0   DOC/DOC   1 8 7 6 5 4 3 2

ISBN   978-0-07-178120-6
MHID   0-07-178120-X

e-ISBN 978-0-07-178121-3
e-MHID   0-07-178121-8

This publication is designed to provide accurate and authoritative information in regard to the subject matter covered. It is sold with the understanding that neither the authors nor the publisher are engaged in rendering legal, accounting, securities trading, or other professional service. If legal advice or other expert assistance is required, the services of a competent professional person should be sought.

> —*From a Declaration of Principles Jointly Adopted by a Committee of the American Bar Association and a Committee of Publishers and Associations*

McGraw-Hill books are available at special quantity discounts to use as premiums and sales promotions or for use in corporate training programs. To contact a representative, please e-mail us at bulksales@mcgraw-hill.com.

This book is printed on acid-free paper.

Library of Congress Cataloging-in-Publication Data
Phillips, Jack J.
   Measuring leadership development : quantify your program's impact and ROI on organizational performance / by Jack Phillips, Patti Phillips, Rebecca Ray
       p. cm.
   ISBN 978-0-07-178120-6 (alk. paper) -- ISBN 0-07-178120-X (alk. paper)
   1. Leadership. 2. Organizational effectiveness. 3. Rate of return. 4.
Leadership--Case studies. 5. Organizational effectivess--Case studies. 6.
Rate of return--Case studies. I. Phillips, Patti. II. Ray, Rebecca. III. Title.
   HD57.7.P494 2012
   658.4'092--dc23
                                                                2011048923

Contents

Preface

As we write this book, we see leadership development facing many challenges. On a positive note, almost all leaders acknowledge that what are needed now to build and sustain success in our global organizations are great leaders who mold and mentor future leaders. Most people would agree that consistent, effective leadership behavior is critical throughout an organization.

Leadership development is alive and well, but critics of leadership development question its value. Even top executives have weighed in and need to see value. In our own work at the ROI Institute, we are evaluating very expensive, high-profile leadership development programs, some offered by the most prestigious organizations in the world. Clients who want to see value for money are the people who drive these evaluations. They want to see the difference resulting from these programs, comparing various theories and approaches to determine which one is most effective for their specific organizations.

With resources being scarce, every expenditure needs to be evaluated to determine its value. Leadership development has grown more expensive. The cost of travel and taking employees away from their jobs add to the total cost of the process. Consequently, program value should be clearly understood.

Concerning investment in leadership development, three basic bodies of work have been explored, as depicted in Figure P-1. At the base of the pyramid are logic and intuition. These are often referred to as the intangibles, meaning leader behavior is needed and can be developed and even changed radically for an organization. Logically and intuitively, leadership development is an essential investment for an organization to be successful.

Unfortunately, some executives want to see more, which leads to macro studies. These studies examine the relationship between variables. Many studies have shown the correlation between investing in people and subsequent outcomes in terms of profitability and productivity, customer satisfaction, and

Figure P-1 Analysis of Leadership Development Investments

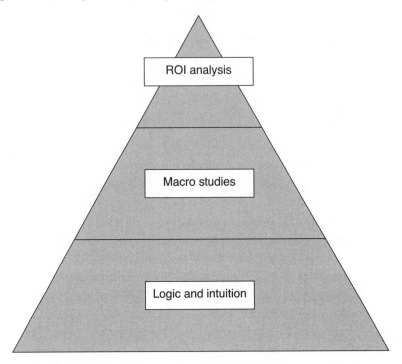

even employee turnover. Only a few of these studies involve leadership development, but the message is becoming quite clear: Investment in this area will probably reap benefits across the organization.

Still, many executives want to know about the payoff of particular programs, even those initiated by them. They also want to know which methods are most effective and which model or theory works best, which means they need an evaluation on a program-by-program basis. This leads us to the third body of knowledge—the ROI analysis, which is a micro-level assessment.

This book does not focus on logic and intuition; others do that quite well. Nor does it focus on correlations between investing in leadership development and outcomes; others are working on that. What makes this book unique is that it shows the value of a particular leadership development program. When every program is evaluated at some level, organizations can see a snapshot of the performance of the entire leadership development function.

This book presents the most-used evaluation system in the world, as it has been adopted by more than 4,000 organizations. It is ideally suited for leadership development, as up to six types of data are collected to show program success:

1. Reaction to the program
2. Learning the skills and behaviors needed for success
3. Application of skills and competencies
4. Business impact related to the program
5. Financial return on investment, showing cost versus benefits
6. Intangible benefits connected to the program

Along the way, the process has conservative standards that are CEO and CFO friendly. We think you'll find this book extremely valuable as you uncover the success of leadership development.

The book also has a slant toward a results-based approach. Processes are advocated and steps are included to show the results of leadership programs. Consequently, following this prescribed methodology ensures that the program will add the desired business value.

ACKNOWLEDGMENTS

We wish to acknowledge all the great clients we've worked with over the years who have helped revise, refine, and implement this ROI Methodology. In our ROI Certification, we've been fortunate to see up to 70 leadership programs annually, all of them taken to the impact and ROI levels. We know what makes programs successful, but success has been built on the work of many others who use the methodology and work with us to make our standards acceptable, realistic, and usable. To name these pioneers would not be practical; some of the best companies in the world have used the ROI Methodology. We can now count over half the Fortune 500 companies and many similar organizations around the world, including the United Nations, which use this process to show the value of all types of programs, including leadership development. To all of these clients, we owe a huge debt of gratitude for endorsing this methodology and making it much better.

From Patti and Jack

We're pleased to partner with one of the best leadership practitioners in the world to produce this book. Rebecca Ray has implemented literally hundreds of programs during her career in business. She understands the value of leadership development and the success it brings. We are grateful for her input and willingness to join us for this important contribution.

We also want to thank our staff at the ROI Institute, who have endured the stresses and strains of a growing global business. We appreciate the efforts of Linda Arnall, who initially worked on this book. Rebecca Benton was able to finish the work in a timely manner. Rebecca has been part of our institute for many years, and we value her continuing efforts. Rachel Robinson did a great job finalizing this book. We greatly appreciate her work.

From Rebecca Ray

I am deeply grateful for the opportunity to have learned leadership lessons at several wonderful institutions and companies over the years; I've learned from strong and inspiring leaders as well as from the numerous teams I've had the honor to lead. Any success I've had in my leadership journey is due in large part to their gifts of wisdom and insight. On a personal note, I would like to thank both Jack and Patti Phillips for the opportunity to partner with them on this project, which has been a professional privilege. I would also like to thank my muse.

PART ONE

Measuring Leadership Development

Leadership Development Has Never Been More Critical

I N   A   W O R L D of strident shareholder demand, shifting business prior-ities, disruptive innovation, rapidly changing demographic and geopolitical forces, regulatory changes, and increasingly competitive business environ-ments, leaders who envision and execute today's strategy as well as antic-ipate and prepare for tomorrow's challenges are more critical than ever. Leaders are expected to demonstrate a deep understanding of their organi-zation's business as well as its products and services, master the nuances of global markets, and conduct themselves in ethical ways. They must respond quickly to competitive maneuvers, foster innovation, communicate a com-pelling vision, and develop not only their globally distributed teams but also the next generation of leaders, all while delivering long-term value measured by short-term results. Becoming such a leader is like reaching the Mt. Everest of leadership development—and attainment is elusive. The results of failure to produce such leaders are often public, usually pronounced, and always profound.

Yet, strong leaders *can* be developed *if* organizations, business leaders, and those who head leadership development functions create the systems, processes, leader involvement, and accountability that are crucial to success. Some organizations seem to have reached the summit. Others struggle against the vertical climb. Still others remain unable to gain a foothold. It's not going to get any easier.

What Do We Mean by Leader, and How Do We Define Success?

What makes an effective, successful leader? What does it take to be successful, and how is that success determined? Is the success to be evaluated quarterly and based on results delivered to the satisfaction of analysts and shareholders? Is it to be judged by results delivered during the tenure in the role, over the course of a lifetime of leadership, or ultimately by the future success of the company, business unit, or team after the leader has departed? What role does character play in this examination of business impact? What character-istics and competencies of a leader distinguish the "best" from the merely "very good"?

As a core criterion, the expectation of leaders has always been to "get the job done" by managing assets and people. Often missing has been a more holistic view of the process in terms of how to motivate, engage, reward, and lead employees.

Twentieth-century research began to crystallize the way effective orga-nizational leaders are viewed and subsequently developed. Few depictions of effective leadership have withstood the test of time as well as that of Peter Drucker, who articulated the eight core practices of the effective leaders he worked with over a 60-year career. According to Drucker, effective leaders:

1. Ask, "What needs to be done?"
2. Ask, "What is right for the enterprise?"
3. Develop action plans.
4. Take responsibility for decisions.
5. Take responsibility for communicating.
6. Are focused on opportunities rather than on problems.
7. Run productive meetings.
8. Think and say "we" rather than "I."

As he saw it, these questions "gave them the knowledge they needed . . . helped them convert this knowledge into action . . . [and] ensured that the whole organization felt responsible and accountable."[1]

One researcher answered the question by offering that in addition to IQ and technical skills, these emotional intelligence attributes characterize the true leader:

1. Self-awareness
2. Self-regulation

3. Motivation
4. Empathy
5. Social skill[2]

Another offered a profile of Level 5 leaders who credit others with success yet assume personal responsibility for failure. These leaders are characterized by humility and a will to succeed that does not tolerate mediocrity; they are quietly and calmly determined to succeed.[3]

Over the years, we've seen the "one-minute manager" joined by the "situational leader" and the "servant leader" and by those leaders who are values driven, principle centered, or searching for "true north." While definitions will undoubtedly continue to evolve, the fundamental description of a leader as one who delivers results in a way that affirms, engages, inspires, and respects others is unlikely to fade from view.

Why Is Effective Leadership Critical?

Effective leadership is critical to the success, and often the survival, of corporations. In recent years, we have witnessed the demise or serious crippling of companies because of the inability of leaders to competently and ethically lead, creating a breach of trust with the public as well as with employees. Newspaper headlines and, in some cases, high-profile trials remind us of the failures of leadership. They are not confined to a particular region or industry, as scandals surrounding such companies as WorldCom, Satyam Computer Services, Adelphia, Parmalat, Tyco International, Clearstream, Enron, Global Crossing, and Arthur Anderson can attest. While most companies are not in the headlines for their leadership failures, they are *all* accountable for business results.

CEOs Care About Leadership

In the wake of a crushing global crisis, companies and their leaders are shifting from survival mode to a business growth approach. It is no wonder that leadership development was on the minds of CEOs around the world when they responded to the Conference Board's annual CEO Challenge survey. When asked to rank their top challenges for the coming 12 months, they ranked business growth first. The surprise was that, after an absence from the 2009 and 2010 "top 10" findings, talent emerged as the second most important global challenge; Asian CEOs ranked it number one, ahead of business growth. CEOs thought talent, innovation, and cost optimization would fuel business growth. When asked about the strategies CEOs would implement to address the talent challenge, these were the top 10:

1. Improve leadership development programs; grow talent internally.
2. Enhance the effectiveness of the senior management team.
3. Provide employee training and development.
4. Improve leadership succession planning.
5. Hire more talent in the open market.
6. Promote and reward entrepreneurship and risk taking.
7. Raise employee engagement.
8. Increase diversity and cross-cultural competencies.
9. Flatten the organization, and empower leadership from the bottom up.
10. Redesign financial rewards and incentives.

Even a cursory read of the top strategies indicates a focus on internal leadership (improving the existing internal leadership base, especially at the top of the house; up-skilling all employees; improving leadership succession) before fighting for talent in the open market. In Asia, where talent was scarce before the global financial crisis, "hiring more talent in the open market" was ranked eleventh, with an internal development and retention focus being preferred, as qualified talent is both scarce and expensive.[4] Asian leaders understand that they must build leaders faster than the global competition. Two things distinguish the approach of Asian companies: (1) attention to the specific developmental needs of the individual leader and (2) the speed with which they accelerate the development of key talent through experience, exposure, and custom training programs.[5]

Customers and Consumers Care About Leadership

We live in an age where maintaining an organization's reputation and brand management is a constant challenge. Of the many ways corporate reputations are made and lost, few are more important than the quality of their leaders. Consumers are negatively influenced by headlines of errant and unethical behavior and positively influenced by lists of most-admired companies, especially those touted for their strong managerial practices. Consumers and customers have strong brand affiliations, product dependencies (e.g., prescriptions or replacement parts), and business affiliations that would be difficult to replace, and they take note of leadership behaviors. Knowing that raw materials are harvested in a sustainable way, that clothing is not manufactured by the use of child labor, that executives are not "tone deaf" to the average citizen, and that the stock market is still a fair and level playing field is important to consumers. In a world of choices, they will provide feedback by remaining loyal to a brand or by choosing a competitor for essentially the same product. They often share their thoughts and feelings among the members of their social networks with messages and postings that seem to never fade from the Internet.

Shareholders Care About Leadership

Those shareholders whose investment dollars and pension funds balance on the edge and are subject to mismanagement, lost revenue, and missed opportunity costs pay close attention. They are looking for superior returns and believe that those returns are the result of well-run companies led by ethical leaders. Analysts agree. There is mounting evidence of a direct correlation between effective leadership and business results. In their examination of CEO performance at publicly traded companies, researchers found that the "best-performing CEOs in the world" came from many countries and industries, and, on average, those CEOs delivered a total shareholder return of 997 percent (adjusted for exchange-rate effects) during their tenure. On average, these top 50 CEOs increased the wealth of their companies' shareholders by $48.2 billion (adjusted for inflation, dividends, share repurchases, and share issues). Compare that to the 50 CEOs at the bottom of the list who delivered a total shareholder return of –70 percent during their tenure and presided over a loss of $18.3 billion in shareholder value. Industry, country, and economic factors were accounted for, and each CEO's background and the situation he or she inherited were certainly factors in judging success. Many on the list of successes are familiar names; numerous others are relatively unknown but tend to be selected internally and have served longer in the role than the current average tenure of CEOs.[6]

Internal Stakeholders Care

In an era of increased scrutiny of virtually all expenditures, accountability for the development of leaders, particularly at the top, will only increase.

Significant resources continue to be devoted to developing leaders. The American Society for Training & Development (ASTD) estimates that, even in the midst of a global financial crisis, U.S. companies alone spent just under $126 billion per year on employee learning and development; slightly more than 10 percent of that expenditure was devoted to developing leaders and managers, and an additional 4 percent was expended on executive development.[7] The inability to determine whether or not resources have been expended wisely cannot be sustained in most corporate environments, even when we intuitively believe that leadership development (along with all employee development) is a noble pursuit.

Current and Prospective Employees Care

Effective leaders create a culture that serves as a magnet for attracting top talent. With each generation entering the workplace, a greater emphasis is placed on continual development as these new employees know that they are unlikely to stay more than a few years; it's about what they can develop and acquire to take to the next stop in the career journey. We know that effective leaders are one of the most important influences on levels of engagement. Recent research reaffirms the correlation between engagement and the leaders' ability to:

- Develop a positive and significant relationship with each employee
- Provide constructive performance feedback often
- Coach employees
- Provide opportunities to grow and develop
- Set a clear direction—at whatever level is appropriate
- Communicate not only corporate strategy goals but also progress toward those goals
- Act in ways that are consistent with words

Higher rates of engagement translate into higher rates of retention, an important factor in retaining talent in an increasingly competitive job market.[8] In a world in which fewer than one in three employees is engaged, trust in executives can have a significant impact on engagement.[9]

Other Stakeholders Care

In an increasingly interconnected world, there are many stakeholders whose fortunes and fates are inextricably linked to successful leaders and the leadership development (LD) programs that create and support them:

- The families of employees who have offered their talents and energy in return for current compensation and, in many cases, future retirement and security
- Taxpayers called upon to "bail out" specific companies, as well as entire industries when economic stability hangs in the balance
- Industries that are enhanced by the reputation for good stewardship by outstanding executives or forever tarnished by the action of a few highly visible transgressors
- Communities that stand to be the beneficiaries of business profits that are poured back into the community in the form of goods and services purchased from local companies, as well as scholarships, endowments, and sponsorships
- National governments whose ability to gather tax revenue from profitable, well-run companies can mean the difference between national solvency and national bailouts

Current Status of Leadership Development

There is no doubt that leadership development is important, and it has changed dramatically in the past decade. Starting many years ago as typical classroom training on the principles of leadership, it has evolved into a critical part of organizational growth and development. How leaders are selected for programs and the specific ways in which programs are offered and structured are significant issues that define the current status.

How Leaders Are Selected for Development

Because leadership development can be one of the most expensive types of development (multiples of 4 or 5 times the expenditure made for other employees is not uncommon), selection is usually a thoughtful process.

At higher levels in the organization, participants in LD programs are often selected by one or a combination of the following methods:

- Nomination by a manager
- Cumulative data from performance management systems and/or past talent review discussions
- Assessment results
- Individual assessment (including a 360-degree instrument and/or psychological profiles) and custom developmental plans based on the outcomes of that assessment

- Participation in an "assessment center" exercise
- Testing (the test needs to be subjected to validity and reliability checks to determine the value of administration)
- Behavioral or structured interviews

At lower levels, participants are often "selected in" versus "screened out" and enter into an LD program by virtue of a promotion or a change in job title. For example, all new supervisors may be automatically enrolled in a particular program.

How Leaders Are Developed

Lewis Carroll, in *Alice's Adventures in Wonderland*, wrote: "If you don't know where you are going, any road will get you there." This is also true with leadership development. Unless there is a clear road map, it is indeed a lovely journey but one without a destination or committed travelers. The methods for development are varied, and many are combined into programs and initiatives of infinite variety:

- Formal training usually in a classroom (a virtual or "brick-and-mortar" one)
- Informal learning including self-guided or structured content (books, online learning, audio/video podcasts, etc.)
- Action learning (with a focus on strategic planning or innovation)
- Job shadowing
- Coaching (either internal or external)
- Mentoring
- Experiential learning
- Stretch assignments
- Simulations
- Community involvement
- "Community of practice" or network involvement
- Short-term rotational assignments
- Long-term international assignments

Years ago, researchers created *assignmentology*, a way of mapping standard leadership competencies to specific opportunities for development, such as serving on a taskforce, chairing a major initiative or assuming a role with a greatly expanded scope. The science of knowing what developmental experiences will result in specific competency improvements (and, by extension, what will not) is an extraordinary global positioning system in a world of increasingly fewer marked paths.

How Leadership Development Programs and Initiatives Are Structured

There will always be a need for a structured process of developing leaders. Simply dropping talented and successful individual contributors into the "manager's chair" robs them of the opportunity to continue to be successful in a completely new situation. It also runs the risk of doing not only professional harm to the individual, but also organizational harm to those he or she impacts. This critical juncture in a career should be carefully managed, and all stakeholders need to be involved for mutual success to occur. Deploying new leaders to different environments or challenging situations without careful planning and support is not a recipe for success. Simply hiring a new CEO from the outside without considering the cultural assimilation challenges, as well as the internal communications and talent implications, is terribly shortsighted.

Most programs have one or more of these goals in mind for their leadership development programs and initiatives:

- Assess the bench strength of the current leadership and develop targeted plans to address deficiencies or placement issues for individuals as well as organizational talent gaps that could impact the execution of the strategy.
- Identify possible successors for critical roles.
- Enhance the effectiveness of current leaders with the business and with people by building specific competencies and/or reducing the potential for "derailers."
- Accelerate the development of high-potential and emerging leaders.
- Develop a strong leadership bench.
- Set standards of behavior and cultural norms.
- Leverage leaders' ability to develop and engage their employees, leading to increased levels of productivity, engagement, and retention.

The structure and effectiveness of LD programs is highly variable and, on the whole, disappointingly ineffective. Research indicates that these programs are "immature," according to a leadership development maturity model:

- "Inconsistent management training" at the lowest level of maturity reflective of a lack of development process, no involvement of business leaders but where content is available and viewed as a "benefit" to employees (47 percent)
- "Structured Leadership Training," which is characterized by the development of competencies and a clearly defined curriculum and where management begins to embrace and support initiatives and programs (27 percent)
- "Focused Leadership Development" that is culture-setting and future-focused, where individuals are assessed and thought of as corporate assets and where the organization's leadership needs are factored into the process (16 percent)
- "Strategic Leadership Development," where development is championed by executives who take their own development seriously and all aspects of talent management are integrated (11 percent).[10]

So, is anyone implementing leadership development well? Research highlights many companies and their "best practices" approaches to leadership development, characterized by:

- Strong executive involvement
- Use of tailored leadership competencies
- Alignment with the business strategy
- A "leaders at all levels" approach
- An integrated talent management strategy in which leadership development plays an integral role[11]

These findings are echoed in *Fortune* magazine's 2011 list of the world's most admired companies, which provides insight into the choices these companies make about leadership development. It also reveals that:

- 90 percent expect employees to lead, whether or not they have a formal position of authority
- 100 percent manage a pool of successors for mission-critical roles
- 90 percent collect leadership development best practices from subsidiaries and share them across the organization
- 100 percent give all employees the opportunity to develop and practice the capabilities needed to lead[12]

The structure of leadership development will naturally shift to reflect the organizational models it supports. As command and control hierarchies intersect with social networks and team organizational structures, so will formal, rigid development programs morph into more flexible, customizable solutions to developing leaders. Rick Lash, director of the Hay Group's Leadership and Talent Practice and coauthor of the 2010 "Best Companies for Leadership" study, notes the "significant shift away from hierarchical organizational operating models. . . . Leadership in the twenty-first century is about leading at all levels, not restricting it to title. As organizations become flatter, the best leaders are learning they must check their egos at the door and become increasingly sensitive to diversity, generational, and geographical issues."[13]

One such customized approach can be seen at Bristol-Myers Squibb, which has found ways to customize leadership development through the use of blended learning, coaching, mentoring, and social networking.[14]

Common Challenges in Implementing Leadership Development

For those of us who have labored in the leadership development field for years, the challenges of getting it "right" at any company are at once unique and yet quite common. The details may be different at each organization, but these common challenges are ubiquitous:

- No clear vision of what individual leadership looks like at the organization now
- No clear vision of what organizational capacity looks like now
- No clear vision of what leadership should look like in the future
- Failure to gain consensus and commitment from senior leadership about the leadership model, behaviors, and pertinent corporate policies
- Absence of accountability of leaders to develop others and lead by example
- Lack of specific, descriptive behavioral anchors that help leaders clearly understand what is expected and accepted
- A patchwork of leadership development programs that do not link to each other or to other talent management practices
- Lack of clear definition of success of a program or initiative
- Absence of executive sponsorship, particularly by the CEO
- The perception that this is an "HR" thing

- Disconnection of leadership development from conversations and presentations about the strategic direction and/or key performance indicators
- Lack of adequate resourcing to fully execute programs and initiatives
- An inability to articulate the impact of programs, initiatives, and resource deployment of LD programs in business terms

What Does the Future Hold for Leadership Development?

The ability to develop leaders more quickly and efficiently will become a competitive advantage for those companies who do this successfully. This concept of flexible and adaptive leadership is well suited for our turbulent times. One of the best crucibles for developing adaptive leaders is the military. Four principles have served military leaders well:

1. Create a personal link, which is crucial to leading people through challenging times.
2. Make good and timely calls, which is the crux of responsibility in a leadership position.
3. Establish a common purpose, buttress those who will help you achieve it, and eschew personal gain.
4. Make the objectives clear, but avoid micromanaging those who will execute on them.[15]

Another core skill for future leaders will be the ability to thrive (not simply survive) in a permanent crisis; this VUCA world (VUCA is a term that originated in military circles, which means *volatile, uncertain, complex,* and *ambiguous*), this "new normal" corporate environment, means a never-ending series of strategy refreshes, setbacks, and unexpected opportunities. Many believe that effective leaders in this environment will need to foster adaptation, embrace disequilibrium, and generate leadership at all levels of the organization.[16]

Where will we find such leaders? Some suggest that we expand our search to include different markets, emerging economies, and differing cultural values; finding leaders who have forged their leadership skills in the crucible of resistance to apartheid, the growth trajectory of emerging markets, and the experience gained during stints with mission-driven entities addressing humanitarian crises around the world.[17] The models are there; India provides leadership lessons in terms of where and how they focus their energy and their emphasis on being transformational leaders.[18] So many of these types of experiential learning are finding their way into the corporate leadership development programs at industry-leading companies such as UBS and IBM.

Leadership development will morph and adapt, just as the leaders it attempts to create must do. But one thing will remain constant: the need to articulate the impact of such a major investment. The journey is always the same for leadership development; at the end of the day, learning to effectively lead people remains a transformational process. It is always about how willing someone is to make himself or herself the lesser so that someone else can be the greater.

Many approaches can be successful, given the right support, the right timing, and the right alignment with corporate imperatives. While setting the course is difficult, attaining the results is even more challenging. One study of leadership competencies that matter most for growth (which, according to the authors, comprise "the Holy Grail of corporate strategy") reveals that great leaders are very rare indeed.[19]

Some companies have found the way. There is no one path; there is no one correct answer. There are, however, correct questions:

- What are you trying to accomplish?
- How aligned are you with the organizational strategy?
- Who will be the champion(s)?
- What specifically will you do? For how long? In what way? What methods will you use?
- Who will be selected to participate, and on the basis of what criteria?
- How integrated is this into every other aspect of talent management?
- How will you measure success?
- How will you articulate success?

Can the Impact of Leadership Development Initiatives Be Measured?

We believe LD initiatives can and *should* be measured. What counts, however, are not our opinions but those of the business leaders who support all human capital that professionals need. Increasingly, C-Suite level leaders such as CEOs and CFOs will want to know the return on their investment in leadership development, particularly the most expensive and higher profile LD programs. In a recent survey of Fortune 500 CEOs, 92 of 96 said that they were interested in learning the business impact of such programs, but only

8 percent see that happening at their companies now.[20] Other business leaders are increasingly interested in "people metrics" and the alignment between people-related data and business priorities, sales performance data, and revenue.[21]

Early research in human capital analytics paved the way for its application in the workplace. Some studied the impact of the consulting psychologist as a path to developing leaders who impact business results.[22] Others found that without the ability to articulate the business impacts of programs and initiatives, the human resources function would have a very difficult time playing a strategic role.[23] One conducted research for the Conference Board with leading multinational firms, including BP, Colgate-Palmolive, Bayer, Unilever, AstraZeneca, and UBS, to determine the ways in which the profession could articulate the business value of leadership development.[24] Two others state that even intangibles can be measured and used to support the impact discussion.[25] Research supports the critical need to demonstrate the return on investment of LD initiatives.[26]

This shift to analytics is well underway. At UPS, the use of metrics and data have driven decision making about programs and their effectiveness, as well as business impact.[27] Google's metrics-driven approach and analysis have helped create the culture-specific leadership model that is now the foundation for leadership development.[28] Companies as varied as Harrah's Entertainment, Starbucks, Procter & Gamble, Limited Brands, and Best Buy have determined that they can compete on talent analytics and win.[29]

This book is a primer on the ways in which the impact and return on investment (ROI) of leadership development can be measured and articulated. It is not only possible to do this; it is necessary for survival.

How This Book Is Organized

Incorporating recaps of various initiatives, this book plots a course to bring accountability to leadership development. It shows how to measure success in ways top executives will recognize, appreciate, and ultimately require. The next chapter explores success factors for leadership development, resulting from many studies that have shown the shortcomings. Identifying failures can quickly translate into process improvement, or at least the success factors that lead to the improvement. Next is the introduction to the ROI Methodology™ and its connection to leadership development. This is the most validated, documented, and utilized system in the world, aptly suited for leadership development because of its significant history in this critical field. The issues of business alignment and preparation for ROI analysis are explored next. One of the key issues is connecting leadership development directly to the business before, during, and after the programs are offered. The next few chapters represent the heart of the book, showing how data are collected, analyzed, and reported to various audiences. Following that, the book details the ways in which this methodology can be sustained over a long period of time. Finally, the book concludes with a sample of case studies.

2

Failure and Success of Leadership Development

T HIS JOURNEY OF accountability will begin with a reflection on the critical elements of successful leadership development. Success factors are often derived from identifying causes of failure. These two issues go hand in hand, and this chapter provides details on the main reasons why leadership fails to meet its potential, as well as the corresponding success factors that are developed from these failures. The conclusions here are based in part on a significant amount of experience in conducting ROI studies on leadership development and observing the reasons for success and failure in these studies. Some new research and a current literature review add to the data.

How Success and Failure Are Identified

The success factors for leadership development are identified from the barriers and enablers of successful leadership development. When leadership development is successful, the enablers to that success are identified and isolated. When leadership development fails, the barriers that caused the failure are isolated as well. A failure does not necessarily mean that the program did not deliver a positive return on investment or even influence significant business impact measures. A failure is described as a program not living up to its expectations—not achieving the established impact or ROI objectives. It could have been more successful if adjustments or changes had been made; it will achieve success if changes are made going forward.

The data in this chapter are identified in a variety of sources. The most important sources are the ROI studies conducted by officers, consultants, associates, and partners of the ROI Institute. Each year this team is involved with approximately 100 to 150 leadership development studies, and each study reveals important issues about failure and success factors. In the case of disappointments, the data show the cause of the disappointment (i.e., barriers that must change in the program to generate more success). From time to time, the ROI Institute conducts reviews of these studies to determine the barriers and enablers to success. Failure is divided into three categories. In the worst-case scenario, the studies are negative, delivering less value than the cost of the program. These are failures that present serious disappointments, and the lessons learned are very clear. The second category is when success has not been achieved at the minimal targets defined by the impact and ROI objectives. While these programs have positive results, they do not meet expectations; there are opportunities for improvement that will drive more success. A third category consists of programs that exceed the objectives and show additional potential. While these programs are successful, if adjustments are made, they can be more so. These adjustments are vital because maximization of the value delivered is always a goal of success.

These distinctions are made because the impact of leadership development, when properly designed and implemented, can be considerable, sometimes ranging from 300 to 1,000 percent return on investment. Consider the impact created when a leader changes his or her behavior and it affects the entire team. For example, for a first-level team leader in a call center with 20 direct reports, the impact would be the improvement of the team. If productivity (e.g., call volume) improves because of the leadership development, the team's productivity is measured. When the monetary value from the team's improvement is compared to the cost of formal learning for an individual, the ROI value can be significant. In our experience at the ROI Institute, when this leverage or multiplicative effect is explained to chief financial officers, they get it. Consequently, we should expect high returns on investment from leadership development; if they are not there, we should determine what can be done to improve them.

In addition to examination of ROI studies, research began with an examination of the literature, probing into both the failures and the success factors of leadership development. Next, a survey was conducted with LD organizers: those who organize, coordinate, or facilitate leadership development and are often aware of the causes of failure. The survey data from 32 respondents are presented in this chapter and the next. The ranking of barriers from most significant to least significant is presented at the end of the chapter. For the most part, these results parallel what the ROI Institute team has uncovered in the analysis of studies.

The remainder of the chapter presents the reasons for failure (or lack of success). The specific success factors are presented in italics.

Alignment Issues

The beginning point in understanding the success (or failure) is the alignment issue. A significant, and unfortunately common, cause of failure is the lack of alignment at the initial stages. Specific failures in the alignment piece are identified. The following are four areas to address.

What Results? (Lack of Business Alignment)

Based on the ROI Institute's review of studies, the number one reason for lack of business results from leadership development is that the program has not been aligned to business needs in the very beginning. For example, the ROI Institute was asked to evaluate a series of LD programs for a large telecommunications organization. The project required five ROI studies on five different leadership programs, and the financial return on investment was required. These programs had already been conducted, and their status had come into question. We did not have the luxury of planning the ROI analysis before a program was implemented; we had to rely on what had already occurred. The difficulty in that evaluation was understanding the business impact. The project became a challenging search mission, as the team sought specific business measures that were or could have been influenced by programs. Struggling to find the data, the team quickly concluded that the program was not connected to the business from the very beginning.

Most LD programs begin with leader behavior (i.e., competencies) that should be developed, with little consideration of the business impact. The assumption is that changes in leader behavior will positively affect the business. Unfortunately, that assumption is not always valid; executives want a clearer path between an investment in leader behavior and the business impact. It is possible to connect leadership development to a business need at the beginning of the program, as Chapter 5 will describe; however, not every program should be evaluated at the business impact or ROI level. There must be a connection to the business if there is a desire and need to evaluate at that level. The issue is simple: if the program is designed to drive business results and there is a critical reason to measure the success, the program needs to be aligned to the business measure in the beginning. It is accomplished routinely by progressive organizations.

Success factors identified are based on the assumption that when these factors are in place for the LD program it will drive improvements and be successful, particularly at the business level. Here's the first success factor:

Success Factor 1: Align the program to business measures in the beginning.

It's Leadership! How Can It Not Be Needed?
(Not Assessing Current Leader Behavior)

There is an old saying that a little training never hurt anyone. When stated in the leadership development context, the saying becomes, "A little *leadership development* would never hurt anyone." While this is true, the goal of leadership development is not to avoid being hurt, but to add value, and part of the value is a clear understanding of necessary leadership behaviors. For example, in our work with a very large agency at the United Nations (UN) involved in humanitarian relief, directors for the various countries had asked the learning and development function to stop offering leadership development. The conclusion from this group was that programs offered focused on competencies or skills that were already in place instead of those actually needed. Canned approaches were taken based on someone else's assessment.

Too often, leadership development is based on a particular book, a popular leadership model, or a successful program, and these competencies may not be appropriate. A clear understanding of the behaviors needed is very critical. Perhaps one of the most important ways to determine needs is the use of the 360-degree feedback from various sources, who indicate if the intended leaders are behaving in accordance with expected leadership dimensions or competencies. Because 360-degree feedback can be expensive, it is not routinely pursued. This leads to the second success factor:

Success Factor 2: Identify specific behavior changes needed for the target audience.

Don't They Know That Already? (Not Assessing Learning Needs Properly)

The learning and development field has a perpetual problem with learning solutions: they may not be needed. Just because a particular behavior is not in place does not necessarily mean that the leaders do not know how to use the effective behavior. A learning solution may not be needed. Instead, it is sometimes a matter of expectations, role modeling, rewards, and any number of other solutions to drive the particular behavior. This issue can be pinpointed by asking leaders in the program if they know how to do this *now*. If they were given no other choice and they were told, "Now you have to use these behaviors," could they do it? If the answer is yes, a learning solution is not needed. If the leaders already have the knowledge or skills but are not using them, chances are they will not use them now. Unfortunately, learning solutions are implemented without clear understanding of the current knowledge or skills. This not only wastes resources and time but also leaves the impression that leadership development is a waste of time, which results in complaints that behaviors already known are being repetitively presented. Simple processes can be used to connect the leader behavior to lack of knowledge or skills. Sometimes, leaders will admit in anonymous surveys what they can and cannot do well, clearly identifying what they need to learn and what they already know. This leads to the third success factor:

Success Factor 3: Identify learning needs for the target audience.

Do Participants Know What They Must Accomplish?
(Failure to Create Application and Impact Objectives)

The learning and development profession generally has excellent capability for developing learning objectives. Learning objectives are written from a performance perspective, which suggests that participants should be able to perform in some way, often under certain conditions and even with a criterion representing quality, accuracy, or time. Regrettably, when it comes to leadership development, even learning objectives are unclear. Even worse, application and impact objectives are almost nonexistent. Application objectives define what participants are expected to do with what they learn. Impact objectives describe the consequences of application, expressed as a business measure.

For example, in a recent review of a leadership program for an electric utility, ROI Institute team members were surprised to find that a one-week leadership development program did not have learning objectives—just an agenda—and there were certainly no application or impact objectives. Obviously, without objectives the participants were unsure about what they were expected to do and the impact the program would deliver. The expectations were perceived as a mystery: participants were unaware of how this program would help them, their teams, their departments, and their functions.

While learning objectives are an absolute necessity these days, it is important to expand that to application objectives (detailing how participants use the competencies) and impact objectives (detailing the business consequences of the application). The root of this problem usually can be traced to those who develop the content of leadership development. They are often not tuned into writing clear, precise objectives, particularly for application and impact levels. Some people suggest that the impact of leadership development should not be detailed. For example, in our work with the United Nations, we were surprised at the reaction to a leadership guru who had written over 40 books on leadership development. In a team meeting where a new leadership program was being developed by representatives of the different UN agencies, the leadership expert suggested that the program should not have application and impact objectives, although top executives at the United Nations mandated that the program show the impact within the UN system. Alternatively, this well-known expert suggested a variety of learning objectives. One of these objectives was that participants should be able to "release the corporate energy of the team." The team quickly asked for a meaning of this objective, as not one individual in the group understood what it meant. The concern: if the human resources manager doesn't understand the objectives, how can participants understand them?

Unfortunately, the experts who have developed much of the leadership material have not stepped up to this challenge. The progress made is often delivered by clients asking for the value of the leadership development. The good news is that developing objectives can be an easy part of the process. We recommend that 60 to 70 percent of the LD programs implemented should have application and impact objectives, although a much smaller number may actually be evaluated at these levels. The fourth success factor is simple:

Success Factor 4: Establish application and impact objectives for LD programs.

Design Issues

While the alignment is often the principal culprit, programs can also fail as a result of improper program design. The design includes issues such as content, process flow, communication, target audience, and implementation. Collectively, the ROI Institute has identified five areas that cause programs to fail from a design perspective.

Who Should Be Involved? (Not Including the Right Participants)

Leadership development is a popular topic, and several factors cause individuals to want to pursue leadership development. If top executives are pushing leadership development and encouraging everyone to be involved, there is a tendency for everyone to want to enroll—or feel that they need to. Some leadership development programs are often expensive and prestigious, and participation is considered an honor. This may cause individuals who probably do not need leadership development to pursue involvement. Also, when the target participation group is vague and very broad, all types of individuals may attend. For example, in a recent study involving leadership development of a Fortune 500 technology company, over 40 percent of participants had no direct reports, although the program was aimed at those in leadership positions who had direct reports. In another leadership program at a government agency, the ROI Institute found that almost 30 percent of the participants were in their last year of employment before retirement. These individuals were developing skills that could be applied in their next career, which is not what the agency wanted. When leadership program participant selections are made by higher-level managers, those whom the managers can least afford to lose working time are sometimes selected. The approach follows this logic: "Let's send the person who's not so busy now or who manages an area that's not so important." These individuals may not need, appreciate, or benefit from the leadership development program.

The challenge is to ensure that the appropriate individuals are available at the right time and are motivated to learn. This brings up the issue of voluntary versus involuntary participation. Although some programs may be mandatory to ensure that everyone has the same leadership competencies, others are offered on a voluntary basis. We have found in our work that those who volunteer to attend leadership programs achieve much more success than those who do not. This probably comes as no surprise, but it is particularly critical for open enrollment programs and leadership coaching. For example, if managers pursue coaching on their own, with some very specific impact measures to improve and with the expectation of results, they can achieve amazing outcomes. Nonvolunteers sometimes feel that they are prisoners involved in a process that they find undesirable or unwarranted. With leadership development, if the person does not want to become a different or better leader, then he or she will not develop those leadership competencies. The fifth success factor is straightforward:

Success Factor 5: Involve the right people at the right time.

Is This the Right Path? (Improper Program Design)

Sometimes the design of the program is the problem. Participants have different styles, and they learn in different ways. Their experiences, needs, and levels of performance vary. While the lack of proper content can be a design issue, problems often surface when the design is dysfunctional in terms of convenience, support, expectation, delivery, and facilitation. Managers in these programs want their facilitators to be knowledgeable about leadership. The facilitator must gain participants' respect to inspire them to learn and apply. The program must meet schedule needs while addressing how people learn. Sometimes participants want to learn in pieces or modules and do not want to be involved in long-term leadership development efforts. Many leaders want to learn quickly and at the time they need it, which poses a problem with some leadership development programs. "Just for me," "just enough," and "just in time" are the requests.

Thoroughly analyzing the needs of the target group and ensuring that the design meets those needs is critical to success. In the ROI Institute's evaluation of a virtual leadership project, most of the individuals appeared online when asked or scheduled. It *was* a mandatory program, and they seemed to do well in some of the exercises, completing the program with seemingly new knowledge and skills. However, the virtual learning approach provided little opportunity to work with skills. In the follow-up evaluation, little success was achieved with application and impact. Essentially, participants did not think this program should be presented in a virtual format. While a different audience would have been more acceptable to the virtual leadership program, it was not appropriate for this group. The sixth success factor addresses several design issues:

Success Factor 6: Design leadership development for successful learning and application.

The critical part of this factor is to ensure that there is a focus on application, and that requires application objectives. These higher levels of objectives should probably be involved in every program, as underscored in the fourth success factor.

What Expectations? (Failure to Secure Commitment from Participants)

Several issues are involved in setting participant expectations. Leadership development participants are like other people involved in a learning activity.

They do not want surprises. They must be made aware of the requirements and expectations as soon as possible. Also, like other participants, they want to know what they must do to make the program work. Program designers must provide the details, let participants know what they should be doing, and define ultimate success. Because participants are leaders, they expect to be treated professionally. This means taking the mystery out of the process to avoid misunderstanding. The professional approach is what they expect from leadership development providers.

For example, in a leadership development program of a large European bank, the ROI Institute used probing interviews to clearly understand what participants had achieved with their leadership development. We posed questions about what was achieved in terms of improvements and behavior changes, impacts in their work units, and any data that would validate business improvements. The pushback from the entire group was that they did not know that there was any particular expectation of what they should do with what they had learned. They thought that application was "optional," and they stated that they did not know that they should be tracking a business improvement—consequently, that had no corroborative impact data.

With proper business alignment, the mystery of application and impact can be removed, and participants are often reminded of those issues when application and impact objectives are developed. However, without these, it is not unusual for participants to struggle with expectations. This issue is significant for two major reasons. The first reason is the need for data from this group. For leadership development, the sources of data for improvements are more likely to be the participants themselves. After all, they provide data for reaction and learning, so it becomes easier for them to provide data on application and impact. The impact measures they drive may be unique to them and their particular functional areas. Data collection associated with application and impact should not be a surprise to the group. They should know it in advance of the program, be reminded of it during the program, and often use tools as built-in data collection such as action planning to make it work.

The second reason involves the expectation of the business impact, if appropriate for the program. Participants should realize that if they change only behavior and there are no corresponding business results, the legitimacy of the program may be called into question; that is, if there is behavior change with no corresponding business value, it may appear as though there has been activity with *no business impact consequences*. Success may require participants to focus on those business measures and attempt to make changes in them using the competencies of the program, working with their teams. Without the business connection, the desired success will probably not occur.

Clarifying the expectations early in the process is one of the best ways to drive significant program results and appropriate amounts of data. This leads to the seventh success factor:

Success Factor 7: Create expectations to achieve results and provide data.

This Won't Work in My World!
(Failure to Remove or Minimize Barriers to Application)

One of the most important causes of failure is barriers to the transfer of the learning to the job. While this has been a classic issue in learning and development for decades, it becomes critical for leadership development, as there are many reasons why participants do not use leadership skills. Typical reasons for lack of application are that it does not fit in their world, they did not have time, it was not supported by their team, it was not applicable to what they do, or they prefer their current approaches or skills. These and other barriers can bring any use of new leadership skills to a halt.

For example, in a leadership development project involving a government agency, the participants were exposed to a variety of leadership approaches. These leaders were seasoned executives who were quite comfortable with their current styles and were unwilling to change. Basically, they said, "I already like what I am doing and do not see a need to change anything." Neither the expectations for change in behavior nor the rationale for change was communicated clearly. Consequently, no new behaviors were developed.

The challenge is to address these barriers early—even during the initial needs assessment—to determine what would prevent newly desired behaviors from transferring to the job. Also, the barriers must be revisited often and problems addressed as they are uncovered, even to the point of asking individuals involved in a program what specific barriers will prevent leadership development from working in their world. The eighth success factor is a classic problem:

Success Factor 8: Address the learning transfer issue early and often.

My Manager Didn't Support This!
(Failure to Secure Management Support for the Program)

Lack of management support can impede learning from transferring to the job. While this may not be expected with leadership development, it is an issue. Imagine if a first-level manager attends a one-week leadership development program and, upon returning to the job, he or she says nothing at all about the program. Most would agree that there will be no application of the learning to the job. Some would argue that leaders should be more accountable than subordinates, and they should accept the responsibility to apply what they have learned. Because of their position, they should not necessarily require management support to make it work. Unfortunately, they do.

For example, in a study involving five leadership programs in a large telecommunications company, an interesting observation was made from the results. The programs were designed for each level, from the first level to the top executive group. Among the reasons for the lack of success was that managers did not support the programs. Each managerial level was blaming the next level for not supporting the process, all the way to the top. When the chairman and CEO reviewed the data, he exasperatedly made the comment, "It looks like someone in the chain of command should take responsibility and not wait for the previous manager to support it."

New leader behavior represents change, and applying any new skills or competencies often involves extra steps and effort. Behavior change requires a very supportive environment from the immediate manager, who must be involved and encourage, support, and sometimes even require application of skills. To prevent a barrier from arising, the next level of manager must be in the loop and ideally given an active role, not only in the expected changes but also in the expected results. After all, the number-one critical step for ensuring the application of leadership development to the job is to have the immediate manager set specific goals prior to the program participation. The second most critical item is the follow-up from the immediate managers to determine if those results have been achieved. Obviously, the immediate manager is in a very critical role, which brings us to the ninth success factor:

Success Factor 9: Establish supportive partnerships with key managers.

Data Collection and Analysis

Sometimes the analysis of what is accomplished (or not) is an important issue that can reveal the success of the program. Determining the cause of failure or success of the program may rest on the proper approach to data analysis. This ranges from data collection to isolating the impact of the program and involves five areas.

What Data? (Not Identifying the Right Data for Analysis)

One of the first issues that arises when leadership development at the impact and ROI levels is evaluated is that sponsors and participants are unsure of the data to be collected. They ask, "Can you tell us what data will be influenced?" Obviously, the impact data influenced by the program depend on the individuals and the program.

There are basically two scenarios for connecting leadership development to business data. First, if the leadership program is developed for all participants to work on one or two measures (e.g., employee turnover and employee engagement), then those measures are clearly identified in the beginning and are easily tracked and analyzed. A problem often surfaces when the selected impact data do not apply to all participants—that is, participants are attending from all functional areas and they all have different measures. They may not have a turnover or engagement issue in their particular world.

The second approach suggests that business measures should be identified by the participants, perhaps through additional discussion with program organizers and the participants' immediate manager. (The different ways will be discussed later in this book.) It is critical for these data sets to be identified and properly addressed throughout the program.

The issue of the right data also surfaces at the application level—what are the right data to seek? Application is often behavior—someone's observation of behavior or the participant's perception of his or her own leadership behavior. Sometimes specific actions or tasks must be completed, such as conducting or eliminating meetings or the completion of checklists or other documents. The data sets for application are often defined in the initial analysis and are monitored through the data collection process to the application level. They should also be defined in the application objectives.

For learning, the right data are straightforward, a matter of skills and knowledge acquired or improved. The right data are the amount of learning acknowledged (various leadership models or theories) or new skills that are demonstrated, observed, and rated. The data sets for reaction are measures that are often tailored to the group and must include items such as relevance to the job context, importance to success, intent to use the skills, recommendation of the program to others, and the practicality of content. These are all content-related questions that represent reaction to the program from the participants' perspective. The tenth success factor is simplistic:

Success Factor 10: Select the proper data sets for the desired evaluation level.

They Won't Provide Me the Data!
(Not Building Data Collection into the Process)

Perhaps one of the greatest problems with evaluating leadership development is not being able to secure the appropriate amount and quality of data. As mentioned earlier, participants are perhaps the best individuals to provide the data, and the challenge often involves building data collection into the program and positioning data collection as application tools. In leadership development, one of the best methods to measure the application and impact, and collect data necessary for the ROI evaluation, is to use an action planning process. This process provides an opportunity for participants to identify specific actions they will take to improve a selected business impact measure. Plans are developed during the session and are positioned as application tools for participants to chart the success of using what they have learned. It provides them a way to guide their application in an efficient manner and see the results achieved in terms of business impact and even monetary value. The data collection becomes a very easy task when this is properly built in, and participation, completion, and return rates of the action plans are greatly enhanced.

The ROI Institute recently received a query from a pharmaceutical company complaining about the lack of data received about the success of the leadership program. Our first question pertained to the method of data collection. The response was a questionnaire, prompting the follow-up question, "Did you let participants know in advance that the questionnaire would be used to track their success with the program?" The answer was "No." Our next question was, "Did anyone review the questionnaire at the end of the session?" Again, the answer was "No." For the most part, this explains the low response rate. When a questionnaire is used for data collection, it must be planned in advance and participants need to have the expectation that they will need to provide data, primarily for them to see the success that they and others have had. A variety of techniques must be used to secure an appropriate response rate. At least 25 techniques used to secure improved response rates will be presented in later chapters.

The important point is that data collection needs to be built in and advance notice must be provided to elicit a successful response rate, as summarized in the eleventh success factor:

Success Factor 11: Build data collection into the process positioned as an application tool.

What Are the Other Influences?
(Taking All the Credit for an Improvement in Business Impact)

One of the most challenging issues in evaluation of leadership development is to sort out the influence of the leadership development program from other factors that may be driving business results. In this book, this issue is described as isolating the effects of the program from other influences. Others call it "attribution analysis" or "contribution analysis." While isolation can be considered for application (i.e., sorting out the different influences for changes in leadership behavior), it is more critical for business impact. A typical approach to most evaluations of leadership development is to ignore the issue altogether by taking all the credit of any business impact measure remotely connected to the program. Another is to suggest that this step cannot be accomplished. Either option leaves a study that is not credible. Sponsors of leadership programs want to see some effort to address this issue.

At the beginning of the recent global recession, a leadership development supplier sent us a case study for potential publication. The program, which was designed to address a high turnover rate among critical talent, was launched just before the recession hit that particular industry. Six months after the program, the turnover rate disappeared, evidenced by some dramatic changes in the numbers. No attempt was made to isolate the effects of the program. The authors of the study claimed all of the success for the leadership development program, completely ignoring the effect of the recession. Our input is that the recession probably caused a major part, if not all, of the improvement in turnover. Consequently, the study was not credible and was not published. This important issue is described in Chapter 6. The twelfth success factor is critical to producing a credible study:

Success Factor 12: Always isolate the effects of the program on impact data.

I'll Do Return on Investment Analysis When I Am Asked to Do It!
(Waiting for the Request for Impact and Return on Investment Analysis)

Although it may seem logical to do so, one of the worst things that providers or organizers of leadership development can do is to wait for a top executive to ask about the impact or return on investment for a particular leadership development program. Unfortunately, it happens in most of the cases in our involvement with leadership development. The argument: "This is difficult to do, and my results may not be what I want them to be, so why should I bring this on myself? Why should I create a problem that I may not have? I'll wait for the executive to request it."

Unfortunately, waiting for the request can cause disastrous results. It often comes with a timeline, and that timeline is usually very short. The request frequently is made after discussions by executives about the program, resulting in questions or concerns about accountability. This places the leadership development team in a reactive or defensive mode. The issue is now an action item on the executives' agenda—and that's not good news.

Waiting for the request can lead to disaster, as we have seen in several situations. For example, at a well-respected European broadcasting company, the leadership development team implemented a new leadership program for all its leaders. The program, developed and implemented by a prestigious leadership development provider in Europe, was expensive. Since the leadership program was requested by the sitting CEO, the team did not engage in efforts to connect the program to business impact. The approach of the team was low risk: "Don't pursue this type of data unless there is a request." The CEO who initially requested the program was fired by the board, and the new CEO began to question the large expenditure for the leadership program, which was half completed. When he asked about the business impact of the program, the team reported that no plans had been made to collect any data and no business results were available. Business impact objectives were not developed, and business alignment to connect to business needs was not pursued. The only response from team members was that perhaps the program could be aligned to the business going forward and the success could be measured at that point. That was not what the CEO wanted to hear. He canceled the program and eliminated the leadership development team.

As this example illustrates, the thirteenth success factor (to be proactive), which is a simple one, is often ignored. The extreme case just mentioned actually happened, and shows an adverse reaction when a leadership development team waits for an executive request. Unfortunately, the request often comes from the executive's perception that the process is not working or is not adding value, which makes it more difficult to show the value in a short time.

Success Factor 13: Be proactive and develop impact and ROI analyses for major programs.

What Do We Do with the Data?
(Not Using the Data Routinely for Process Improvement)

With this methodology, data are collected along a chain of impact (see Figure 2-1) that must exist for the program to add value. If data are collected, adjustments are made. At Levels 1 and 2, when an adverse reaction or lack

Figure 2-1   Chain of Impact

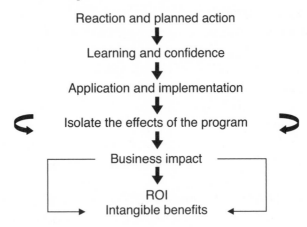

of learning is revealed, adjustments are made. At Level 3, application, indicators may suggest that the participants are not using what they have learned. Again, adjustments must be made. At Level 4, business impact, where the business measures are monitored, data are collected to determine what should be adjusted, if necessary. Return on investment is then calculated and the results should be reported to the proper groups.

This reporting is critical to provide recognition, improve processes, show contributions, build support, increase influence, and initiate a variety of other actions needed as data are collected and reported. Collecting data and not using them properly to drive improvement and funding, or to build respect and influence, is like planting seeds and failing to fertilize them. The yield will not be as great. The last success factor, number fourteen, is just as important as the first:

Success Factor 14: Use the data collected at different levels to make adjustments and improvements.

A large telecommunications organization had us conduct a study involving a group of leaders. The results showed that they were not using the skills at all and the ROI study was negative. The evaluation focused on Levels 3 and 4, although a review of Levels 1 and 2 indicated some problems, as the participants did not view the skills as relevant to their needs, and thus did not plan to use them. There was no indication that they even acquired any new skills, yet the program continued, and the results were disappointing at Levels 3 and 4. When we reported the data to the client, we were asked not to report them to anyone else, including the sponsor who funded the project and the

Table 2-1 Reasons for Leadership Development Program Failures

Reason Cited	Ranking	Percentage
Not building data collection into the process	1	74%
Not using the data routinely for process improvement	2	53%
Failure to create application and impact objectives	3	51%
Not assessing current leader behavior	4	49%
Failure to secure commitment from participants	5	48%
Not identifying the right data for analysis	6	47%
Failure to secure management support for the program	7	46%
Failure to remove or minimize barriers to application	8	43%
Not assessing learning needs properly	9	42%
Lack of business alignment	10	39%
Improper program design	11	24%
Taking all the credit for an improvement in business impact	12	17%
Waiting for the request for impact and ROI analysis	13	16%
Not including the right participants	14	13%

facilitators who conducted it. As far as our client was concerned, the project was complete. The client was fearful that this evaluation would reflect unfavorably on them. Unfortunately, they let the program continue, although it was clear that it was not adding value. Prolonging an ineffective program wastes resources, demotivates the individuals involved, and ultimately hurts the leadership development function.

Any evaluation of leadership development should be taken in the spirit of process improvement, not performance evaluation for the team. An entire chapter is devoted to communicating results to the right audience (see Chapter 10).

Summary of Successes and Failures

While this chapter has outlined the failures and reasons for them, it is helpful to summarize, particularly in terms of the frequency in which they occur. Table 2-1 shows the results of a recent survey of leadership practitioners. A

Table 2-2 Success Factors for Leadership Development

1. Align the program to business measures in the beginning.	☐
2. Identify specific behavior changes needed for the target audience.	☐
3. Identify learning needs for the target audience.	☐
4. Establish application and impact objectives for LD programs.	☐
5. Involve the right people at the right time.	☐
6. Design leadership development for successful learning and application.	☐
7. Create expectations to achieve results and provide data.	☐
8. Address the learning transfer issue early and often.	☐
9. Establish supportive partnerships with key managers.	☐
10. Select the proper data sets for the desired evaluation level.	☐
11. Build data collection into the process and position it as an application tool.	☐
12. Always isolate the effects of the program on impact data.	☐
13. Be proactive and develop impact and ROI analyses for major programs.	☐
14. Use data collected at different levels for adjustments and improvements.	☐

total of 232 responses were received. The most significant reason for failure is not building data collection into the process, followed by not using the data for process improvement.

Final Thoughts

The success factors for leadership development have been presented throughout the chapter. Table 2-2 presents them in checklist form, listed in the order in which they normally occur in the LD process. Leadership development facilitators, developers, organizers, and supporters can use this checklist to ensure that the proper processes are in place for success. The factors are developed from literally hundreds of studies on leadership development and through other research. Not all of the success factors need to be addressed. Usually, three to six items are missing for any given program design, and these are often critical enough to inhibit the results.

To be safe, it is helpful to focus on all these factors. They represent a solid design for increased accountability, particularly when the impact and return on investment are desired. The next chapter discusses why the ROI Methodology is the most credible tool for measuring leadership development in various organizations.

Leadership Development and the ROI Methodology

THIS CHAPTER MAKES the business case for using return on investment as a part of the measurement process. The paragraphs that follow present the rationale for the use of the ROI Methodology, explore its fundamental components, and present the ROI standards, which are essential for building the methodology's credibility and respect as a viable tool for measuring the success of leadership development.

Why ROI Methodology?

The ROI Methodology compares the benefits of LD programs to the costs of those programs. Although other types of analyses show the general relationship between investing in human capital and such outcomes as talent retention, profits, and productivity, most executives need a tool to show the impact of a particular program. The methodology generates the data needed to convince senior management of the program's contribution. Return on investment is a new addition to the LD manager's measurement toolkit; it is essential for showing the connection of this development to the bottom line and the impact of specific programs.

A Rationale for Return on Investment

Several features about return on investment make it an effective measure for leadership development:

1. **Return on investment is the ultimate measure.** In the range of measurement possibilities, return on investment represents the ultimate— a comparison of the actual cost of a program to its monetary benefits by using the same standard ratio that accountants have used for years to show the return on investment for equipment and buildings.

2. **Return on investment has been the elusive measure.** Many leadership development managers have long assumed that it was impossible to measure return on investment in that arena. Recognizing that investment is essential and that human potential is an unlimited power, many leaders have argued that return on investment cannot and should not be applied to leadership development. The concept of return on investment, therefore, has been surrounded by misconceptions, myths, and mysteries that have prevented many executives from pursuing it. Because of the increase in evidence to the contrary, it is no longer an elusive measure.

3. **Return on investment has a rich history of application.** The ROI Methodology is not a fad passing through the organization. It is a measure of accountability that has been in place for centuries. Wherever there is a significant expenditure, there is a need to know the financial impact of the expenditure. Return on investment will continue to be an economic measure in the future.

4. **Operating managers understand and relate to return on investment.** Most managers in an organization have special training on how to manage the business. Some have business or management degrees or even master's degrees in business administration. These managers understand return on investment and routinely use it to value other investments. They have a desire to have ROI data for major programs. They know how to use it, appreciate it, and support it.

5. **Return on investment builds excitement among stakeholders.** One of the most important sources of pride and satisfaction comes when the LD function organizes, implements, or operates a program that results in a positive ROI calculation. No other measure can generate the amount of energy, excitement, and enthusiasm as return on investment can, particularly when the ROI value exceeds expectations. Most stakeholders involved in leadership programs intuitively believe that the programs add value; return on investment, as a measurement tool, confirms this intuition using a credible, validated process.

6. **Return on investment is a top executive requirement.** Thanks in part to the popular press and media attention to return on investment

as an evaluation tool, executives are suggesting, asking, requiring, and sometimes demanding that return on investment be calculated for certain programs. Often, leadership development rises to the top of consideration. Previously, executives assumed that return on investment could not be developed based on logical and persuasive arguments from the HR team. Now, these executives see many examples in which return on investment is becoming an important part of the measurement mix. The global recession has intensified this issue to the point that executives now suggest that return on investment be required for human capital expenditures, treating them the same as other business functions. Gone are the days of blindly increasing human capital investments with no clue as to their payoff.

These six factors sway many executives and LD organizers to pursue ROI evaluation. It is the ultimate level of evaluation that not only is needed but is also required by some key stakeholders. More important, return on investment provides different stakeholder groups important, balanced information about the success of a leadership development program.

Current Status

In a survey of leadership development practitioners in summer 2011, 368 surveys were sent out and 232 were received for a response rate of 63 percent. Several lists of current practitioners were used to choose recipients who were actively involved in leadership development. In every case, the job title included leadership development or reflected a manager or director responsible for leadership development. Most of the organizations were global, representing both public and private sectors.

Table 3-1 shows where leadership development is being evaluated, using the levels of evaluation as a reference. These levels are described in more detail in the next section. As this table shows, a surprising number of these evaluations are at the business impact and ROI levels, exceeding expectation. Part of this could be a function of the global recession. The recession has led some organizations to step up their evaluation efforts, pushing the evaluation up the chain of impact to the impact and ROI levels.

Figure 3-1 shows today's ROI reality, as recipients responded to the question: "Is there an emphasis on ROI?" Surprisingly, 88 percent said yes. This dramatically underscores the concern about ROI during a global recession.

Table 3-1 Levels of Evaluation for Leadership Development

Level of Evaluation	Percent of Programs Evaluated at This Level
1. Reaction—Measures reaction to, and satisfaction with, the experience, contents, and value of the program	88.9%
2. Learning—Measures what participants learned in the program: information, knowledge, skills, competencies, and contacts (takeaways from the program)	59.1%
3. Application/implementation—Measures progress after the program: the use of information, knowledge, skills, competencies, and contacts	33.9%
4. Business impact—Measures changes in business impact variables such as output, quality, time, and costs linked to the program	21.3%
5. Return on investment—Compares the monetary benefits of the business impact measures to the costs of the program	11.3%

N = 232

Figure 3-2 shows the drivers for ROI evaluation and represents data only from those who indicated there is a current emphasis on return on investment. Perhaps as anticipated, increased pressures for cost efficiencies dominated the rationale for ROI evaluation, which for the most part is a function of the current global competitive situation and the remnants of the economic recession. The cost of the program is the second driver, which is consistent with the work at the ROI Institute. An impressive 29 percent indicated that top executives are requiring this now, which is also consistent with ROI Institute data. This survey clearly shows that the need for ROI evaluation is here, and many organizations are stepping up to the challenge of showing the value of their programs up to the impact and ROI levels.

Figure 3-1 Today's ROI Reality

Is there an emphasis on ROI?	Response, %
Yes	88
No	12

N = 232

Figure 3-2 Drivers for ROI Evaluation

Drivers for ROI evaluation	Response, %
Top executive requirement	29
The costs of the program	62
Increased pressures for cost and efficiencies	81
Competitive pressures for funding	48
Lack of success in previous efforts to show the value	38
Client requires it	14

$N = 204$

Types of Data for the ROI Methodology

At the heart of the ROI Methodology is the variety of data collected throughout the process and reported at different intervals. Some of the data are assigned a level because they reflect a successive effect in which one type of data affects the next.

The concept of levels is an age-old one. There are very logical steps of succession in any particular project or program. Their use in a sequence can be traced back a few centuries. For example, John Quincy Adams wrote, "If your actions inspire others to dream more, learn more, do more, and become more, you are a leader." This quote easily breaks into logical steps and levels of outcomes, as shown in Figure 3-3.

The good news is that the ROI Methodology works extremely well in all types of environments and programs, particularly in leadership development. A program would likely be unsuccessful if an adverse reaction occurred, so the first level is critical. Also, participants must learn what to do to make a program successful; thus, an element of learning is required in programs. Regardless of the type of initiative involved, those participating usually acquire knowledge and skills. Of course, some programs require significant skill development. However, learning does not guarantee success. Follow-up is needed to ensure that participants use the knowledge and skills appropriately. Application and implementation are critical for success; failure in these areas is typically what causes a program to fail. Participants simply do not do what is expected of them.

Figure 3-3   Early Description of the Steps and Levels of Evaluation

	Steps	Levels
1.	Dream more.	Reaction
		⇩
2.	Learn more.	Learning
		⇩
3.	Do more.	Application
		⇩
4.	Become more.	Impact

The most important data set for those who fund programs is the impact, the consequence of application, often expressed in business terms as output, quality, costs, and time. For some executives, showing the impact of a program isn't enough. They want to know something else, which pushes evaluation to the ultimate level of accountability: return on investment. The return on investment is the amount of the improvement at the impact level (attributed to the program), converted to money and compared to the cost of the program.

Table 3-2 describes seven types of data that can be used to measure the complete success of LD programs. As the evaluation moves to the higher levels, the value ascribed to the data by the client increases. However, the degree of effort and cost of capturing the data for the higher levels of evaluation generally increase as well. With proper program planning and design, costs can be minimized. The following sections describe the various qualitative and quantitative measures listed in Table 3-2 and are basic to the ROI Methodology.

Program Cost Data

This type of data reveals the cost of the LD program, representing a fully loaded cost profile. It reflects all direct costs (e.g., program materials) and indirect costs (e.g., participant time in the program).

Table 3-2 Types and Levels of Evaluation Data for Leadership Development Programs

Level/Type	Measurement Focus
Costs	Measure the fully-loaded costs of the program
1. Reaction	Measures the participant's reaction to the program and captures planned actions, if appropriate
2. Learning	Measures changes in knowledge and skills related to the program
3. Application/implementation	Measures changes in behavior or actions as the program is applied, implemented, and/or utilized
4. Business impact	Measures changes in business impact variables
5. Return on investment (ROI)	Compares monetary benefits to the costs of the program
Intangible data	Impact measures that are not converted to monetary values

Reaction Data

The first category of outcome data collected from a program is basic reaction data (Level 1 evaluation). This type of data represents an immediate reaction to the program from a variety of key stakeholders, particularly those charged with the responsibility to make it work. At this level, a variety of basic satisfaction and reaction measures are taken, often representing five to fifteen separate measures to gain insight into the value, importance, relevance, and usefulness of the program.

Learning Data

As participants become involved in a program, they must acquire information, absorb new knowledge, and learn new skills. In some cases, as they learn skills, they must gain confidence in using those skills in the workplace. This level of measurement (Level 2) focuses on the changes in knowledge and skill acquisition and details what participants have learned to make the program successful. Some solutions have a high learning component, such as those involved in comprehensive long-term development. Others may have a low learning component, such as brief virtual modules.

Application and Implementation Data

Application and implementation are key measures that show the extent to which participants have changed their behavior or implemented the LD program (Level 3). This type of data reflects how participants take actions, make adjustments, apply new skills, change habits, implement specific steps, and initiate processes as a result of the program.

This is one of the most powerful categories of data because it uncovers not only the extent to which the program is implemented but also the reasons for lack of success. At this level, barriers and enablers to application and implementation are detailed, and a complete profile of success at the various steps of implementation is provided.

Business Impact Data

Behavior change or actions taken in application and implementation have a consequence. This consequence can be described in one or more measures representing an impact on the leader's own work environment, as an impact directly on his or her team, or as an impact in other parts of the organization.

This level of data (Level 4) reflects the specific business impact and may include measures such as output, quality, costs, time, job satisfaction, and customer satisfaction that have been influenced by the application and implementation of the program. A direct link between business impact and the program must be established for the program to drive business value. At this level of analysis, a technique must be used to isolate the effects of the program from other influences that may be driving the same measure. Answering the following question is imperative: "How do you know it was the leadership development program that caused the improvement and not something else?"

Return on Investment Data

This level of measure compares the monetary value of the business impact measures to the actual cost of the program. It is the ultimate level of accountability and represents the financial impact directly linked with the program, expressed as a benefit/cost ratio (BCR) or return on investment percentage. This measure is the fifth level of evaluation (Level 5). It requires a step to convert the business impact, linked to the program, to monetary value and get the benefits stream.

Intangible Data

Intangible data consist of measures that are not converted to monetary value. In some cases, however, converting certain measures to monetary values simply is not credible with a reasonable amount of resources. In these situations, data are listed as intangibles, but only if they are linked to the program.

Figure 3-4 shows five of the seven types of data arranged as levels in a chain of impact that is necessary if the program is to drive business value. Reaction leads to learning, which leads to application, which leads to business impact, and ultimately to return on investment. At the business impact level, the effects of the program must be isolated from other influences. Also, business impact data must be converted to monetary value and compared to the cost of the program to develop the return on investment. All stakeholders should understand this chain of impact. It is a novel yet pragmatic way to show the consequences of leadership programs.

An Example

The following example helps explain how the chain of impact works by describing the different types of data and their importance. Table 3-3 shows data collected from an evaluation of a leadership program for 25 first-level managers. This example represents a typical program at this level, a four-day

Figure 3-4   Chain of Impact of a Leadership Development Program

Chain of Impact

Participants **react** favorably to the program.

⇩

Participants **learn** new skills and knowledge needed to implement the program.

⇩

Participants apply new skills or take actions to **implement** the program.

⇩

The consequences of application are captured as **business impact** measures.

⇩

A **return on investment** is calculated as program costs are compared to monetary benefits.

Table 3-3 Chain of Impact of a Leadership Development Program

First-Level Leadership Development

Type of data	Data collection method	Data source	Timing	Results
Reaction (Level 1)	Questionnaire	Participants (first-level managers)	At the end of the four-day program	4.3 out of 5 rating on relevance, importance, intent to use
Learning (Level 2)	Questionnaire	Participants	At the end of the four-day program	4.1 out of 5 rating on skill acquisition for all skills
Application and implementation (Level 3)	Questionnaire	Participants	Three months	4.2 on extent of use 4.1 on frequency of use 4.4 on success with use
Business impact (Level 4)	Action plan, two measures per participant	Participants (from records)	Four months	$278,000
Cost	Monitor records	Cost statements, staff	End of program	$121,500
ROI (Level 5)	—	—	—	129%
Intangibles	Questionnaire	Participants	Three months	Increased communications, job engagement, teamwork

schedule with significant skill building. Participants identify two business measures to improve using the skills with their teams. The table reflects how the data are developed through the chain of impact. At Level 4 (business impact), the results look very promising, with $278,000. At Level 5, the return on investment is 129 percent.

The ROI Methodology

The ROI model encompasses the seven types of data in a consistent and systematic way. Figure 3-5 shows the systematic approach for capturing data, processing and analyzing data, and reporting results.

As can be seen in the figure, the activities comprising the ROI Methodology are divided into four basic categories:

- Evaluation planning
- Data collection
- Data analysis
- Reporting

The first step in planning is to develop objectives that reflect all the various types of data. Ideally, for major leadership programs, objectives should be set at each level and linked to baseline data, if available. The challenge is to push the objectives to higher levels beyond reaction and learning objectives to include application, impact, and even return on investment. Objectives provide the necessary focus for program designers and the direction needed for program organizers. In addition, objectives show the participants what specifically should be accomplished with the program. Higher levels of objectives also provide program sponsors with meaningful data needed to judge the feasibility and initial effectiveness of the program.

The second part of the planning process involves developing the planning documents. Three documents are recommended, although they can be combined into a single plan. The three documents include a data collection plan, an ROI analysis plan, and a communication and implementation plan. Additional detail on evaluation planning is presented in Chapter 4.

Data Collection

As Figure 3-5 reveals, data collection involves four different types of data that reflect the first four outcome levels of evaluation (see Table 3-3). Reaction

Figure 3-5 The ROI Process Model

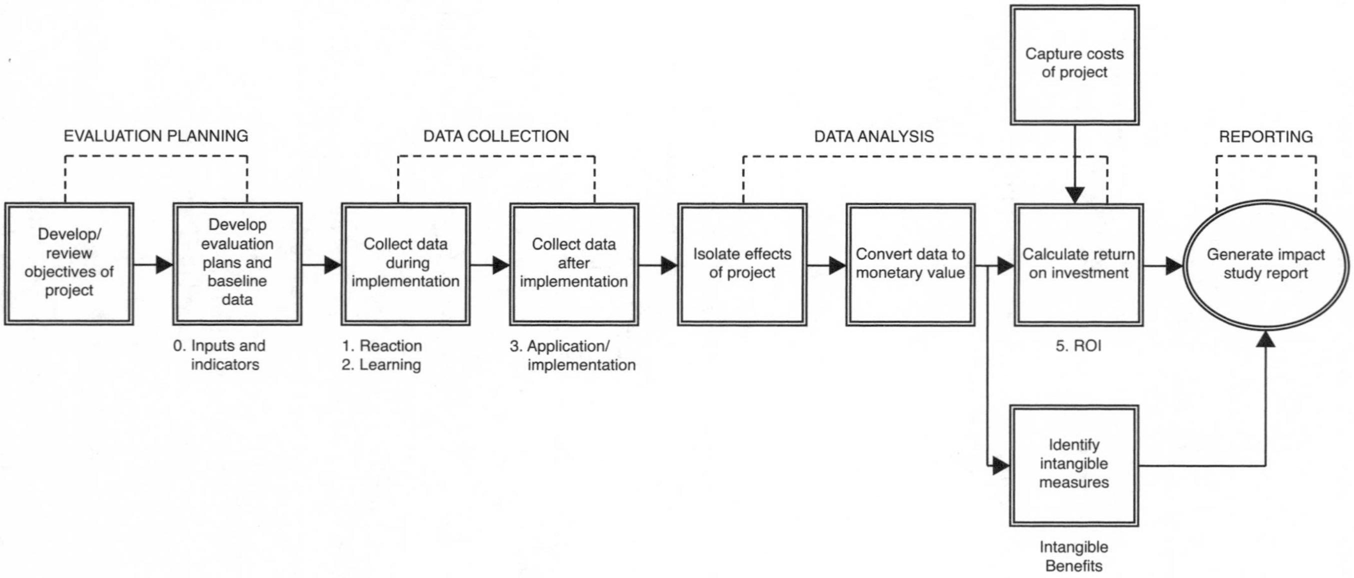

and learning data are collected during the early stages of implementation. After the program is executed, application, implementation, and business impact data are captured in a follow-up evaluation. Data collection methods used to capture the first four levels of data include questionnaires, observations, interviews, focus groups, action plans, and business performance monitoring. These common collection methods capture a variety of qualitative and quantitative data. Additional information on data collection is presented in Chapter 5.

Data Analysis

Analyzing the collected data requires isolating the effects of the program, converting the data to monetary values, tabulating program costs, calculating ROI, and identifying intangible measures. Each step is described briefly here.

Isolating the effects of the program. Although sometimes challenging, it is necessary to determine the business contribution of the LD program. Fortunately, there are many ways by which this can be accomplished. The typical methods used to isolate the effects from other factors include the use of control groups, time series analysis, and expert estimation. Some of these techniques are research focused, whereas others are more subjective but nonetheless valuable. These techniques are described in more detail in Chapter 6.

Converting data to monetary values. Another important challenge is converting business data to monetary value. If the actual return on investment is needed, either hard or soft data must be converted to monetary value. A variety of techniques are available to make this conversion, including standard values, which are almost always available, as well as records, expert input, external databases, and estimations.

For short-term programs, only the first year's benefits are used to represent one year of improvement. For long-term programs, longer time periods are used. The important challenge is to use the most conservative approach, even one that is more conservative than that used by the CFO. Chapter 7 offers more details on these issues.

Tabulating costs. Monitoring the cost of the program is essential and must be represented by a fully loaded cost profile. Fully loaded costs should represent both direct and indirect categories, including costs for analysis and development, implementation, time for participants to be involved in the program, and overhead. Cost data are developed using cost statements, cost guidelines, benchmark data, and estimations. More details on costs are included in Chapter 8.

Calculating return on investment. The return on investment may be calculated using either the benefit/cost ratio or the ROI formula. The benefit/cost ratio (BCR) is defined as the total monetary benefits for the period of time selected divided by the fully loaded costs of the program:

$$\text{Benefit/Cost Ratio (BCR)} = \frac{\text{Program Benefits}}{\text{Program Costs}}$$

The return on investment, although similar to the benefit/cost ratio, uses net benefits divided by costs. (The net benefits are the program benefits minus program costs.) In the formula form, the return on investment is:

$$\text{ROI (\%)} = \frac{\text{Program Benefits} - \text{Program Costs}}{\text{Program Costs}} \times 100$$

or

$$\text{ROI (\%)} = \frac{\text{Net Program Benefits}}{\text{Program Costs}} \times 100$$

This is the same basic formula used for evaluating capital investments where the return on investment is traditionally reported as earnings divided by investment. In the context of leadership development, earnings equate to net program benefits (in monetary benefits), and investment equates to the fully loaded program costs.

The benefit/cost ratio and the return on investment present the same general information but with slightly different perspectives. An example illustrates the use of these formulas. A program designed to reduce turnover of critical talent produced benefits of $732,000 at a cost of $314,000. Therefore, the benefit/cost ratio is:

$$\text{BCR} = \frac{\$732,000}{\$314,000} = 2.33 \text{ (or } 2.33{:}1)$$

As this calculation shows, for every $1 invested, $2.33 in benefits is returned. In this example, net benefits are $418,000. Thus, the return on investment is:

$$\text{ROI\%} = \frac{\$732{,}000 - \$314{,}000}{\$314{,}000} \times 100 = 133\%$$

This means each $1 invested in the program returns $1.33 in net benefits after recovering costs. The benefits are usually expressed as annual benefits for short-term programs, representing the amount saved or gained for a complete year after the program has been implemented. Although the benefits may continue after the first year, the impact usually diminishes and is omitted from calculations in short-term solutions. For long-term projects, the benefits are spread over several years. This conservative approach is used throughout the application of the ROI Methodology. Additional information on the ROI calculations is presented in Chapter 8.

Identifying intangible measures. Intangibles are measures directly linked to the program and developed at different time frames. Although intangible benefits are not converted to monetary value, they represent important data, often having as much perceived value as the tangible ROI calculation. Typical intangible data include measures such as job satisfaction, organizational commitment, job engagement, teamwork, reputation, image, brand, customer service, conflicts, and stress. This list is not meant to imply that these measures cannot be converted to monetary value. In most organizations, these items are not converted because the conversion cannot be accomplished credibly, with a reasonable amount of resources. Additional details on intangibles are presented in Chapter 9.

Reporting. The final step in the ROI Methodology involves reporting to the many stakeholders who need the data. The challenge at this step is to determine the appropriate target audience, the information needed, the communication media that fit the situation and the timing of presentation. Collectively, you must address these issues to have a systematic process for reporting data. Chapter 10 presents additional detail on reporting.

Return on Investment Standards

Every process or model must have operating standards to be reproducible, accurate, credible, and sustainable. The operating standards for this process show how data are developed, processed, utilized, and reported using very conservative principles. The conservative approach builds respect, credibility, and buy-in from the management group. The operating standards for the ROI Methodology are labeled "Guiding Principles," which support decision making and replication of the methodology. The 12 Guiding Principles of the ROI Methodology are:

1. **When a higher-level evaluation is conducted, data must be collected at lower levels.** A balanced data set is needed that represents all seven types of data and provides a complete profile of success using both qualitative and quantitative data. Some data represent lower levels of evaluation, while other data represent higher levels. Lower-level data are needed to understand the dynamics of the process and provide insight into problem areas and opportunities. For example, an adverse reaction at the first level can cause the program to fail from the beginning, but this will not be known unless an adequate amount of reaction data is collected. Also, many leadership development projects have a tendency to deteriorate during application and implementation. Collecting data at this level provides insight into the barriers and enablers so adjustments can be made.

2. **When an evaluation is planned for a higher level, the previous level of evaluation does not have to be comprehensive.** This resource-saving principle is designed to keep costs at a minimum. No organization has unlimited resources for funding measurement and evaluation projects. Shortcuts must be used, costs must be controlled, and steps must be taken to keep time commitments to a minimum. When shortcuts are taken, as a general rule, taking them at lower levels is best. The corollary to this principle is to use the most comprehensive analysis at the highest level of evaluation pursued. For example, when a program is evaluated at the application level, tracking the use of skills with a 360-degree feedback instrument, the method to measuring learning does not need to be very comprehensive. A self-assessment during or at the end of the program will usually suffice.

3. **When collecting and analyzing data, use only the most credible sources.** Credibility is a substantial concern with leadership development measurement and evaluation. When data are presented, credibility must be addressed to build respect and support for an impact study. One critical determinant of credibility is the source of the data. Sources must be identified that are most credible for the data needed, and this level of credibility can vary with studies and with groups.

4. **When analyzing data, choose the most conservative method among alternatives.** Some studies uncover more than one way to conduct a specific analysis. For example, when the effects of a program are being isolated, more than one method may be used. In these cases, the most conservative method (the one that generates the lowest ROI) is recommended. This principle assumes that both processes are equally credible. The net effect of this principle is to eliminate doubt and error by understating rather than overstating results.

5. **At least one method must be used to isolate the effects of the program.** This principle represents a critical challenge with leadership development. The amount of improvement in a specific data item related to the program must be isolated from other influences. Although a variety of techniques can measure isolation, at least one technique must always be used. Otherwise, the impact study is not credible because there is no direct linkage between the program and business impact. The default method for isolation is the use of estimates from individuals who know the process best. When all else fails, estimation may be the method used in the majority of settings.

6. **If no improvement data are available for a particular population or from a specific source, it must be assumed that little or no improvement has occurred.** Having no data equals having no improvement. This is perhaps the most conservative of the Guiding Principles. If participants do not respond to questionnaires, surveys, action plans, or other data collection methods, it is assumed that they have achieved no value from the program. Also, if participants are no longer in their job assignments or in the organization, it is assumed they did not achieve success with the program. Realistically, some value may have been developed by the nonrespondents, particularly if they are still on the job. When there is a departure, the employee may have been successful before he or she left the organization. This

principle exerts much pressure to obtain as much data as possible from credible sources, a factor that is at the heart of the implementation of the ROI Methodology.

7. **Estimates of improvement should be adjusted (discounted) for the potential error of the estimate.** Estimates will have some error, and the amount of error is addressed in the analysis. By using confidence estimates, an error range is created and the low side of the error range is used, thus discounting for any doubt or error associated with the estimate. This is accomplished with the use of a confidence estimate. This Guiding Principle builds credibility, because the results are understated instead of overstated.

8. **Extreme data items and unsupported claims should not be used in ROI calculations.** Occasionally, extreme data items (sometimes called "outliers") appear to be connected to the program or, in some cases, may be directly connected. Because they are extreme, they are omitted from the ROI analysis. It is important to protect the integrity of the ROI calculation and for key stakeholders to understand that the payoff is not generated on extreme values. Extreme data items are reported in other parts of an impact study but not in the ROI calculation. Unsupported claims are not used in the ROI analysis. For example, if participants do not show the source of data (when asked) or how they developed monetary value (when asked), the claim is omitted from the ROI calculation. It may, however, be included in the impact study in another section. These two issues in this Guiding Principle add credibility to the analysis.

9. **Only the first year of benefits (annual) should be used in the analysis of short-term programs and solutions.** Return on investment is an annual concept, so one year's worth of benefits is always needed. To be conservative, only the first year is used for short-term programs. *Term* is defined as the length of time it takes to implement the program with a particular participant. If conducting a new leadership development program takes five days for a participant, then it is a short-term program, and the return on investment should be developed based on one-year benefits from the time the impact occurs. However, a two-year continuous mentoring and coaching process is a long-term solution, and a longer analysis period is needed. The point is to be conservative by using a number of years that is fair and at the same time as short as possible. The number of years should

be established before the study is initiated and with input from the finance and accounting staff, if possible.

10. **Use fully loaded program costs for the ROI analysis.** Costs represent the denominator of the ROI calculation. Both direct and indirect costs should be included. Indirect costs are not normally included by some stakeholders. For example, the chief financial officer may argue that the use of meeting room space for meetings connected with a program implementation should not be charged because the meeting room is a fixed cost. However, a conservative approach is to account for all expenditures, even on an allocated or prorated basis. Including this cost in the analysis may not materially affect the ROI calculation, but it is an important gesture that may be necessary to gain additional respect for the methodology.

11. **Intangible benefits are measures that are purposely not converted to monetary values.** An important issue that can affect the ROI calculation and the credibility of an ROI study is converting data to monetary values. Some data are considered to be soft (or intangible) and cannot (or should not) be converted to monetary value. If the conversion cannot be made on a credible basis in the specific setting with a reasonable amount of resources, the data item is left as an intangible benefit. The primary issue surrounds the method used to make the conversion. Specific rules are developed to help evaluators decide when a measure should be converted to monetary value or when it should be left as an intangible. These rules make the process consistent.

12. **Communicate the results of the ROI analysis to all key stakeholders.** Communicating data to the appropriate audience groups is critical. The first step is to identify the key stakeholders and then ensure that these and other groups receive the desired information using the most effective medium at the right time with the appropriate content. Four key stakeholder groups should be included in the communications: (1) the participants charged with using the leadership program and reporting the data; (2) the immediate managers of the participants; (3) the key client or sponsor of the program; and (4) other members of the leadership development team.

These macro-level Guiding Principles ensure that the ROI Methodology is consistent, routine, and standardized. At the same time, they keep costs low and credibility high. They are essential for obtaining the appropriate buy-in and support needed for the methodology. The Guiding Principles are explained in more detail throughout the book.

Final Thoughts

This chapter began with the reasons for implementing the ROI Methodology. Next, the different types and levels of data were explained, which provide the framework for the ROI analysis. Step by step, the ROI Methodology was explored, showing how the seven types of data are generated, analyzed, and communicated. Finally, the Guiding Principles of ROI were described, showing how consistency and standardization are used to make the process realistic, replicable, and credible. The next chapter focuses on the planning and preparation needed to conduct an ROI study.

Business Alignment and Preparation for Return on Investment Analysis

PREPARING THE ORGANIZATION and the LD team for ROI measurement invites a few challenges. One of the early decisions is the appropriate level of evaluation for each program or project. While every program should be evaluated at some level, ROI analysis should be reserved for the most important LD programs. This chapter explores how to select programs for ROI analysis and the steps necessary to begin each ROI study.

When to Use Return on Investment Analysis

Every leadership program should be evaluated in some way, even if that involves only reaction data collected from participants. While reaction data alone may be sufficient for evaluating many LD programs, the challenge is to collect additional data at higher levels, when appropriate and feasible.

Appropriate evaluation is usually determined when the program is initiated, recognizing that the evaluation level may change throughout the life of the program. For example, a leadership program for nonsupervisory professionals can be evaluated with reaction (Level 1) and learning (Level 2) data. The objective at this point is to ensure that participants learn what they need to know to be successful and grow and have the appropriate impressions about being a leader. Later, a follow-up evaluation may be implemented to determine whether participants are using the information provided in the program and whether they are progressing appropriately based on what they have learned. This follow-up is an application/implementation evaluation (Level 3).

If the cost of this program increases and enrollments surge, some managers may question the value of the process and push the evaluation to higher levels. To carry out a Level 4 or 5 evaluation, a program redesign may be needed to connect it to business measures. The important point is that during the life of a particular program, the desired level of evaluation may change. Because of the resources required and the realistic barriers for ROI implementation, ROI analysis is used only for certain programs applying several criteria as outlined in the following pages.

Recommended Programs for Evaluation at Lower Levels

Reaction evaluation (Level 1) can suffice as the only level of evaluation for short programs, such as briefings, policy introductions, and general information distributed to participants. If reaction to the program is critical, ongoing assessment of reaction may be appropriate. For example, a leadership ethics briefing is measured at Level 1, capturing the extent to which participants perceive the program as fair, responsive, appropriate, and helpful.

Learning evaluation (Level 2) is appropriate when participants need to acquire specific knowledge or skills. With most LD programs, learning evaluation is important. For example, in leadership coaching, it is helpful to know whether the participant is learning from his or her coach. Learning evaluation is also important when participants must know critical policies such as diversity.

Application and implementation evaluation (Level 3) is necessary when participants must perform or behave in a particular way as a result of the program. For example, most leaders are required to deliver a certain level of new-leader behavior after completing an LD program. Evaluation at Level 3 may be necessary to measure success. Periodic observations from a variety of sources can ensure that they are using correct behavior on the job. Other methods are available to evaluate key programs at Level 3, which is essential to make certain that leaders are doing what they are supposed to do or reacting properly under particular circumstances.

Deciding which level of evaluation is appropriate is not only a test of the ideal but also a trade-off with resources available and the amount of disruption allowed in the organization. Because most data collection at this level may disrupt work or inconvenience participants in some way, the evaluation must be balanced with the time, effort, and resources that can be committed to the process. Most organizations fall short of the ideal evaluation and settle for a feasible approach within existing constraints.

Recommended Programs for Impact and Return on Investment Analysis

Programs taken to the levels of business impact and ROI analysis are special; it's important to understand the contributions they make to the organization. The criteria for selecting programs to evaluate with business impact and ROI data are described next.

1. **Expected life cycle of the program.** The first criterion is the length of time the program is in existence (life cycle). Some programs are one-time opportunities designed to react to a particular issue or tackle a particular problem in the organization. These programs are intended to be brief, and ROI analysis may not be necessary. For example, a program on ethics and integrity for leaders that is for all managers and executives may be a one-shot program. Evaluation at this level may not be necessary. Conversely, some programs seem to exist forever. For example, leadership development for new first-level managers will always be needed. Consequently, at some point in the life cycle of this program, conducting a comprehensive analysis may be helpful.

2. **Linkage to strategic initiatives or objectives.** Strategic programs are those designed to address specific strategic objectives. They're so important that they should be subjected to a high level of scrutiny. For example, a major pharmaceutical company devised a program to support a strategic goal that would transform the organization. The program became a candidate for ROI analysis because it was linked to this strategic initiative. Other programs may be operationally focused, adding significant impact to the organization's bottom line. For example, workout programs similar to those instituted at General Electric, where managers tackled particular issues and problems in a formal development effort, may be suitable candidates for ROI analysis. These programs are designed to add value and, consequently, should be subjected to ROI analysis to see whether they are adding appropriate value as intended.

3. **Cost of the program.** Expensive programs need a comprehensive level of analysis to ensure that they are adding appropriate value. The more expensive the program, the greater the need for ROI analysis.

For example, in a large Canadian commercial bank, an expensive LD program costing $100,000 per candidate was subjected to ROI analysis to show the actual value, using a sample of participants. The board of directors wanted this evaluation because of perceived excessive program costs. Of 450 executives who participated, the first 22 were targeted for ROI evaluation. The executives did not question the need for the program and the design; they were concerned about the costs.

4. **Time commitment.** Programs that involve much time are also candidates for business impact and ROI analysis. If participants must take significant time away from their jobs to attend meetings and learning sessions, it can be helpful to determine if the process is adding value. For example, at Allied Irish Bank, senior executives questioned the value of a 360-degree feedback process because it required so much of the managers' time. The managers complained about filling out the many forms, receiving feedback data, and attending training sessions and meetings to analyze and understand the process. This excessive time caused executives to question the value of the program and ultimately led to an ROI study.

5. **Visibility of the program.** Highly visible or controversial programs often generate a need for accountability at higher levels. For example, a large South African electric utility conducted a two-week program, the Leadership Challenge, each year for middle-level managers who were destined to be top executives. Extensive reporting and publicity made it high profile, highlighting the "chosen ones." Middle managers who were not selected for the program questioned the value of the high-profile program. They even considered it a waste of resources. The concern elevated the evaluation to the business impact and ROI levels.

6. **Management interest.** The extent of management interest is often the most critical issue in driving programs for impact and ROI analysis. Senior executives have concerns about some programs but not all of them. Based on feedback they receive or their own perceptions of the program, they want this level of accountability applied. For example, executives at a wireless technology company questioned the impact of a coaching program. These executives were concerned that the coaches were used improperly, amid reports that some managers delegated their "people issues" to the coaches. Senior executives wanted to know whether the program added business value to the company and therefore commissioned a detailed study.

7. **Client requirement.** Particularly since the global recession, funders of LD projects ask for their results. Today, more executives are concerned about every expenditure. For major and significant programs, they may require an ROI calculation. For example, a major European oil company required an impact study of an executive leadership program developed by a prestigious university on the west coast of the United States. The top executives said, "We must see results from this program because it takes a lot of time, commitment, energy, and resources." In another example, the executive vice president of sales and marketing wanted to see the value of a sales manager development program that consisted of a variety of managerial and leadership tools. This top executive wanted a proof of concept all the way to the ROI level to be convinced that this program would add value before it was implemented. These days, the clients are fully in charge of the evaluation requirement. They are now specifying evaluation early and often for major programs.

The good news is that there are only a few programs where these concerns exist. Even if the other criteria do not apply, it may be helpful or even necessary to elevate the evaluation to these levels to satisfy executive concerns. So-called soft programs that deal with leadership, motivation, empowerment, and communication are often scrutinized closely by executives who are not clear about the programs' value to the organization.

Table 4-1 lists programs often taken to these levels of analysis. Although this book focuses on leadership development, the ROI Methodology is used in all these areas. The table represents both impact and ROI analysis, but reviewing the distinction between the two levels is helpful. Sometimes the business impact of the program is desired without the subsequent ROI analysis. For example, a program designed to improve job satisfaction may be evaluated only at the business impact level. In that case, the direct link between the program and job satisfaction is established. The ROI Methodology requires monetary benefits of the program and compares them to the costs of the program. Because of the difficulty in converting job satisfaction data to monetary value credibly with minimal resources, the organizer may not wish to pursue ROI analysis in this example.

Programs Unsuitable for Return on Investment Analysis

To determine which programs are not suitable candidates for impact and ROI analysis, the criteria are essentially the opposite of those used to select

Table 4-1 Programs Suitable for Return on Investment or
Business Impact Analysis

Leadership development	Recruiting strategies
Career development	Talent retention
Competency systems	Safety and health
Organizational development	Self-directed teams
Orientation systems	Empowerment
Executive coaching	Flexible work systems
Management development	Skill-based compensation
Success sharing	Technology and systems
Employee relations	Process improvements
Diversity	Wellness/fitness
Recognition and rewards	Green

programs for higher levels of analysis. However, other factors help sort out those that should not be considered. In some cases, developing an ROI value could send an unintended negative signal. For example, consider a leadership program targeted to nonsupervisory female employees who have potential for leadership roles. The program would probably generate a negative return on investment, at least in the short term, because they are not yet in a supervisory role. Reporting a return on investment in monetary terms may give the impression that the organization is only pursuing this program because there is a monetary payoff, ignoring the fact that investment in female leadership development is needed. Therefore, LD organizers carefully consider the decision of whether to conduct a business impact evaluation or an ROI analysis.

Programs required by executive mandate are often not good candidates for ROI analysis. For example, a series of leadership tools such as leader guides, leadership tips, and action notes are sent to all leaders from top executives. These are reinforcing tools that are unlikely to generate a positive return on investment, making evaluation at this level frustrating or pointless. With limited resources for this level of analysis, the mandated programs are typically not subject to ROI evaluation unless senior executives want to pursue it for some reason.

Programs of short duration also are inappropriate for impact and ROI analysis. For a program to add value, a change in behavior or a significant action must take place. Short-duration programs do not typically drive this type of change. For example, a string of one-hour virtual LD modules will not usually drive a significant behavior change.

Leadership programs that involve only a small group of people are not necessarily good candidates for this analysis. The time and costs for the program may be insignificant to warrant a study. For example, a leadership retreat for managers in the legal department may not be a very good candidate for ROI evaluation.

Job-related programs may also be inappropriate candidates for ROI analysis. These programs include critical skills necessary for the job or programs covering basic leadership policies, practices, and procedures. These types of programs are necessary for job success, and their value rarely comes into question.

Finally, programs that are important to the value systems of the organization or those designed to make social and political statements are usually not good candidates for ROI analysis. For example, a program to help top executives become socially responsible leaders would not be an ideal project for ROI evaluation. These programs are in place for a variety of noneconomic reasons, and the actual payoff to the organization in the short term is often not an issue.

Selecting the First Project for Return on Investment Analysis

New to many organizations, ROI analysis can be extremely powerful; it requires skills that must be developed through trial and practice. With these factors in mind, a few requirements for first-time projects are often helpful. The first requirement is simplicity; it is helpful to tackle a very simple project for which the issues are few and the scope is narrow. This focus helps the LD team achieve early success and undertake ROI analysis for more complicated issues later.

Another issue is perception of the project in terms of current success. It is best to undertake projects that appear from current feedback to be successful. Leadership programs that are already considered to be successful help ensure that the first ROI study has a positive return on investment. Nothing is more discouraging than having the initial study generate a negative ROI, possibly deflating the enthusiasm of the LD team.

Avoiding programs that are controversial, political, or sensitive in nature is prudent. These programs often have hidden agendas and political issues that make success difficult. A study organizer may get caught in the crossfire between feuding executives. Although these programs can be addressed later with the process, excluding them in the early stages is wise.

Finally, LD practitioners should not take on a program that is a pet project of a senior executive. The program may have critics or supporters that can influence the data, conclusions, and recommendations.

Considering these additional criteria can help avert the frustration that may result from the first use of ROI analysis and build confidence in a methodology that can eventually be used to assess any type of program, in any setting and in any environment.

Initial Analysis: The Beginning Point of the Return on Investment Analysis

The basis for a leadership program adding value rests on the rationale for its existence and the extent to which it relates to a specific business need. This fundamental concept requires much more attention on the initial analysis that leads to the LD program or the continuation of the program. This is the beginning point in the ROI Methodology.

The Most Common Reason for Failure

As highlighted in Chapter 2, the authors have conducted an analysis of hundreds of impact studies involving virtually every type of program, including those in private and public sector organizations, revealing that the top reason for lack of success is the failure to align the program with business or organizational needs from the very beginning.

Although most leadership directors are confident in the analysis used to decide whether a program is needed, in many cases the process is not rigorous enough to make a real connection to the business need. If there is no business need in the initial rationale for the program, there is often little or no improvement in the business impact measures, which makes it impossible to achieve a positive return on investment. Thus, for most organizations a more comprehensive approach is necessary for the initial analysis leading to LD programs or at least an occasional analysis to see if the program is still necessary. Unfortunately, this initial analysis is often perceived as unnecessary and inappropriate.

The Analysis Dilemma

The up-front analysis of problems or issues leading to specific programs and solutions creates a dilemma for the organization. Analysis is often misplaced, misunderstood, and misrepresented. The process conjures up images of complex problems, confusing models, and a plethora of data involving complicated statistical techniques. Analysis is often not pursued to necessary detail for five reasons:

1. **Employee needs and problems appear to point to a solution.** When employee needs and problems are examined, several potential solutions are connected to those needs. The solutions, however, may be inappropriate. If managers are not treating their employees fairly, for example, a leadership program may not be the answer. Perhaps the managers know how to treat employees fairly and with respect but are not required or encouraged to do so. Consequently, training is not necessarily the appropriate solution.

2. **Solutions appear to be obvious.** Some solutions appear obvious when examining certain types of data. If the base pay of a particular group is lower than a competitor's pay for the same group, the obvious solution to an employee turnover problem is to increase base pay. Nevertheless, pay is not always the principal reason for departure. Leader development may be the solution. Low turnover rates can be achieved in organizations with lower-than-average salaries. The cause of the problems must be thoroughly analyzed to ensure that funds flow to the right solution, yielding a positive effect on the problem.

3. **Everyone has an opinion about the cause of problems.** Almost every executive who wrestles with problems has an opinion about their actual causes. Other stakeholders may have opinions as well. It is tempting to use the highest-ranking input (usually from the most senior manager) and move forward with a solution. Unfortunately, this practice often leads to allocating resources to an inappropriate solution.

4. **Analysis takes too much time.** Up-front analysis takes time and consumes resources; however, the consequences of no analysis can be more expensive. If solutions are implemented without determining the cause, time and resources may be wasted and results can be more damaging than doing nothing at all. If incorrect solutions are implemented, the consequences can be devastating. When planned properly and pursued professionally, an analysis can be completed within any organization's budget and time constraints. The key is to focus on the right tools for the situation.

5. **Analysis appears confusing.** Determining the causes of problems may appear to be complex and confusing. In reality, analysis need not

be very complicated. Simple, straightforward techniques can uncover the causes of many problems and achieve excellent results.

Alignment and Analysis Steps

For many LD programs, the first step in analysis is to examine the actual business need. Too often, programs are implemented based on behavioral issues or perception of a problem that may or may not be connected to a business need. Figure 4-1 shows a needs assessment process that begins with potential payoff and develops through preferences. Table 4-2 shows an example for a program, basic leadership skills for team leaders, in which participants focus on an absenteeism problem. The example shows the links of the levels between needs assessment, objectives, and evaluation.

Payoff Needs

The analysis begins with initial feasibility issues. The primary question here—whether the problem is worth solving or the opportunity is worth pursuing—addresses the ROI issue. Is a positive return on investment possible? Sometimes a problem cannot be solved, or the monetary value of the measure may not move enough to overcome the potential expense of the solution. This initial analysis may be brief but examines the overall viability of confronting the issue. In Table 4-2, the client is suggesting that unplanned absenteeism is causing disruptions and is very expensive. That conclusion is all that may be needed to move forward. Due to limited resources, a detailed analysis (and potential solutions) should be reserved for issues that really make a difference.

Figure 4-1 Levels of Needs Analysis

Levels	Needs assessment	Key question
5	Payoff needs ⇩	Is the problem worth solving?
4	Business needs ⇩	What business measures reflect the problem?
3	Performance needs ⇩	What should change in the work environment that will enhance the business measures?
2	Learning needs ⇩	What skills or knowledge must be developed to meet the performance need?
1	Preference needs	How should the solution be structured and perceived?

Table 4-2 Linking Needs Assessment with Evaluation

Level	Needs assessment	Program objectives	Evaluation	Level
5	Absenteeism is very expensive and disruptive	Achieve 25% ROI	Compare costs vs. benefits	5
4	An absenteeism problem exists (9% compared to 5% benchmark)	Weekly absenteeism rate will lower to 5% in six months	Monitor absenteeism data for six months	4
3	Discussions between team leader and team member are not occurring when there is an unplanned absence	Counseling discussions conducted in 95% of situations when an unexpected absence occurs	Follow-up questionnaire to participants will verify frequency of discussions in three months	3
2	Deficiency in counseling/ discussion skills	Counseling discussion skills will be acquired/ enhanced	Skill practice sessions during program will confirm skills	2
1	Team leader prefers the program to be brief, relevant, and useful	Program receives favorable rating of 4 out of 5 on duration, relevance, and usefulness	Reaction questionnaire at the end of the program	1

Business Needs

The next step of analysis is the connection to the business need. Is an actual business measure not performing as well as it should? The good news is all organizations have many business measures that either need to be addressed or that represent opportunities for improvement. Identifying the business measure(s) is an easy step in the process. Typical business measures include hard data categories of output, quality, costs, and time, as shown in Table 4-3, and soft data categories such as work climate, attitudes, customer service, and image, as shown in Table 4-4. The challenge is to connect the proposed LD program to a business measure. This is not very difficult. The next few pages explain the different approaches.

Table 4-3 Examples of Hard Data

Output	Time
Units produced	Downtime
Items assembled	Overtime
Tons manufactured	Supervisory time
Money collected	Time to proficiency
Students graduated	Learning time
Tasks completed	Lost-time days
Output per hour	Equipment downtime
Incentive bonus	On-time shipments
Completion rate	Time to project completion
Work backlog	Processing time
Sales	Cycle time
Forms processed	Meeting schedules
Loans approved	Repair time
Inventory turnover	Efficiency
Patients served	Work stoppages
Applications processed	Order response time
Productivity	Late reporting
Projects completed	
Shipments	
New accounts opened	

Costs	Quality
Budget variances	Scrap
Unit costs	Rejects
Cost by account	Error rates
Shelter costs	Dropout rates
Treatment costs	Time card corrections
Project cost savings	Agency fines
Variable costs	Rework
Fixed costs	Shortages
Overhead costs	Deviation from standard
Operating costs	Product failures
Number of cost reductions	Inventory adjustments
Accident costs	Percent of tasks completed properly
Sales expense	Accidents

Table 4-4 Examples of Soft Data

WORK HABITS

Tardiness

Visits to dispensary

Violations of safety rules

Communication breakdowns

Excessive breaks

WORK CLIMATE/SATISFACTION

Grievances

Discrimination charges

Employee complaints

Job satisfaction

Organization commitment

Employee engagement

Employee loyalty

Intent to leave

Stress

CUSTOMER SERVICE

Customer complaints

Customer satisfaction

Customer dissatisfaction

Customer impressions

Customer loyalty

Customer retention

Customer value

Lost customers

EMPLOYEE DEVELOPMENT/ADVANCEMENT

Promotions

Capability

Intellectual capital

Programs completed

Requests for transfer

Performance appraisal ratings

Readiness

Networking

(continued on next page)

Table 4-4 Examples of Soft Data *(continued)*

CREATIVITY/INNOVATION
Creativity
Innovation
New ideas
Suggestions
New products and services
Trademarks
Copyrights and patents
Process improvements
Partnerships
Alliances
IMAGE
Brand awareness
Reputation
Leadership
Social responsibility
Environmental friendliness
Social consciousness
Diversity
External awards

Performance Needs

One of the most difficult steps in the analysis is establishing performance needs in which the actual cause of the business need improvement is determined. At this level of analysis, the basic issue is to determine what is—or is not—occurring in the job context that is influencing the business measure.

This analysis focuses on the root of the problem or opportunity, detailing what must change to improve the business measure. This is the upfront linkage to the business measure and is the step that is often omitted or assumed. This step may involve traditional data collection methods such as questionnaires, surveys, interviews, and focus groups to uncover underlying linkage to business measure improvement. It can also encompass probing of analytical techniques such as brainstorming sessions, problem-solving tools, fishbone diagrams, and other techniques. This level of analysis may unveil other solutions. Many of the problems that appear to be related to manager learning and development may be associated with other issues, such as technology, environment, systems, and processes, which are beyond the influence and control of the LD team. The solution must be matched to the cause.

Learning Needs

The next level of analysis is the learning gap analysis, which focuses on what individuals need to know to correct the performance gap. Sometimes the learning gap is the actual solution; the primary cause of the performance gap is that the team leaders do not know how to do something. Even when other solutions prevail, the solution usually calls for a learning component. For example, if a reward system is implemented, the learning need involves knowing how to use the actual reward system and understanding the processes that make it work successfully. Learning is a minimal part of the actual solution to the performance gap. For leadership development, learning is an important and significant component.

Too often, organizations implement learning solutions even though they did not conduct previous analyses, and they assumed that a deficiency in learning caused the performance gap. This disconnect creates problems when resources are misappropriated and the problem is not addressed; the performance gap remains. In addition, a negative image of learning is created when it is not needed or is misapplied.

Preference Needs

The final level of analysis is the preference for the solution. In this analysis, participants and other key stakeholders define their preferences for the implementation of a particular LD solution. Preferences may include the stakeholders' perception of the solution in terms of relevance, importance, necessity, and value. They may also encompass the location, nature of the delivery, extent of the implementation, and who is involved. Because preferences sometimes shape the actual design and rollout of the solution, they should be addressed after the solutions are clearly defined.

These steps in the analysis are critical, but they should be applied sparingly. If a problem or opportunity is minor in scope, inexpensive, and not very visible, then it might be better to reduce the analysis to input at the lower levels only. The entire five levels should be reserved for those situations when projects are strategic or important to operational issues; the perceived cost of the solution is high; the expected solution is highly visible, perhaps controversial; and the accountability of the solution will attract management's interest. These are almost the identical criteria for considering programs for impact and ROI analysis.

Linkage to Evaluation

Figure 4-2 shows the linkages of the needs assessment or front-end analysis with evaluation levels. These linkages are critical because they often explain some of the important concepts and reveal many of the problems with dysfunctional processes. The objectives of programs represent a transition from the needs to evaluation at that same level. This parallel thinking along the levels is an excellent way to approach needs and programs. The analysis at the different levels leads to development of objectives at different levels that in turn drive evaluation data to be collected at different levels.

Connecting Leadership Development to Business Impact

Although the previous steps clearly show how to connect any type of solution to a business need, leadership development deserves some special attention.

Figure 4-2   The V Model for Connecting Needs Assessment with Evaluation

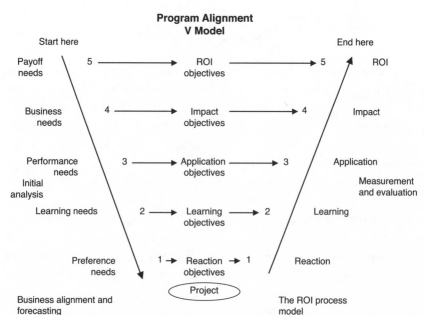

Many LD directors have a difficult time understanding how something as soft as LD can be connected to business measures. They often try desperately to make the connection after the program has been implemented, totally disregarding the up-front analysis necessary to connect it to business. When faced with this situation, they often say, "Well, how is this done?" Here are three basic approaches.

Linking Leadership Development to Classic Human Resources Measures

Perhaps one way to connect LD to business is to attempt to link it to one or more classic HR measures. Typically, these are:

- Talent retention (talent turnover)
- Job engagement
- Job satisfaction
- Employee complaints

The assumption is that if the skills and competencies of leaders are improved, then these measures should also improve. However, the difficulty arises when the LD program is offered to all leaders and these measures are essentially forced on them under the assumption that every leader has a problem with these measures. Unfortunately, that is not the situation with most LD programs.

While turnover may be an issue, it is not an issue in every area, and job satisfaction and job engagement can be very high in the organization yet leadership development is implemented. This approach should be taken only if one or more of these measures are a problem, and if the process described in the previous situation is followed, there is a connection between lack of leadership skills or competencies and that particular measure. Unfortunately, this is an approach taken in many ROI studies. It is very narrowly focused and often delivers disappointing results.

Connecting Learning and Development to an Operational Measure

Another approach is to use LD to improve an operational measure that is creating a problem. The concern is that this measure needs to improve, and leadership development is a solution. In this case, the analysis used would apply equally well when the business measure is fully identified. The next two steps (performance needs and learning needs) must clearly show that the measure is not where it needs to be because of leader behavior on the job and a lack of knowledge or skills about being an effective leader. In other words, the reason the measure is not where it should be is a lack of leadership actions and knowing about the leadership behavior. This approach is more narrowly focused and can be a proper option.

The difficulty is connecting a business performance measure to leadership behavior. Table 4-2 showed an example of this approach, where unplanned employee absenteeism was linked to a skill the first-level team leaders were not comfortable using. In that case, the leadership program is the right solution, because the team leaders were not comfortable with coaching and counseling discussions needed to improve unplanned absenteeism. Consequently, there is a way to link the leadership development to a business measure.

Connecting Leadership Development to One to Three Business Measures

Because most LD programs are developed for cross-functional implementation, the business issue becomes a little more confusing. Program participants can come from a variety of organizational functions, so they all have different business measures; thus, trying to connect the behavior to these different measures frequently seems confusing, at least to some. For example, a manager in a call center is attending a leadership program along with a manager from an accounting function, a manager from logistics, and a manager from operations. They all have different measures. An attempt to connect leadership development to all of their needs seems difficult—but maybe it isn't.

Cross-functional participation is common in LD programs. The approach is to connect the program to measures that matter to participants. In essence, participants identify one, two, or three measures that need to improve in their immediate work units. The measure could be a goal that must be achieved; a problem that must be solved; a key performance indicator that's necessary for a bonus, or an item on the scorecard that needs improvement. Whatever the situation, participants select two measures that matter to them (e.g., business needs). To connect these measures to the LD program, participants are asked to place two conditions on the selection of the measures. First, the measure must be within the control of the team. Improvements in the measure can be made by the team itself. Second, the measure can be improved using the proposed leadership skills or competencies offered in a program. Participants examine that program's objectives, the list of skills covered, the topics explored, the competencies offered, and other details about the proposed program. Then they make the decisions as to whether the measure can be improved by the team using these competencies.

Sometimes the connection is as simple as providing a particular example. If there's a quality issue in service delivery that is under the control of the team, then the participant would examine the competencies such as problem solving, goal setting, counseling, brainstorming, and other potential topics to see if those skills or competencies can be used to correct a problem. If the participant suggests that it can, then that becomes the business measure.

The next issue is to ensure that leaders/participants do not know these competencies now. In other words, if they already know the skills and competencies, then they should not participate in the program. When this is complete, the participant is essentially making these conclusions:

1. There is a clear business measure, maybe two or three.
2. There is something he or she is not doing with the group that could be accomplished using the skills and competencies in the proposed leadership program.

This approach lets the participant complete the needs assessment, which was described earlier. The processes will be the same, but the measures will be completely different. When this is suggested to a group of LD organizers, there is often a lot of resistance. The concern is that all of these business measures are different. For example, if each participant in a group of 25 in a proposed leadership program selects 2 measures, there could be as many as 50 different measures. This situation looks like an unmanageable nightmare for analysis, but it is manageable because ultimately improvements in a business measure can be converted to money. Although the 50 different measures cannot be combined in a meaningful way, if they are converted to money, they can clearly be totaled for a total monetary contribution. Techniques to accomplish this will be covered in Chapter 7. While this approach often creates a concern, it does have some very positive approaches. The first concern is the ability of participants to make this connection. In our experience, they can do this. After all, it's a measure that matters to them, and the program content is often generic, easy-to-understand leadership competencies.

The second concern is that of having too many measures. The number of measures is actually a plus for participants, as it provides the ultimate customization. Just imagine, a participant is planning to attend an LD program and has the opportunity to improve measures that matter to him or her. This is a very common approach for other programs, such as Six Sigma and Lean Six Sigma. For example, in a Lean Six Sigma program, a participant is asked to identify a particular project for improvement, and that project ultimately develops a monetary value. In the beginning of the process, the participants have the complete autonomy of selecting whatever project they need to improve. There isn't any restriction that everyone must tackle one particular measure. They have complete freedom to select any measure. This is what makes Lean Six Sigma work in those diverse applications. We are using the same process with a soft-skills approach (i.e., leadership development). An actual case study is presented next to show this initial alignment piece in action.

A Case Study

Profile

International Car Rental (ICR) (the actual name has been changed at the client's request) operates in 27 countries with 27,000 employees. The U.S. division has 13,000 employees and operates in most major cities. The auto rental business is very competitive, and several major companies have been forced into bankruptcy in the past few years. Customer service is critical in such a price-sensitive industry. Operating costs must be managed carefully to remain profitable. Senior executives are exploring ways to improve ICR; they perceive that developing leadership competencies for first-level managers would be an excellent way to achieve profitable growth and efficiency.

The Need

A recent needs assessment for all functional areas conducted by the learning and development (L&D) staff determined that several leadership competencies were needed for first-level managers. The needs included typical competencies such as problem solving, counseling, motivation, communication, goal setting, and feedback. Attempting to address the needs, the L&D staff developed a new program, the Leadership Challenge, designed for team leaders, supervisors, and managers responsible for those who actually do the work (i.e., the first level of management). Program participants may be located in rental offices, service centers, call centers, regional offices, and headquarters. Most functional areas are represented, such as operations, customer service, service and support, sales, administration, finance and accounting, and information technology (IT).

The L&D staff attempted to link the competencies to job performance needs and business needs. However, the senior management team did not want the L&D staff to visit all locations to discuss business needs and job performance issues. Senior executives were convinced that leadership skills were needed and that these skills would drive a variety of business measures when applied in the work units. The L&D team was challenged to identify the measures influenced by this particular program. Additionally, top executives were interested in knowing the impact and ROI for two groups of U.S. participants in this program.

This challenge created a dilemma. The L&D staff members realized that for a positive ROI to be generated, the program should be linked to the business needs. However, in reality they did not have the time, resources, or encouragement to conduct a more comprehensive analysis linking the need for the leadership development to business needs. They thought that perhaps the participants themselves could help with this task.

The Leadership Challenge involves four days of off-the-job learning with input from the immediate manager who serves as a coach for some of the learning processes. Before attending the program, participants must complete an online prework instrument and read a short book. Because few senior executives at ICR have challenged the L&D staff to show the business impact of this program, two groups were evaluated with 36 participants (i.e., 18 in each group).

Business Alignment

In order to link the program to business needs and job performance needs, prior to attending the program each manager was asked to identify at least two business measures in the work unit that represent an opportunity for improvement. The measure should come from operating reports, key performance indications, cost statements, or scorecards. The selected measures had to meet an additional three-part test:

1. Each measure should be a measure that matters to the manager.
2. Each measure has to be under the control of the team when improvements are to be considered.
3. Each measure has to have the potential to be influenced by team members with the manager using the competencies in the program.

A description of the program was provided in advance, including a list of objectives and skill sets.

While there was some concern about the thoroughness of the needs assessment, it appeared appropriate for the situation. The initial needs assessment on competencies uncovered a variety of deficiencies across all the functional units and provided the information necessary for job descriptions, assignments, and key areas of responsibility. Although very basic, the additional steps taken to connect the program to business impact were appropriate for a business needs analysis and a job performance needs analysis. Identification of two measures needing improvement is a simple business needs analysis for the work unit. Restricting the selected measures to only those that can be influenced by the team with the leader using the skills from the program essentially defines a job performance need. In essence, the individual leader is identifying something that is not currently being done in the work unit that could be done to enhance the business need. Although more refinement and detail would be preferred, the results of the assessment process should suffice for this project.

Objectives

The L&D staff developed the following objectives for the program:

1a. Participants will rate the program as relevant to their jobs.
1b. Participants will rate the program as important to their job success.
 2. Participants must demonstrate acceptable performance of each major competency.
 3. Participants will utilize the competencies with team members on a routine basis.
 4. Participants and team members will drive improvements in at least two business measures.

The Role of Objectives for Leadership Programs

The previous section presented the linkage between needs assessment and evaluation, with the objectives serving as a transition. At the higher levels, the objectives provide focus, guidance, and direction. Because objectives are a critical part of the process, they merit further exploration.

Developing Objectives

Ideally, objectives are developed directly from key issues identified in the initial analysis. The objectives are arranged in a hierarchy, often showing the chain of impact that should be developed after the program is implemented.

Reaction objectives are defined that clearly identify the important issues for acceptance of the leadership program. Measures such as usefulness, appropriateness, relevance, importance, and fairness are critical issues that can be explored directly in an objective. The goal is to have an acceptable level of agreement with a particular measure. A typical example of a reaction objective is "participants will perceive the leadership program to be important to their success." Table 4-5 provides more detail for developing reaction objectives.

Learning objectives are classic in their design. They focus on skills and knowledge that should be acquired as the LD program is launched. A learning objective often has a clearly defined statement with a criterion, possibly even with a condition. For example: "Demonstrate the four steps for active listening within five minutes of the conversation." Table 4-6 provides more detail for developing learning objectives.

Application objectives are developed much the same way as learning objectives are, but the context is positioned to the job. The application measure may go beyond typical behavior change and include tasks, steps, processes, and procedures that are either implemented or adjusted. Sometimes a specific criterion is used and the conditions are detailed. An example of an application objective is "participants will use at least three positive feedback skills every day." Table 4-7 provides more detail for developing application objectives.

Impact objectives are very measurable and often cover both hard and soft data categories. Hard data categories include output, quality, cost, and time. Soft data categories include issues such as employee satisfaction and customer satisfaction. The measure may be broad (e.g., "Increase sales or improve quality") or specific (e.g., "Decrease turnover of critical talent from 38 percent to 25 percent in six months"). The specificity depends on the situation. Table 4-8 provides more detail for developing impact objectives.

ROI objectives are developed when the analysis is conducted at level 5. The objective is stated as a desired or acceptable ROI percentage or a benefit/cost ratio (BCR). Additional information on establishing ROI objectives is presented in Chapter 8.

The Power of Higher-Level Objectives

Ideally, objectives are established directly from the up-front analysis. When application and impact objectives are developed, much of the design, development, and implementation of the leadership program can be influenced by the objectives. For program designers, these objectives provide guidance and direction as they develop various scenarios and support tools that will become

Table 4-5 Developing Reaction Objectives

Measuring Reaction and Planned Action

Reaction objectives are critical in this measurement chain because they:

- Describe expected immediate satisfaction with the program
- Describe issues that are important to the success of the program
- Provide basis for evaluating the beginning of the measurement chain of impact

The best reaction objectives:

- Identify issues that are important and measurable
- Are perception based, clearly worded, and specific
- Underscore the linkage between perception and the success of the program
- Represent a satisfaction index from key stakeholders
- Have the capability to predict program success

Key questions are:

- How relevant is this program?
- How important is this program?
- Are the facilitators effective?
- How appropriate is this program?
- Is this information new?
- Is this program rewarding?
- Will you implement this program?
- Will you use the concepts and advice?
- What would keep you from implementing objectives from this program?
- Would you recommend the program to others?

Examples of Level 1 objectives:

At the end of this program, participants should rate each of the following statements 4 out of 5 on a 5-point scale.

- The program content was important to my success.
- The program was motivational for me personally.
- The program content was relevant to my work.
- The program contained new information.
- The program represented an excellent use of my time.
- I will use the material from this program.

Table 4-6 Developing Learning Objectives

Measuring Knowledge and Skills Gained

Learning objectives are critical to measuring learning because they:

- Communicate expected skills and knowledge outcomes from the program
- Describe competent performance that should be delivered by the program
- Focus on what participants must know or do to make the program successful

The best learning objectives:

- Describe behaviors that are observable and measurable
- Are outcome based, clearly worded, and specific
- Specify what the participant must do as a result of the program
- Have three components:
  - Performance—what the participant will be able to do in the early stages of the program
  - Condition—circumstances under which the participant will perform the task
  - Criteria—degree or level of proficiency necessary to perform the desired task

These types of learning objectives are:

- Awareness—familiarity with terms, concepts, and processes
- Knowledge—general understanding of concepts, processes, etc.
- Performance—able to demonstrate the skill (at least at a basic level)

Examples of Level 2 objectives:

After completing the program, participants will be able to:

- Successfully complete the leadership simulation in 15 minutes
- Demonstrate the use of each skill in three minutes
- Use problem-solving skills, given a specific problem statement
- Identify the six features of the new ethics policy
- Explain the five categories for the value of diversity in a work group
- Document suggestions for award consideration
- Identify at least 9 out of the 10 leadership challenges
- Identify five trends explained at the conference
- Name the six pillars of the division's new strategy

Table 4-7 Developing Application Objectives

Application and Implementation

Application objectives are critical to measuring application of skills and knowledge because they:

• Give expected intermediate outcomes

• Describe performance in routine work settings connected to the program

The best application objectives:

• Identify behaviors that are observable and measurable

• Are outcome based, clearly worded, and specific

• Specify what the participant will change as a result of the program

• May have three components:

  – Performance—what the participant will change or accomplish at a specified follow-up time

  – Condition—circumstances under which the participant performed the task

  – Criteria—degree or level of proficiency under which the task was performed

Key questions:

• What new or improved knowledge will be applied on the job?

• What is the frequency of the skill application?

• What new tasks will be performed?

• What new steps will be implemented?

• What new action items will be implemented?

• What procedures will be implemented or changed?

• What new guidelines will be implemented or changed?

• What new processes will be implemented or changed?

Examples of Level 3 objectives:

When the program is implemented:

• The average 360-degree leadership assessment score will improve from 3.4 to 4.1 on a 5-point scale

• At least 99.1 percent of team leaders will be following the correct sequences for counseling employees who violate procedures

• Ninety-five percent of high-potential employees will complete all steps in their individual development plans within two years

• Sexual harassment activity will cease within three months after the zero-tolerance policy is implemented

• Eight percent of participants will use one or more of the three actions in the leading strategically module each week

• By November, all managers will communicate the transformational shift to all employees

Table 4-8 Developing and Measuring Business Impact Objectives

Measuring Business Impact
Impact objectives are critical to measuring business performance because they:
• Describe expected business outcomes
• Specify the business unit performance that should be improved by the program
• Provide a basis for measuring the consequences of the application of skills and knowledge
• Place an emphasis on achieving bottom-line results
The best impact objectives:
• Must contain measures that are linked to the program
• Describe measures that are easily collected
• Are results based, clearly worded, and specific
• Specify what the participants are to have accomplished in their work unit as a result of the program
Four types of impact objectives involving hard data are:
• Output
• Quality
• Cost
• Time
Common types of impact objectives involving soft data are:
• Customer satisfaction
• Work climate/job engagement
• Image/reputation
Examples of Level 4 objectives:
• The Metro Hospital employee engagement index should rise by 1 point during the next calendar year.
• After nine months, grievances should be reduced from three to no more than one per month at the Golden Eagle tire plant.
• The average turnover rate at Great Western Bank should decrease from 32% to 15% in one year.
• Tardiness for prison guards should decrease by 20% with the next calendar year.
• There should be an across-the-board reduction in overtime for front-of-house managers at Tasty Time restaurants in the third quarter of this year.
• Employee complaints should be reduced from an average of three per month to an average of one per month at Guarantee Insurance headquarters.
• By the end of the year, the average number of product defects should decrease from 214 per month to 153 per month at all Amalgamated Rubber extruding plants in the Midwest region.
• Teamwork at the United Food Agency should increase by the fourth quarter.

part of the program implementation. For facilitators involved in conducting programs, higher-level objectives give them direction so they can relate their own experience or motivation with the desired outcomes. For participants struggling to make the program work, the higher levels of objectives provide specific goals they often need to be successful. Application and impact objectives take the mystery out of the value the program will deliver. Finally, the individuals who sponsor or support programs often find higher-level objectives helpful and even essential in describing the impact. They provide more value than do traditional reaction and learning objectives. In some cases objectives are not clearly defined for a program, yet the program must be evaluated at the higher levels: impact and ROI. In these cases, objectives must be developed to reflect the actual or perceived impact of the program. This approach involves securing input from a variety of experts to clearly define the expected outcome of the program, recognizing all the consequences, both negative and positive.

Planning for Return on Investment Projects

Leadership professionals realize the importance of planning for almost any type of undertaking. Most agree that thorough planning can lead to more effective implementation. These are understatements when it comes to ROI analysis. Careful planning for ROI analysis not only saves time and effort but can also make a difference in the success or failure of the entire project. Planning involves three documents described in detail in this section:

1. Data collection plan
2. ROI analysis plan
3. Communication and implementation plan

Data Collection Plan

Figure 4-3 shows a completed data collection plan for an executive coaching program. This initial planning document builds on the revised program objectives and defines key issues for data collection. Defining the objectives through the different levels, including return on investment, is vital. The measures are defined, if clarification is needed. This column is particularly relevant for application and impact objectives. For example, a productivity measurement is vague, and therefore, defining it is necessary.

Figure 4-3 Data Collection Plan

DATA COLLECTION PLAN

Program: Coaching for Business Impact   Responsibility: _____   Date: _____

Level	Objective(s)	Measures/data	Data collection method	Data sources	Timing	Responsibilities
1	**REACTION/SATISFACTION** • Relevance to job • Importance to job success • Value-add • Coach's effectiveness • Recommendation to others	• 4 out of 5 on a 1 to 5 rating scale	• Questionnaire	• Executives	• Six months after engagement	• NHLO staff
2	**LEARNING** • Uncovering strengths and weaknesses • Translating feedback into action • Involving team members • Communicating effectively • Collaborating with colleagues • Improving personal effectiveness • Enhancing leadership skills	• 4 out of 5 on a 1 to 5 rating scale	• Questionnaire	• Executives • Coach	• Six months after engagement	• NHLO staff
3	**APPLICATION/ IMPLEMENTATION** • Compare and adjust action plan • Identify barriers and enablers • Show improvements in skills	• Checklist for action plan • 4 out of 5 on a 1 to 5 rating scale	• Action plan • Questionnaire	• Executives • Coach	• Six months after engagement	• NHLO staff
4	**BUSINESS IMPACT (3 of 5)** • Sales growth • Productivity/efficiency • Direct cost reduction • Retention of key staff members • Customer satisfaction	• Monthly revenue • Varies with location • Direct monetary savings • Voluntary turnover • Customer satisfaction index	• Action plan	• Executives	• Six months after engagement	• NHLO staff
5	**Return on investment** 25%	*Comments: Executives are committed to providing data. They fully understand all the data collection issues prior to engaging in the coaching assignment.*				

The data collection methods are detailed here to correspond to the different levels of objectives using a range of options described in the next chapter. Next, the data sources are identified. In many cases, data are collected from organizational records. In other cases, data are collected by program participants. In some cases, the managers of participants provide data.

Timing is important to determine specifically when data are collected from the different sources for each level. During implementation, data often come directly from participants involved in the solution implementation. In other situations the follow-up can be determined based on when the program is operational and successful.

Finally, the responsibilities are detailed, outlining specifically who will be involved in the data collection.

Return on Investment Analysis Plan

Figure 4-4 shows the completed ROI analysis plan for the same program described in Figure 4-3. This plan is connected to the previous plan through business impact data. The first column on this plan is the detailed definition of each impact data measure. The next two columns refer to each specific data item.

The second column defines the method for isolating the effects of the program on each data item, using one or more of the specific techniques available. The method of converting data to monetary values is listed in the third column, using one or more available techniques.

The next column defines the cost categories for the specific program or solution. Using a fully loaded cost profile, all the categories are detailed here. Completing this action during planning is helpful in determining if specific cost categories need to be monitored during the program implementation. The next column defines the intangible benefits that may be derived from this program. When listed here, the intangible benefits are only anticipated; they must be measured in some way to determine if they have been influenced by the program. Finally, the other influences or issues that may affect implementation are specified along with any additional comments.

Communication and Implementation Plan

The communication and implementation plan details how the results will be communicated to various groups. It also details the specific schedule of events and activities connected to the other planning documents. The targets for

Figure 4-4 Simple Return on Investment Analysis Plan

Program: __Coaching for Business Success__   Responsibility: _____   Date: _____

Data items (usually Level 4)	Methods for isolating the effects of the program	Methods of converting data to monetary values	Cost categories	Intangible benefits	Communication targets for final report	Other influences/ issues during application	Comments
Sales growth Productivity/ operational efficiency Direct cost reduction Retention of key staff members Customer satisfaction	Estimates from executive (Method is the same for all data)	• Standard value • Expert input • Executive estimate (Method is the same for all data items)	• Needs assessment • Coaching fees • Travel costs • Executive time • Administrative overhead • Communication expenses • Facilities • Evaluation	• Increased commitment • Reduced stress • Increased job satisfaction • Improved customer service • Enhanced recruiting image • Improved teamwork • Improved communication	• Executives • Senior executives • Sponsors • NHLO staff • Learning and development council • Prospective participants for CBI	A variety of other initiatives will influence the impact measure, including our Six Sigma process, service excellence program, and efforts to become a great place to work.	It is extremely important to secure commitment from executives to provide accurate data in a timely manner.

communication identify the specific groups that will receive the information. The plan should also include the method of communicating, the content of the communication, and the timing for the communication.

This plan defines the rationale for communicating with the group and anticipated payoffs, along with the individual responsibility for monitoring actions from the evaluation. It clearly delivers the information to the right groups to ensure that action occurs; in almost every impact study, there are significant actions that can be taken.

Resources and Responsibility for Planning

Typically, the person responsible for the impact study (usually someone on the HR team) is the one who completes the planning process. In smaller organizations, the leadership development organizer probably has the responsibility for planning. Planning may take an hour for a simple program evaluation or it may require a full day for more complex programs. Although this seems to be a significant time investment, it may be the best time spent for the entire project.

Consider planning for ROI analysis early in the process. For programs that are already in operation, planning shows what is involved for collecting, analyzing, and reporting data. For a program that is not yet developed, planning can actually define what would occur in an ideal situation and then drive design and implementation as the program focuses on results.

Final Thoughts

This chapter explored a variety of issues involved in the preparations for ROI analysis. It described in detail when and how ROI analysis should be considered as a process improvement tool. The initial analysis—the beginning point of the ROI Methodology—was explored in terms of what must be accomplished or developed to have a successful ROI evaluation.

The initial needs assessment is important for impact and ROI evaluation. Five levels of needs were identified; all levels should be addressed for a program evaluation at the ROI level. Special attention was focused on how to connect leadership development to the business with an example.

Objectives are also critical to evaluation. This chapter covered how and when objectives are developed and offered several examples of them. Finally, the role of planning for an ROI project was presented, detailing all the key steps in the process and the actual planning documents. The next chapter addresses issues surrounding data collection.

5

Data Collection Issues

D ATA COLLECTION BEFORE, during, and after program im-plementation is the most time-consuming and potentially disruptive step of the ROI Methodology. This chapter defines the sources of data and timing of data collection; it also outlines useful and widely accepted approaches for collecting data.

Sources of Data

An array of possible data sources is available to provide input on the success of an LD program. Six general categories are described here.

Organizational Performance Records

Perhaps the most useful and credible data source for impact and ROI analysis are the records and reports of the organization. Whether individualized or group based, these records reflect performance in a work unit, department, division, region, or overall organization. Performance records include all types of measures. Collecting data from performance records is preferred for impact and ROI evaluation because these records usually reflect business impact data and are relatively easy to obtain. However, inconsistent and inaccurate record keeping may complicate the task of locating performance reports.

Program Participants

Perhaps the most widely used data source for an ROI analysis is participants in the LD program. Participants are frequently asked about reaction (Level 1), learning (Level 2), and how skills, knowledge, and procedures have been applied on the job (Level 3). Sometimes they are asked to explain the impact or consequence of those actions (Level 4). Participants are a rich source of evaluation data at the first four levels of outcome data.

Participants are credible because they are involved in the program and are expected to make it successful. Also, they know the most about other factors that may influence results. The challenge is to find an effective, efficient, and consistent way to capture data from this important source to minimize the time required to provide input.

Participants' Managers

Another important source of data is the individuals who directly supervise or manage program participants. Managers often have a vested interest in the evaluation process because they approve, support, or require the participants to become involved in the program in the first place. In many situations, they observe the participants as they attempt to make the program successful by applying their new learning.

Because of this, the managers are able to report on the successes linked to the program, as well as the difficulties and problems associated with application. Although manager input is usually best for application evaluation (Level 3), it is sometimes helpful for impact (Level 4) evaluation. The challenge is to make data collection convenient, efficient, and not disruptive.

Direct Reports

Because most LD programs involve supervisors, managers, and executives, their direct reports can be important sources of data. Direct reports can report perceived changes since the program was implemented. Input from direct reports is usually appropriate for application (Level 3) data. For example, in a 360-degree feedback program, comments from direct reports are perhaps the most credible source of data for changes in leadership behavior.

Team/Peer Group

Individuals who serve as team members or occupy peer-level positions in the organization are a source of data for some programs. Team/peer group members are usually a source of input for 360-degree feedback. In these situations, peer group members provide input on perceived changes since the program has been implemented. This source is appropriate when all team members participate in the program and, consequently, when they can report on the collective efforts of the group.

Internal/External Groups

In some situations, internal or external groups such as the LD team, program facilitators, coaches, mentors, expert observers, or external consultants may provide input on the success of the individuals when they learn and apply the skills and knowledge covered in the program. Sometimes expert observers or assessors may be used to measure learning. This source may be useful for on-the-job application (Level 3).

Timing for Data Collection

The timing of data collection can vary. When a follow-up evaluation is planned after the program, determining the best time for data collection is critical. The challenge is to analyze the nature and scope of the application and implementation and determine the earliest time that a trend or pattern will evolve. This occurs when the application of skills becomes routine and the implementation is progressing properly. When to collect data is a judgment call. Collecting data as early as possible is important so that potential adjustments can still be made. At the same time, evaluations must allow for behavior changes so that the application of skills can be observed and measured. Two factors will usually determine the routine use of skills: The complexity of the skill and the opportunity to use the skill. In programs spanning a considerable length of time for implementation, measures may be taken at three- to six-month intervals. This provides successive input on progress and clearly shows the extent of improvement, using effective measures at well-timed intervals.

The timing for impact data collection is based on the delay between application and the consequence (the impact). Subject-matter experts familiar with this situation will have to examine the content of the application and implementation and, when considering the context of the work environment, estimate how long it will take for the application to have an impact. In some situations, such as the use of new tools or procedures, the impact may immediately follow the application; in other processes, such as the use of complex leadership skills, the impact may be delayed for some time. For example, managers involved in an LD program to improve talent retention (essentially keeping critical talent from leaving) will have to learn to work more closely with the team, demonstrating increased caring for the group; assisting team members in achieving individual and professional goals; providing challenging assignments; and allowing team members to learn, grow, and develop. A mere change of behavior will not necessarily result in an immediate reduction in turnover of critical talent. There will be some lag between the new behavior and the corresponding increase in retention; however, the impact will usually occur in the time frame of one to six months in most LD programs. The key is to move as quickly as possible to collect the impact data as soon as it occurs.

Convenience and constraints also influence the timing of data collection. Perhaps the participants are conveniently meeting in a follow-up session or at a special event. These would be excellent opportunities to collect data. Sometimes constraints are placed on data collection. Sponsors or other executives are eager to have the data, and to make decisions about the program. So they move data collection to an earlier-than-ideal time. If it's too early, another, later data collection will be necessary.

Responsibilities for Data Collection

Measuring application and impact includes the responsibility and work of others. Because these measures occur after the program has been implemented, an important question may surface in terms of who is responsible for this follow-up. Many possibilities exist, from the LD team to the client staff, and perhaps even external, independent consultants. Sometimes in a large organization the local or division HR or LD team may be responsible for collecting the data. This matter should be addressed in the planning stage so no misunderstandings about the distribution of responsibilities occur. More importantly, those who are responsible must understand the nature and scope of their roles and what is needed to collect data.

Business Performance Monitoring

One of the more important methods of data collection is monitoring the organization's records. Performance data are available in every organization to report on impact measures such as outputs, quality, costs, time, job engagement, and customer satisfaction. In most organizations, performance data are available to measure the improvements from an LD program. If not, additional record-keeping systems must be developed for measurement and analysis. At this point, the question of economics arises. Is developing the record-keeping system necessary to evaluate the program economically? If the cost of developing and collecting the data is greater than the expected value for the data, then developing the systems to capture the data is meaningless.

Using Current Measures

The recommended approach is to use existing performance measures, if available. Performance measures should be reviewed to identify the items related to the proposed program objectives. Sometimes, an organization has several performance measures related to the same objective. For example, a new leadership program may be designed to increase productivity from the team, which could be measured in a variety of ways:

- Team output (products, services, projects, etc.)
- Individual output
- Output per unit of time
- Gross productivity (revenue per person)
- Time savings (when the saved time is used on other productive work)
- Fewer hours worked (with the same output)
- Few team members (with the same output)

Each of these measures, in its own way, gauges the efficiency or effectiveness of the team. All related measures should be reviewed to determine those most relevant to the LD program.

Occasionally, existing performance measures are integrated with other data, making it difficult to isolate them from unrelated data. When this occurs, all existing related measures should be extracted and retabulated to be compared appropriately in the evaluation. At times, conversion factors may be necessary. For example, the number of items produced per month (or services delivered) may be a routine performance measure for the department. In addition, the average cost for producing the item is also reported. Finally, the number of hours worked for the team is reported. However, with the evaluation of a program, the average cost per person is needed (labor cost). The three existing performance measures are used when converting data to average labor cost per item produced.

Developing New Measures

In some cases, data are unavailable to measure the effectiveness of a program. If economically feasible, the LD team must work with the participating organization to develop the measures. Possibly the quality division, the finance department, or the information technology section will be instrumental in helping determine if new measures are needed and, if so, how they will be collected. Typical questions to consider when creating new measures include the following:

- Which function will develop the measurement system?
- Who will input the data?
- Where will the data be captured?
- When and how will the data be reported?

In one example, a coaching program for new employees was implemented across an organization. Several measures were planned, including early turnover (the percentage of employees who left the company during the first six months of employment), which should be influenced by an improved coaching program. At the time of the program's inception, this measure was unavailable, but when the program was implemented, the organization began to collect early turnover figures for comparison.

Questionnaires and Surveys

The most common method of data collection is the questionnaire. Ranging from short reaction forms to detailed follow-up tools, questionnaires are used to obtain subjective information about participants, as well as objective data to measure business results for ROI analysis. With its versatility and popularity, the questionnaire is the preferred method for capturing the first four levels of data (i.e., reaction, learning, application, and business impact). Surveys represent a specific type of questionnaire to capture attitudes, beliefs, and opinions. The principles of survey construction and design are similar to questionnaire design. The development of both types of instruments is covered in this section.

Design Issues

In addition to the types of data sought, the types of questions asked distinguish surveys from questionnaires. Surveys can have yes or no responses if absolute agreement or disagreement is required. Alternatively, a response scale, or Likert scale, allows respondents to select from a range of response points (e.g., strongly disagree to strongly agree) on a survey. In contrast, a questionnaire may contain any or all of the following types of questions, including Likert scale-type questions:

- *An open-ended question* has an unlimited answer. The question is followed by ample blank space for the response.
- *A checklist* provides a list of items where respondents are asked to check those that apply in the situation.
- *A two-way question* has alternate responses (yes/no) or other possibilities.
- *A multiple-choice question* asks the respondent to select the one most applicable response.
- *A ranking scale* requires the respondent to rank a list of items.

Questionnaire design is a straightforward, logical process. There is nothing more confusing, frustrating, and potentially embarrassing than a poorly designed questionnaire. Table 5-1 shows the steps that help develop a valid, reliable, and effective instrument.

Questionnaire Content for Different Levels

The areas of feedback used on reaction questionnaires depend on the purpose of the evaluation. Some forms are simple, while others are detailed and require considerable time to complete. When a comprehensive evaluation is planned, where impact and ROI are being measured, the reaction questionnaire can be simple, asking only questions that provide pertinent information about a participant's perception of the program. However, when a reaction questionnaire is the only means of collecting evaluation data, then a more comprehensive list of questions is necessary.

Table 5-2 presents a list of the most common types of feedback solicited at this level. Objective questions covering each of the areas in the table can help ensure thorough feedback from participants. Most of the questions focus on content and not the experience. Content drives application and impact. This feedback can be useful in making adjustments to a program and assisting in predicting performance after the program, or both.

In most medium to large organizations with significant LD programs, reaction instruments are automated for scanning and reporting. Some organizations use direct input into a website to develop not only detailed reports but also databases, which allows feedback data to be compared to other programs.

Table 5-1 Questionnaire Design Steps

1. Determine the specific information needed for each objective, issue, or level.
2. Secure input for subject matter experts.
3. Involve management in the process, when appropriate and feasible.
4. Decide on the method for returning the questionnaire.
5. Select the type(s) of questions, keeping in mind the time needed for analysis.
6. Choose the first question carefully.
7. Group-related questions.
8. Begin with questions that all participants can respond to.
9. Present the questions in the order of the results chain of impact.
10. Place sensitive questions at the end of the questionnaire.
11. Develop the questions with clarity and simplicity in mind.
12. Draft the questionnaire, checking the flow and total length.
13. Check the reading level and match it to the audience.
14. Design for ease of tabulation and analysis.
15. Be consistent in the visual presentation of the questions.
16. Use color and contrast to help respondents recognize the components of the questionnaire.
17. Avoid clutter and complexity in the question.
18. Develop the revised questionnaire.
19. Test the questions with a small group of individuals knowledgeable about the target audience.
20. Keep responses anonymous or confidential.
21. Finalize the completed questionnaire, and prepare a data summary.
22. Use an existing user-friendly software tool, if feasible.

Collecting learning data with a questionnaire is also common. Most types of tests, whether formal or informal, are based on questionnaires. Simple questions to measure learning can be developed for the reaction questionnaire.

Possible areas to explore on a questionnaire, all aimed at measuring learning, are:

- Knowledge gain
- Skill enhancement
- Ability
- Capability
- Contacts

- Competence
- Awareness

Questions to gauge learning are developed using a format similar to the reaction part of the questionnaire. They measure the extent to which learning has taken place and usually are based on confidence and perception.

Questionnaires are also commonly used to collect postprogram application and impact data. Table 5-3 presents a list of questionnaire content possibilities for capturing these follow-up data. Reaction and learning data may also be captured in a follow-up questionnaire to compare to similar data gathered immediately after the conclusion of the program. Most follow-up issues, however, involve application and implementation (Level 3) and business impact (Level 4).

Testing

Testing can be important for measuring learning in LD program evaluations. Pre- and postprogram comparisons using tests are common. An improvement in test scores shows the change in skill, knowledge, or attitude attributed to the program. Performance testing, simulations, role-plays, and business games are used to measure the extent of knowledge or skill increase related to

Table 5-2 Typical Reaction/Satisfaction Questions

- Appropriateness: Was the program appropriate for the target group?
- Implementation: Was the method of implementation appropriate for the objectives?
- Coordinator: Was the program coordinator/administrator effective?
- Motivation: Are you motivated to apply the content of this program?
- Relevance: Was the program relevant to your needs? The organization's needs?
- Importance: How important is this program to your success?
- Logistics: Were the scheduling and organizing efficient?
- Potential barriers: What potential barriers exist for the implementation of the program?
- Planned implementation: Will you implement this program? How?
- Recommendations for others: What is the appropriate target group for this program?
- Overall evaluation: What is your overall rating of this program?

Table 5-3 Typical Content Areas for Postprogram Questionnaires

* Progress with objectives
* Use of program materials, guides, and technology
* Application of knowledge/skills
* Frequency of use of knowledge/skills
* Success with use of knowledge/skills
* Change in work or work habits
* Improvements/accomplishments
* Monetary impact of improvements
* Improvements linked to the program
* Confidence level of data supplied
* Perceived value of the investment
* Linkage with output measures
* Barriers to implementation
* Enablers to implementation
* Management support for implementation
* Other benefits
* Other possible solutions
* Target audience recommendations
* Suggestions for improvement

a program. Test design and development issues are similar to those presented in the previous section on questionnaires.

Interviews

Another helpful data collection method is the interview, although it is not used in evaluation as frequently as questionnaires. The LD team, the participant's immediate manager, or a third party usually conducts interviews. Interviews can secure data that are not available in performance records or are difficult to obtain through written responses or observations. Also, interviews can uncover success stories that can be useful in communicating evaluation results. Participants may be reluctant to describe their results in a questionnaire, but they may be willing to volunteer the information to a skillful interviewer who uses probing techniques. The interview process can uncover reaction, learning, and impact data, but it is primarily used with application data. A major disadvantage of the interview is that it is time-consuming and requires interviewer preparation to ensure that the process is consistent.

Interviews are categorized into two basic types: structured and unstructured. A structured interview is much like a questionnaire. The interviewer asks specific questions that allow the participant little room to deviate from the menu of expected responses. The structured interview offers several advantages over the questionnaire. For example, an interview can ensure that the questionnaire is completed and that the interviewer understands the responses supplied by the participant. The unstructured interview has built-in flexibility to allow the interviewer to probe for additional information. This type of interview uses a few general questions, which can lead to more detailed information as important data are uncovered. The interviewer must be skilled in the probing process. The design issues and steps for interviews are similar to those of the questionnaire. Preparing the interviewer, trying out the interview, providing clear instruction to the participant, and following a plan are all critical.

Focus Groups

An extension of the interview, focus groups are particularly helpful when in-depth feedback is needed for evaluating application (Level 3). The focus group involves a small group discussion conducted by an experienced facilitator. It solicits qualitative judgments on a planned topic or issue. Group members are all required to provide their input, as individual input builds on group input.

Focus groups have several advantages over questionnaires, surveys, tests, or interviews. The basic premise of using focus groups is that when quality judgments are subjective, several individual judgments are better than one. The group process, whereby participants stimulate ideas in others, is an effective method for generating qualitative data. Focus groups are less expensive than individual interviews and can be quickly planned and conducted. They should be small (8 to 12 individuals) and should portray a representative sample of the target population. Facilitators must have the appropriate expertise. The flexibility of this data collection method makes it possible to explore a program's unexpected outcomes or application.

Focus groups are particularly helpful when qualitative information is needed about the success of a program. For example, focus groups can be used in the following ways:

- To gauge the overall effectiveness of program application
- To identify the barriers and enablers to a successful implementation
- To isolate the impact of a program from other influences

Essentially, focus groups are helpful when evaluation information is needed but cannot be collected adequately with questionnaires, interviews, or quantitative methods. The focus group is an inexpensive and quick way to determine the strengths and weaknesses of HR programs. For a complete evaluation, focus group information should be combined with data from other instruments.

Observations

Another potentially useful data collection method is observation. The observer may be a member of the LD team, the participant's immediate manager, a member of a peer group, or an external party. The most common observer, and probably the most practical, is a member of the LD team.

Observation is often misused or misapplied to evaluation situations, leaving some people to abandon the process. Observations should be systematic, minimizing the observer's influence. Observers should be carefully selected, fully prepared, and knowledgeable about how to interpret and report what they see.

This method is useful for collecting data on leadership systems, compliance, employee training, and performance evaluation. For example, observation is used to provide 360-degree feedback as behavior changes are solicited from the direct reports, colleagues, internal customers, immediate managers, and perhaps self-input. This feedback is taken before participation in an LD program and a few weeks or months after the program is completed to observe changes.

For observation to work, it must be either invisible or unnoticeable. *Invisible* means that the person under observation is never aware that the observation is taking place, as in the case of a mystery shopper. *Unnoticeable* means that although the person under observation may know that the observation is taking place, he or she does not notice it because it occurs over a longer period of time or at random times, as in the case of a 360-degree feedback process.

Five methods of observation can be used, depending on the type of information needed and the context or use. The 360-degree feedback process is using the delayed report method of observation. Table 5-4 summarizes the methods.

Table 5-4 Observation Methods for Data Collection

Observation method	Description
Behavior checklist and coded behavior forms	A behavior checklist is used for recording the presence, absence, frequency, or duration of a participant's behavior as it occurs. Codes are used to abbreviate specific behaviors and steps.
Delayed report method	The observer does not use any forms or written materials during the observation and subsequently attempts to reconstruct what has been observed during the observation period.
Video recording	A video camera records behavior in every detail.
Audio monitoring	Conversations of participants, who are using specific skills as part of the HR program, are monitored.
Computer monitoring	The computer "observes" participants as they perform job tasks.

Use of Action Plans and Performance Contracts

For many LD programs, business data is readily available to the LD team. However, at times data won't be easily accessible to the program evaluator. Sometimes, data are maintained at the individual, work unit, or department level and may not be known to anyone outside that area. Tracking down those data sets may be too expensive and time-consuming. In these cases, other data collection methods, such as action plans and performance contracts, capture data sets and make them available for the evaluator.

Action plans capture application and implementation data; they can also be a useful tool for collecting business impact data. For business impact data, the action plan is more focused and credible than a questionnaire. The performance contract is essentially an action plan with a preprogram commitment. The basic design principles involved in developing and administering action plans are the same for collecting application business impact data. The following steps are recommended when an action plan is developed and implemented to capture business impact data and to convert the data to monetary values. The adjustments needed to convert action plans to performance contracts are described at the end of the section.

Set Goals and Targets

As shown in Figure 5-1, an action plan can be developed with a direct focus on business impact data. The plan presented in this figure requires participants to develop an overall objective for the plan, which is usually the primary objective of the program. In some cases, a program may have more than one objective, which requires additional action plans. In addition to the objective, the improvement measure is defined, along with the current and target levels of performance. This information requires that the participant anticipate the application of skills and set goals for specific performances that can be realized.

The action plan is completed during the program, often with input and assistance from a facilitator. The facilitator actually approves the plan, indicating that the action steps meet the requirements of being SMART: specific, motivating, achievable, realistic, and time-based. Each plan can be developed in a 30-minute time frame and often begins with action steps related to the

Figure 5-1 Sample Program Action Plan

Name _____ Facilitator signature _____ Follow-up date _____

Objective _____ Evaluation period _____ to _____

Improvement measure _____ Current performance _____ Target performance _____

Action Steps	Analysis
1. _____	A. What is the unit of measure? _____
2. _____	B. What is the value (cost) of one unit? $ _____
3. _____	C. How did you arrive at this value? _____
4. _____	
5. _____	D. How much did the measure change during the evaluation period? (monthly value) _____
6. _____	E. List the other factors that have influenced this change. _____
7. _____	F. What percent of this change was actually caused by this program? _____ %
Intangible Benefits:	G. What level of confidence do you place on the above information? (100% = Certainty and 0% = No Confidence) _____ %

Comments: _____

program. These action steps are Level 3 activities that detail application and implementation of program content. All these steps build support for and are linked to business impact measures.

Define the Unit of Measure

The next step is to define the actual unit of measure. In some cases, more than one measure may be used and will subsequently be contained in additional action plans. The unit of measure is necessary to break the process into the simplest steps so that its ultimate value can be determined. The unit may be output data, such as an additional unit manufactured or package delivered, one closed sale, or a 1 percent increase in market share. In terms of quality, the unit can be one reject, one error, or one defect. Time-based units are usually measured in minutes, hours, days, or weeks. Other units are specific to their particular type of data, such as one grievance, one complaint, one absence, or one fewer person on welfare. The point is to break down impact data into the simplest terms possible.

Place a Monetary Value on Each Improvement

During the program, participants are asked to locate, calculate, or estimate the monetary value for each improvement outlined in their plans. The unit value is determined using a variety of methods such as standard values, expert input, external databases, or estimates.

The process used in arriving at the value is described in the instructions for the action plan. When the actual improvement occurs, participants will use these values to capture the annual monetary benefits of the plan. In the worst-case scenario, participants are asked to calculate the value. When participant estimates are necessary, participants must show the basis of their calculations. Space for this information should be provided. The preferred actions are using standard values or having participants contact an expert. Also, the facilitator must be prepared to discuss this issue in the session. More information on converting data to money is included in Chapter 7.

Implement the Action Plan

Participants implement the action plan after the program is conducted. They follow action plan steps (Level 3), and generate the subsequent business impact improvements (Level 4). The results are forwarded to the evaluator.

Provide Specific Improvements

At the end of the specified follow-up period—usually three months, six months, nine months, or one year—participants indicate the specific improvements made, usually expressed as a daily, weekly, or monthly amount. This determines the actual amount of change that has been observed, measured, and recorded. Participants must understand the need for accuracy as data are recorded. In most cases, only the changes are recorded, as those amounts are needed to calculate the monetary values linked to the program. In other cases, before and after data may be recorded, which allows the evaluator to calculate the differences.

Isolate the Effects of the Program

Although the action plan is initiated because of the program, the actual improvements reported on the action plan may be influenced by other factors. Accordingly, the program should not be given full credit for all the improvement. For example, an action plan to implement leadership skills for department managers could only be given partial credit for a business improvement because other variables in the work unit might have influenced the impact measures. While several ways are available to isolate the effects of a program, participant estimation is usually most appropriate in the action planning process. Participants are asked to estimate the percentage of the improvement directly related to the program. This question can be asked on the action plan form or in a follow-up questionnaire, as sometimes it's beneficial to precede this question with a request to identify all the other factors that might have influenced the results. This allows participants to think through the relationships before allocating a portion to this program. Additional detail on methods to isolate the effects of programs is presented in Chapter 6.

Provide a Confidence Level for Estimates

Isolating the amount of the improvement directly related to the program is not a precise process. Because it is an estimate, an error adjustment is made. Participants are asked to indicate their levels of confidence in their estimates using a scale of 0 to 100 percent—where 0 percent means no confidence and 100 percent means the estimates represent absolute certainty. The confidence estimate serves as an error discount factor.

Collect Action Plans

An excellent response rate is essential, so several steps may be necessary to ensure that the action plans are completed and returned. Usually, participants will see the importance of the process and develop their plans during the program. Some organizations use follow-up reminders by mail or e-mail. Others call participants to check progress. Still others offer assistance in developing the final plan. These steps may require additional resources, which must be weighed against the importance of having more precise data. Specific ways to improve response rates were discussed in Chapter 6.

Summarize the Data and Calculate the Return on Investment

If developed properly, each action plan should have annualized monetary values associated with improvements. Also, each individual should have indicated the percentage of the improvement directly related to the program. Finally, participants should have provided a confidence estimate expressed as a percentage to reflect their uncertainty with the estimates and the subjective nature of some of the data they provided.

Because this process involves estimates, it may not appear to be accurate. Several adjustments during the analysis make the process credible and more accurate. These adjustments reflect the Guiding Principles of the ROI Methodology. The following adjustments are made:

Step 1. For those participants who do not provide data, the assumption is that they had no improvement to report. This is a very conservative approach.

Step 2. Each value is checked for realism, usability, and feasibility. Extreme values are discarded and omitted from the analysis.

Step 3. Because improvement is annualized, the assumption is that the program had no improvement after the first year (for short-term programs). Some add value in years 2 and 3. More on this issue can be found in Chapter 7.

Step 4. The new values are adjusted by the percentage of the improvement related directly to the program using multiplication. This isolates the effects of the program.

Step 5. The improvement from Step 4 is then adjusted using the confidence estimate, multiplying it by the confidence percentage. The confidence estimate is actually an error percentage suggested by the participants. The confidence estimate is multiplied by the amount of improvement connected to the program. For example, a participant indicating 80 percent confidence reflects a 20 percent error possibility (100 − 80 = 20). In a $10,000 estimate with an 80 percent confidence factor, the participant suggests that the value can be in the range of $8,000 to $12,000 (20 percent less to 20 percent more). To be conservative, the lower number, $8,000, is used. More information about this can be found in Chapter 6.

Step 6. The monetary values determined in the previous five steps are totaled to arrive at the final program benefit. Since these values are already annualized, the total of these benefits becomes the annual benefits for the program. This value is placed in the numerator of the ROI formula to calculate the return on investment.

Advantages of Action Plans

The action planning process has several inherent advantages as a useful way to collect business impact data. Most of the data are taken directly from participants and often have the credibility needed for the analysis. Also, much of the responsibility for the analysis and evaluation is shifted to participants as they address three of the most critical parts of the process. In effect, they collect data to show improvements, isolate the effects of the program, and convert data to monetary values. This enables the evaluation to be conducted with limited resources and shifts much of the responsibility to those who apply and implement the program.

Converting Action Plans to Performance Contracts

An action plan can easily be converted to a performance contract with minor adjustments. First, the improvement measure, with its current and target levels of performance, is negotiated with the participants' immediate manager. In essence, they agree on how much improvement will occur as a result of this program. Second, the facilitator and/or program leader agrees to this improvement. Third, both the manager and facilitator/program owner sign the document, along with the participants.

In essence, this becomes a three-way contract for performance improvement. Not only do participants have the content to drive improvement but they also will have the support of their immediate managers and the extra efforts and attention of the facilitator to meet the performance target. It is a powerful process that can drive tremendous results, and it is appropriate for LD programs where there is a need to achieve improvement. A word of caution: In some LD efforts, this process may be perceived as performance review and thus could be resisted by some participants. The logic goes this way: If participants do not achieve the target, the immediate manager is disappointed. The disappointment has come as a result of participation in an LD program; consequently, participants might resist these types of programs in the future.

When appropriate, performance contracts are recommended as a very powerful way to drive improvement. In studies where this method had been used, the ROIs are quite large, usually from 500 to 1,000 percent.

Improving the Response Rate for Data Collection

One of the greatest challenges in data collection is achieving an acceptable response rate or a certain level of participation. Requiring too much information may result in a suboptimal response rate. The challenge, therefore, is to tackle data collection design and administration to achieve maximum response rate. This is a critical issue when the primary data collection method hinges on participant input obtained through questionnaires, surveys, action plans, performance contracts, and focus groups.

The following actions may help boost response rates:

Provide advance communication. If appropriate and feasible, participants should receive advance communications about the requirement to provide data. This step minimizes some of the resistance to the process, provides an opportunity to explain in more detail the circumstances surrounding the evaluation, and positions the follow-up evaluation as an integral part of the program and not just an add-on activity.

Communicate the purpose. Participants should understand the reason for the data, and they should know who or what initiated a specific evaluation. They should also know if the evaluation is part of a systematic process or if it is a special request for this program.

Explain who will see the data. It is important for participants to know who will see the data and the results of the data collection. If the input is anonymous, the steps that will be taken to ensure anonymity should be communicated clearly to participants. Participants should know whether senior executives will see the combined results of the study.

Describe the data integration process. Participants should understand how the results will be combined with other data, if applicable. Participants' input may be only one of the data collection methods used. Participants should know how the data are weighted and integrated in the final report.

Keep the data collection as simple as possible. Although a simple instrument does not always provide the full scope of data necessary for an ROI analysis, a simplified approach should always be a goal. When questions are developed and the total scope of data collection is finalized, every effort should be made to keep it as simple and brief as possible. Only ask questions if you intend to act on the results.

Simplify the response process. Make it easy for the participants to respond. If appropriate, include a self-addressed, postage-paid envelope for mailed surveys and questionnaires. E-mail or online questionnaires are preferable in some settings, especially if the questionnaire is being administered at sites in different countries.

Use local manager support. Management involvement at the local level is critical to response rate success. Managers can help with data collection, make reference to data collection in staff meetings, follow up to see if input is provided, and show support for the process.

Let participants know their input is valued. If appropriate, participants should know that they are part of a carefully selected sample and that their input will be used to make decisions regarding a much larger target audience. This action often appeals to a sense of responsibility for participants to provide usable, accurate data for the instrument.

Consider incentives. At least three types of incentives can be used to boost response rates:

- **Offer an incentive in exchange for input.** For example, if participants return questionnaires or participate in interviews or focus groups, they will receive a small gift, such as a mouse pad or coffee mug. If identity is an issue, a neutral third party can provide the incentive.
- **An incentive can be provided to make participants feel guilty if they do not respond.** Examples of incentives are coupons attached

to the questionnaire or a pen enclosed in the envelope. Participants are asked to "take the coupon, buy a beverage, and fill out the instrument" or to "please use this pen to complete the instrument."

- **Obtain a quick response by providing a reward for early completion.** This approach is based on the assumption that quick responses improve response rates. If an individual puts off completing the instrument, the odds of finishing it diminish considerably. Those who complete and submit their responses first may receive a more expensive gift than others or they may be part of a drawing for an incentive. For example, in one study involving 75 participants, the first 25 instruments returned were placed in a drawing for a $500 credit card gift certificate. The next 25 were added to the first 25 for another drawing. After the first 50, there was no incentive. The longer a participant waited, the lower would be the odds for winning.

Have an executive sign the introductory letter. Participants are always interested in who sent the letter with the request. For maximum effectiveness, a senior executive (or top executive) who is responsible for a major area where the participants work should sign the letter.

Use follow-up reminders. A follow-up reminder should be sent a week after the first request, and another reminder should be sent one week after that. Depending on the instrument and the situation, these times could be adjusted. In some situations, a third follow-up message is recommended. Sometimes the follow-up should be sent via different media. For example, the questionnaire can be sent through regular mail, whereas the first follow-up reminder is from the immediate manager and a second follow-up reminder is sent by e-mail.

Send a copy of the results to participants. Even if it is an abbreviated form, participants should see the results of the study. More important, they should understand that they will receive a copy of the study when they are asked to provide the data. This promise often increases the response rate, as some individuals want to see the results of others along with their input.

Make participants know that action will be taken as a result of their responses. When participants provide data, they want some assurance that their information will be used in a productive manner. This assurance can be given by providing information on when actions will be taken as a result of their responses. Providing a particular date shows the significance of the data collection, and participants have a sense of knowing they can make a difference.

Review the questions and issues during the program. Seeing an advance copy of the actual data collection instrument helps participants understand the process. Ideally, the instrument should be distributed and reviewed during the session. Each question should be briefly discussed, and any issues or concerns about the questions should be clarified. Ideally, a commitment to provide data is secured from the participant not only to help the response rate but also to improve the quality and quantity of data.

Consider a captive audience. The best way to have an extremely high response rate is to use a captive audience. In a follow-up session, a routine meeting, or a session designed to collect data, participants meet and provide input, usually during the first few minutes of the meeting. Sometimes a routine meeting (such as a management meeting) can serve as a good setting to collect the data.

Communicate the timing of data flow. Participants should be given specific deadlines for providing the data. They also need to know when they will receive results. The best approach is to determine the last date when the instruments will be accepted, the date when the analysis will be complete, the date that they will receive the results of the study, the date the sponsor will receive the results, and the date that participants will receive a copy of the actions taken based on the feedback. A specific timeline builds respect for the entire process.

Select appropriate media. The medium for data collection (whether paper-based, face-to-face, web-based, or e-mail) should match the culture of the group and not necessarily be selected for the convenience of the evaluator. Sometimes an optional response medium is allowed. The important thing is to make the medium fit the audience.

Consider collecting anonymous input. For surveys and questionnaires, anonymous data are often more objective and sometimes given more freely than nonanonymous data. If participants believe that their input is anonymous, they are more likely to be constructive and candid in their feedback, and their response rates will generally be higher than others.

Keep data confidential. Confidentiality is an important part of the process. A confidentiality statement should be included, indicating that participants' names will not be revealed to anyone other than the data collectors and those involved in analyzing the data. In some cases, it may be appropriate to indicate specifically who will actually see the raw data. Detail the specific steps to be taken to ensure confidentiality. Respondents are told that individual results will not be released and that data will be combined for reporting so that no one person's responses can be singled out.

Conduct pilot testing. Consider using a pilot test on a sample of the target audience. This is one of the best ways to ensure that data collection is designed properly and that questions flow logically. Pilot testing the data collection process can be quick and effective with a small sample size. The findings of a pilot test can be very revealing.

Explain how long it will take to provide data. Although this appears to be a trivial issue, participants need to have a realistic understanding of how long it will take them to provide the data. There is nothing more frustrating to a participant than discovering that an instrument takes much longer to complete than what was estimated. The pilot test should be able to indicate how much time should be allocated for the response.

Personalize the process, if possible. Participants generally respond to personal messages and requests. If possible, the letter accompanying the data collection instrument should be personalized. Personal comments on a note can help. Also, if it is possible, a personal phone call is a helpful follow-up reminder. The personal touch brings appropriate sincerity and responsibility to the process.

Provide an update. In some cases it may be appropriate to provide an update on current response rate and the progress on the entire project. It is helpful for individuals to understand how others are doing. Sometimes this communication creates a subtle pressure and reminder to provide data.

Collectively, these items help boost response rates on follow-up data. Use of all of these strategies can yield a 60 percent to 80 percent response rate for surveys and questionnaires and 90 percent to 100 percent for action plans, performance contracts, and focus groups, even with lengthy processes that might take 45 to 60 minutes to complete.

Selecting an Appropriate Method

This chapter presented a variety of methods to capture postprogram data for an impact analysis. Several issues should be considered when deciding which method is appropriate for a given situation.

Table 5-5 Mehods of Collecting Data

Methods	Level 1	Level 2	Level 3	Level 4
Performance monitoring				✓
Questionnaires/surveys	✓	✓	✓	✓
Tests		✓		
Interviews			✓	
Focus groups			✓	
Observations		✓	✓	
Action plans			✓	✓
Performance contracts			✓	✓

Type of Data

Perhaps one of the most important issues to consider when selecting the method is the type of data to be collected. Some methods are more appropriate for impact, while others are better for application. Still others are more appropriate for reaction or learning evaluation.

Table 5-5 shows the most appropriate type of data for a specific method. Questionnaires and surveys are suited for all levels. Tests are appropriate for Level 2 (learning). Questionnaires and surveys are used at all levels. Interviews and focus groups can be used for Level 3, although they are often expensive. Performance monitoring, action plans, and performance contracts can easily capture Level 4 (business impact) data.

Participants' Time for Data Input

Another important factor when selecting the data collection method is the amount of time participants need to provide their input for data collection. Time requirements should be minimized, and the method should be positioned so that it is a value-added activity (i.e., the participants perceive the activity as valuable so they will not resist). This requirement often means that sampling is used to keep the total participant time to a reasonable amount. Some methods, such as business performance monitoring, require no participant time, whereas others, such as focus groups and interviews, require a significant time investment.

Management's Time for Data Input

The time that a participant's immediate manager must allocate to data collection is another important issue when selecting a data collection method.

Always strive to keep the managers' time requirements to a minimum. Some methods, such as focus groups, may require involvement from the manager prior to and after the program. Other methods, such as performance monitoring, may not require any manager time.

Cost of the Method

Cost is always a consideration when selecting a method. Some data collection methods are more expensive than others. For example, interviews and observations are expensive. Questionnaires and performance monitoring are usually inexpensive.

Disruption of Normal Work Activities

Another important issue is the amount of disruption the data collection will generate. Routine work processes should be disrupted as little as possible. Some data collection techniques, such as performance monitoring, require little time or distraction from normal activities. Questionnaires generally do not disrupt the work environment and can often be completed in only a few minutes or even after normal work hours. On the other extreme, techniques such as focus group and interviews may be too disruptive for the work unit.

Accuracy of Method

Accuracy is a factor to weigh when selecting a data collection method. *Accuracy* refers to the instrument's ability to correctly capture the data desired, with minimum error. Some data collection methods are more accurate than others. For example, performance monitoring usually is highly accurate, whereas a questionnaire is less accurate. If you need data regarding on-the-job behavior, unobtrusive observation is clearly one of the most accurate processes.

Utility of an Additional Method

Because there are many different methods for collecting data, it is tempting to use too many data collection methods. Using multiple data collection methods adds time and cost to the evaluation and may add little value. Utility refers to the added value of using an additional data collection method. When more than one method is used, the question of utility should always be addressed. Does the value obtained from the additional data warrant the extra time and expense of the method? If the answer is no, the additional method should not be implemented.

Cultural Bias for Data Collection Method

The culture or philosophy of the organization can dictate which data collection methods are used. For example, some organizations are accustomed to using questionnaires and prefer to use them in their culture. Other organizations do not use observation because their culture does not support the potential invasion of privacy associated with it.

Final Thoughts

This chapter has provided an overview of data collection methods that can be used in ROI analysis. Study organizers and evaluators can select from many methods according to their budgets and situations. Follow-up questionnaires and surveys are commonly used to collect data for application and impact analyses. Since action plans (and with modification, performance contracts) are very effective in LD evaluation, design and administration issues have been explored. Other methods can help develop a complete profile of success of the LD program and its subsequent business impact. A full array of techniques to obtain an impressive response has been presented, along with tips on selecting the proper data collection method. The next chapter addresses the very important issue of isolating the effects of the program on the data collected.

6

Isolating the Effects of the Program: Tackling the Attribution Issue

IN ALMOST EVERY program, multiple influences drive the business measures. With multiple influences, measuring the effect of the LD program on the business measure is imperative. Without this isolation step, program success will come into question. The results will be overstated if it is suggested that all the change in the business impact measure is attributed to the program. When this issue is ignored, the impact study is considered inconclusive. Evaluators, therefore, face tremendous pressure to show the actual value of their programs when compared to other factors. To emphasize the importance of this issue, a few facts need to be explored.

The Importance of This Issue

Isolating the effects of leadership development on business improvement is the most critical issue for credibility. Sometimes labeled "attribution analysis" or "contribution analysis," this step is a must. Here's why:

1. **Other factors are always present.** In almost every situation, multiple factors create business results. The world does not stand still while LD programs are being implemented. Many other functions, processes, or projects attempt to improve the same metrics that are influenced by the program in question. A situation where no other factors enter

into the process would be almost impossible in today's dynamic work environments.

2. **Proof of business linkage requires isolation of the program effects.** Without taking steps to show the contribution, the business measure change is the only evidence that the program has made a difference. While impact measures have improved, other factors may have influenced the data. The proof that the program has made a difference for the business comes from this step in the analysis: isolating the effects of the program.

3. **Other factors and influences have protective owners.** The owners of other functions, projects, and programs that influence business results are convinced that their processes have made the difference. Perhaps they think the results are *entirely* due to their efforts. They sometimes present a compelling case to management, stressing their achievements.

4. **Achieving isolation requires discipline.** The challenge of isolating the effects of the program on impact data can be met, although it is not always easy for very complex programs, especially when strong-willed owners of other processes are involved. Determination is needed to address this situation every time an impact study is conducted. Fortunately, a variety of approaches is available.

5. **Without the isolation of the effects of leadership development on business improvement, the study is not accurate.** Without addressing this issue, a study is not accurate because other factors are almost always in the mix, and the direct connection to leadership is often not apparent. In every study, three things should never be done:

   - Taking all the credit for the improvement without tackling the issue
   - Doing nothing and attempting to ignore the issue altogether
   - Suggesting that this step is impossible

Any of these things will lower the credibility of the study. The cause-and-effect relationship between a leadership program and performance can be confusing and difficult to prove, but it can be shown with an acceptable degree of accuracy. The challenge is to develop one or more specific techniques to isolate the effects of the LD program, usually as part of an evaluation plan conducted before the program begins. Up-front attention ensures that appropriate techniques will be used with minimum costs and time commitments.

Chain of Impact: The Initial Evidence

Before the techniques for isolating leadership's impact are presented, it is helpful to examine the chain of impact implied in the various levels of evaluation. As illustrated in Figure 6-1, the chain of impact must be in place for the program to drive business results.

Measurable business impact achieved through a program should be derived from the application of skills and knowledge over a specified period of time after a program has been conducted. Successful application of the program should stem from the participants' learning of new skills or acquiring new knowledge in the program so they know what, how, and why to do something differently.

Without the preliminary evidence of the chain of impact, isolation is difficult. Without learning or application, LD directors cannot conclude that the program caused any business impact improvements. Furthermore, if the program is not viewed as relevant or important, participants are unlikely to make an effort to learn and apply the knowledge or skills.

Developing this chain of impact requires data collection at four levels for an ROI calculation. If business impact data are collected, data should be

Figure 6-1 The Chain of Impact

Level 1	Participants react to the program.
	⇩
Level 2	Participants obtain skills/knowledge needed to implement the program.
	⇩
Level 3	Participants apply skills/knowledge and implement the program.
	⇩
Level 4	The consequences of application are reflected in changes in business measures.
	Isolate the effects of the program.
	⇩
Level 5	Return on investment is calculated.

collected for the other levels of evaluation to ensure that the program has produced the business results.

Identifying Other Factors: A First Step

As a first step in isolating leadership development's impact on business performance, all key factors that may have contributed to performance improvement should be identified. Consequently, the credit for improvement is shared with several possible sources—an approach that is likely to gain the respect of the client. Several potential sources are available to identify influencing variables:

1. If the program is implemented at the request of a sponsor, the sponsor may be able to identify other initiatives or factors that might influence the impact measure.

2. Program participants are usually aware of other influences that may have caused performance improvement. After all, with this level of evaluation, the impact of their collective efforts is being monitored and measured. In many situations, they have witnessed previous movements in the performance measures and can pinpoint reasons for changes.

3. The LD program implementation team is another source for identifying variables that impact results. Although the needs analysis will sometimes uncover these influencing factors, designers, developers, and facilitators may be able to identify the other factors as they implement the program.

4. In some situations, the immediate managers of participants may identify variables that influence the business impact measure. This is particularly useful when participants are nonsupervisory employees (e.g., in a professional leadership program) who may not be fully aware of the other factors.

5. Subject-matter experts may identify other factors. These experts often analyze the need for the program, help design a specific solution, and provide specifications for implementation. They are knowledgeable about these issues, and their expertise may help identify the other factors that could affect the program.

6. Other process owners may be able to provide input. For most situations, other processes are adding value to business measures. Could it be technology, restructuring, job design, new processes, quality initiatives, marketing, reengineering, transformation, or change manage-

ment? These are all likely processes inside an organization, and the owners of these processes will know whether their processes are in place or have been implemented during this same time period.

7. Finally, in the area where the program is implemented, middle and top managers may be able to identify other influences. Perhaps they have monitored, examined, and analyzed the variables previously. The authority of these individuals often increases the data's credibility.

Taking the time to focus on these additional factors and variables brings additional accuracy and credibility to the process. This step moves the study beyond presenting results with no mention of other influences—a situation that often destroys credibility. It also provides a foundation for some of the techniques described in this book by identifying the variables that must be isolated to show the effects of a program.

Use of Control Groups

The most accurate approach for isolating the impact of a program is the use of control groups in an experimental design process. This approach involves the comparison of an experimental group of people participating in a program with a control group that is not. The composition of both groups should be as identical as possible and, if feasible, participants for each group should be selected randomly. When this is achieved and both groups are subjected to the same environmental influences, the difference in the performance of the two groups can be attributed to the program.

As illustrated in Figure 6-2, the control group and experimental groups do not necessarily have preprogram measurements. Measurements can be taken during the program and after the program is implemented, and the difference in the performance of the two groups shows the amount of improvement directly related to the program.

Figure 6-2 Use of Control Groups

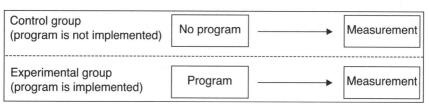

Control group arrangements appear in many settings, including both private and public sectors. A turnover-reduction program for nurses in a hospital chain used a control group and an experimental group. The experimental group included managers in a special LD program designed to reduce turnover. The control group was carefully selected to match up with the experimental group in terms of current turnover rate, tenure with the hospital, age, family status, and performance rating. The control/experimental group differences were dramatic, showing the impact of the retention program.

One concern with the use of control groups is that they are sometimes associated with a laboratory setting, which can make some executives and administrators uncomfortable. To avoid this stigma, some organizations conduct a pilot program using participants as the experimental group. A similarly matched, nonparticipating comparison group is selected but does not receive any communication about the program. The terms "pilot program" and "comparison group" are somewhat less threatening than "experimental group" and "control group."

The control group approach does have some inherent issues that may make it a challenge to apply in practice. The most important issue is the selection of the groups. From a theoretical perspective, having *identical* control and experimental groups is almost impossible. Dozens of factors can affect performance, some of them individual, others contextual. To address this problem on a practical basis, it is best to select four to six factors that will have the greatest influence on performance, using the concept of the Pareto principle. With this principle, only the most important factors are used.

For example, a control group was used in a program for the sales team at Dell Computer. The program involved regional sales managers, account managers, account executives, account representatives, and sales representatives. The output measures were profit-margin quota attainment, total revenue attainment, profit margin, and various sales volumes. An experimental group was involved in the program and was carefully matched with a control group that was not involved. The equivalent number of participants for the control group was selected at random using the company database. To ensure that the control group and the program group were equivalent, selections were made on three criteria: job positions, job levels, and experience.

Control groups are inappropriate in some situations. Withholding the program from one group while it is implemented in another may not be suitable. This is particularly important for critical solutions that are needed immediately. This barrier often keeps many control groups from being implemented. Management is not willing to withhold a solution in one area to see how it works in another.

In practice, many opportunities arise for a possibility of a natural control group arrangement. For example, in a large retail store chain, a new LD program for store managers will take several months to complete. Consequently, there may be enough time for a parallel comparison between the initial group and the last group. In these cases, ensuring that the groups are matched as closely as possible is critical so that the first group is similar to the last. These naturally occurring control groups often exist in major enterprisewide program implementations. The challenge is to address this issue early enough to influence the implementation schedule so that similar groups can be used in the comparison.

Contamination may develop when participants involved in the program group (i.e., the experimental group) communicate with the control group. Sometimes, the reverse situation occurs, when members of the control group model the behavior of the experimental group. In either case, the experiment becomes contaminated as the influence of the experimental group is passed to the control group. Contamination can be minimized by ensuring that the two groups are at different locations (store managers), have different shifts (first-level supervisors), or are on different floors in the same building (engineering team leaders). When separation is impossible, explain to both groups that one group will be involved in the program now and the other will be involved at a later date. Also, it might be helpful to appeal to the sense of responsibility of those involved in the program and ask them not to share the information with others.

Time can be an issue. The longer a comparison of the control group and the experimental group operates, the greater the likelihood of factors influencing the impact measures, which contaminates the results. However, enough time must elapse so that a clear pattern can emerge between the two groups. Therefore, the timing for control group comparisons must strike a delicate balance between waiting long enough for performance differences to show and not waiting too long so that the results become seriously contaminated.

Another issue can develop when the different groups are exposed to different environmental influences. Although the groups may begin the experiment under the same influences, the influences of one group may shift with time. This is usually the case when groups are at different locations. Sometimes, the selection of the groups can help with this issue. Another tactic is to use more groups than necessary and discard those with environmental differences.

Because use of control groups is an effective approach for isolating impact, it should be considered as a technique when a major ROI or impact study is planned. In that situation, isolating the program impact with a high level of accuracy is important, and the primary advantage of control groups is accuracy.

Using Trend-Line Analysis

Another useful technique for calculating the impact of a program is trend-line analysis. With this approach, a trend line is drawn to project the future, using previous performance as a base. After the program is conducted, actual performance is compared to the trend-line projection. Any performance improvement over what the trend line predicted can then be reasonably attributed to program implementation. While this is not an exact process, it provides a credible calculation of the program's impact, if certain conditions are met.

Figure 6-3 shows an example of a trend-line analysis taken from the turnover records of an insurance company. The vertical axis reflects the turnover of critical talent, annualized but reported monthly. Data are presented before and after conduction of a leadership program. The program is designed to reduce the turnover of critical talent, which has been averaging about 31 percent, annualized. As shown in the figure, a slight upward trend on the data begins prior to program implementation. Although the program apparently has had an effect on turnover, the trend line shows that some improve-

Figure 6-3   Trend-line Analysis

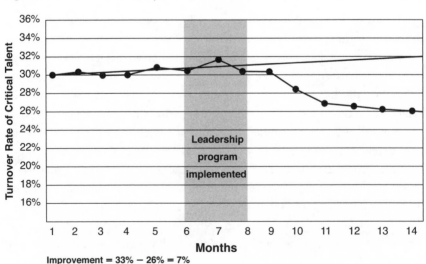

Improvement = 33% − 26% = 7%

ment would have occurred anyway, given the slightly upward trend that had previously been established. Program organizers may have been tempted to measure the improvement by comparing the average prior to the program (31 percent) to the amount in month 14 (26 percent), yielding a difference of 52 percent. However, a more accurate comparison is the 14-month amount (26 percent) compared to the trend-line amount of 32 percent. In this analysis, the difference is 6 percent. Using this more appropriate measure increases the accuracy and credibility of the process to isolate the impact of the program.

To use this technique, two conditions must be met:

1. The trend that had developed prior to the program is expected to continue as if the program had not been conducted. One needs to ask: Would this trend have continued on the same path established before the participants attended the program? The process owners (usually the participants) should be able to provide input to reach this conclusion. If the answer to the question is no, the trend-line analysis will not be used. If the answer is yes, the second condition is considered.

2. No new influences can enter the process during the evaluation period. The key word is *new*; people conducting the program must realize that the trend has been established because of the influences already in place and that no additional influences have entered other than con-duction of the program. If new influences *have* entered the process, another method must be used. If not, the trend-line analysis can do a reasonable calculation of the impact of this program.

Preprogram data must be available before this technique can be used, and the data should have a reasonable degree of stability. The trend line can be pro-jected directly from historical data using a simple routine available with many calculators and software packages, such as Microsoft Excel. If the variance of the data is high, the stability of the trend line becomes an issue. If this is an extremely critical issue and the stability cannot be assessed from a direct plot of the data, more detailed statistical analyses can be used to determine whether the data are stable enough to make the projection.

Forecasting Analysis

A more analytical approach to trend-line analysis is the use of forecasting methods that predict a change in impact measures. This technique represents a mathematical interpretation of the trend-line analysis when other factors enter a situation during the evaluation period. With this approach, the impact measure targeted by the program is forecast based on the influence of other factors that have changed during the evaluation period. There must be a relationship between the other factors and the impact measure driven by the program. The actual value of the measure is compared to the forecasted value. The difference reflects the contribution of the program.

A case study will illustrate this method for isolating program effects. National Computer Company (NCC) sells computers to businesses and consumers. To ensure that customer service and support were sufficient, NCC established customer care centers in six geographic regions. In recent years, NCC care centers had experienced a high employee turnover rate. To reduce turnover, a new LD program was developed to help managers improve employee engagement, appreciate employee concerns and differences, and communicate with employees effectively.

When the impact of the new program on employee turnover was considered, the staff identified an additional factor driving improvement: the change in the unemployment rate. In the area of the customer care center where the program was implemented, the unemployment rate increased from 5 to 6 percent. Figure 6-4 shows the relationship between the unemployment

Figure 6-4 Relationship Between Unemployment and Voluntary Turnover

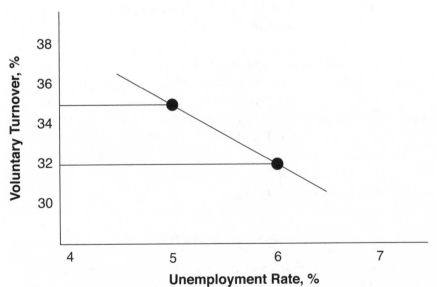

rate and the voluntary turnover rate. The mathematical relationship is $y = 50 - 3x$, where x is the unemployment rate and y is the voluntary turnover rate. As the unemployment rate increased from 5 percent to 6 percent, the turnover rate went down by 3 percent (from 35 percent to 32 percent). The mathematical relationship between the unemployment rate and the turnover rate is used to estimate how much of the reduced turnover was caused by the increased unemployment rate, not the program. In the absence of other factors, the improvement in turnover rate not allocated to increased unemployment is attributed to the program. In this case, it is 8 percent (from 11 percent to 3 percent). When this approach is used, it is important to find the mathematical relationship already developed. Working it out consumes too many resources, and a correlational analysis is beyond the scope of most LD staff expectations in examining programs.

With the forecasting approach, a major disadvantage occurs when several factors enter the process. The complexity multiplies, and the use of sophisticated statistical packages for multiple variable analyses is necessary. Even then, a good fit of the data to the model may not be possible. Unfortunately, some organizations have not developed mathematical relationships for output variables as a function of one or more inputs; without them, the forecasting method is difficult to use.

The primary advantage of this process is that it can accurately predict business performance measures without the program, if appropriate data and models are available. Because of this, it is worth it to ask if there are any credible mathematical relationships between the measure in question and the other influences. If the answer is yes, then try to use them. If the answer is no, then move on to another technique.

Using Estimates

The most common method of isolating the effects of a program is the use of estimates from the most credible sources. Estimating the amount of improvement connected to a particular program might be the least effective method from an analytical viewpoint. Because it is perceived to be the weakest method, every step should be taken to make it as credible as possible. Fortunately, it can be very reliable if some precautions are taken, and these are described in this section.

The beginning point in using this method is ensuring that the estimation is taken from the most credible source, and that is often the participant directly involved in the leadership program. Three other categories of individuals often provide input. The person who provides this information must be able to understand how the program has influenced the impact measures. The managers of the participants may be credible, if they are close to the situation. Customers provide credible estimates in unique situations when they are involved. External experts may also be very helpful. These are all described in this section.

Participants' Estimates of Leadership Impact

An easily implemented method for isolating the impact of a program is to obtain information directly from participants (i.e., the users) during the program. The effectiveness of this approach rests on the assumption that participants are capable of determining or estimating how much of a performance improvement (i.e., impact measure) is related to the program. Because their actions have produced the improvement, they may have highly accurate input on the issue. They should know how much of the change has been caused by using the program content. Although it is an estimate, this value will usually have credibility with executives because they know participants are at the center of the change and improvement. Begin by asking participants this series of questions:

- What other factors have contributed to this improvement in performance?
- What is the link between these factors and the improvement?
- What percentage of this improvement can be attributed to the implementation of this program?
- What confidence do you have in this estimate, expressed as a percentage? (0 percent = no confidence; 100 percent = complete confidence)
- What other individuals or groups could estimate this percentage to determine the amount attributed to this program?

Table 6-1 illustrates this approach with an example of one participant's estimations for one measure in a cross-functional LD program where each participant selects two measures that matter to him or her. Participants who do not provide information on the questions are excluded from the analysis. Also, erroneous, incomplete, and extreme information should be discarded before analysis. To be conservative, the confidence percentage can be factored into the values. The confidence percentage is a reflection of the error

Table 6-1 A Participant's Estimate

Factor that influenced improvement	Improvement caused by factor	Confidence	Adjusted improvement caused by factor
Leadership program	60%	80%	48 %
Process changes	15	70	10.5
Environmental change	5	60	3
System change	20	80	16
Other	—	—	—
Total	100%		

in the estimate. Thus, an 80 percent confidence level equates to a potential error range of plus or minus 20 percent. With this approach, the level of confidence is multiplied by the estimate. In the example, the participant allocates 60 percent of the improvement to the leadership program and is 80 percent confident in the estimate. The confidence percentage is multiplied by the estimate to develop a usable value of 48 percent. This adjusted percentage is then multiplied by the actual amount of improvement (postprogram value minus pre-program value) to isolate the portion attributed to the program. For example, if a service delivery cycle time has been improved by 12 hours, 48 percent (5.76 hours) of this number is attributed to the LD program. The adjusted improvement is now ready for conversion to monetary values and, ultimately, use in the ROI calculation.

Although an estimate, this approach does have considerable accuracy and credibility. Six adjustments are effectively applied to the participant estimate to reflect a conservative approach:

1. Participants who do not provide usable data are assumed to have experienced no improvements.
2. Incomplete, unrealistic, and unsupported claims are omitted from the analysis.
3. Extreme data are omitted from the analysis, although they may be included in the "other" benefits category.

4. For short-term programs, it is assumed that no benefits from the program are realized after the first year of full implementation. (For long-term programs, additional years may be used.)

5. The improvement amount is adjusted by the amount directly related to the program, expressed as a percentage. This is the allocated improvement value.

6. The allocated improvement value is multiplied by the confidence estimate, expressed as a percentage, to reduce the amount of the improvement, adjusting for the potential error.

For the most part, these adjustments follow the Guiding Principles of the ROI Methodology described in Chapter 3.

When presented to senior management, the result of an impact study is usually perceived to be an understatement of the program's success. The data and the process are considered credible and accurate. As an added enhancement to this method, the next level of management above the participants may be asked to review and approve the estimates from participants.

An example will illustrate the process for participant estimates. A restaurant chain initiated a management development program. The program was designed to improve the operating performance of the chain using a variety of empowerment strategies with the employees. Store managers established measurable goals for employees, provided performance feedback, measured progress toward goals, and took action to ensure that goals were met. As part of the program, store managers developed an action plan for improvement. The action plans could focus on any improvement area as long as they considered the performance measure to be important to their goals and related to store success. Each improvement would have to be converted to either cost savings or restaurant profits. Managers learned how to convert measurable improvements into an economic value for the restaurant. Some of the improvement areas were inventory, food spoilage, cash shortages, employee turnover, absenteeism, and productivity.

As part of the follow-up evaluation, each action plan was thoroughly documented, showing results in quantitative terms, which were converted to monetary values. The annual monetary value for each participant's improvement was calculated from the action plans. The managers were asked to identify the other factors that could have caused part of the improvement. Next, realizing that other factors could have influenced the improvement, managers were asked to estimate the percent of the improvement that resulted directly from the program (i.e., the contribution estimate). Restaurant managers are usually aware of factors that influence costs and profits and typically know how much of an improvement is traceable to the program. To help with this, each manager was asked to list the other factors that could have influenced the results. Finally, each manager was asked to be conservative and provide a confidence estimate for the above contribution estimate (100 percent = certainty, and 0 percent = no confidence). The results are shown in Table 6-2.

Estimation of the program's impact can be calculated using the conservative approach of adjusting for the contribution of the program and adjusting for the error of the contribution estimate. For example, the $5,500 annual value for labor savings is adjusted to consider the program contribution ($5,500 × 60% = $3,300). Next, the value is adjusted for the confidence in this value ($3,300 × 80% = $2,640). The conservative approach yields an overall improvement of $68,386 for this group. Participant 5 did not submit a completed action plan and was discarded from the analysis, although the costs for this participant are still included in the ROI calculation.

Another interesting observation emerges from this type of analysis. When the average of the three largest improvements is compared with the average of the three smallest values, the potential for return on investment could be much larger. If all the participants in the program had focused on high-impact improvements, a substantially higher return on investment could have been achieved. This information can be helpful to the management group, whose support is often critical for program success. While an impressive return on investment is refreshing, a potentially greater return on investment is outstanding.

This example illustrates the power of this methodology when individuals in a particular program focus on different measures. This would be the case for many LD programs, such as business coaching, executive development, team building, management development, executive education, mentoring, job retention, communications, process improvements, special assignments, and negotiations. In those situations, the specific impact measure may not be known until the participant identifies it before the program.

For other programs, the specific measure or measures are known and are often just a small number. For example, a program designed to improve retention, sales, quality, or safety performance will focus on one or just a few measures. This isolation technique is effective in all of these.

Manager's Estimate of Impact

In lieu of, or in addition to, participant estimates, the participants' immediate managers may be asked to provide input as to the program's influence

Table 6-2 Estimates of Program Impact from Participants

Participant	Total annual improvement, $	Basis	Contribution estimate from manager (participants), %	Confidence estimate from store managers (participants), %	Conservative value reported, $
1	$5,500	Labor savings	60%	80%	$2,640
2	15,000	Turnover	50	80	6,000
3	9,300	Absenteeism	65	80	4,836
4	2,100	Shortages	90	90	1,701
5	0	—	—	—	—
6	29,000	Turnover	40	75	8,700
7	2,241	Inventory	70	95	1,490
8	3,621	Procedures	100	80	2,897
9	21,000	Turnover	75	80	12,600
10	1,500	Food spoilage	100	100	1,500
11	15,000	Labor savings	80	85	10,200
12	6,310	Accidents	70	100	4,417
13	14,500	Absenteeism	80	70	8,120
14	3,650	Productivity	100	90	3,285
Total	$128,722				$68,386

on improved performance. In some settings, the participants' manager may be more familiar with the other influencing factors; therefore, he or she may be better equipped to provide impact estimates. The recommended questions to ask managers, after describing the improvement, are similar to those asked of the participants. Managers' estimates should also be analyzed in the same manner as participants'. To be more conservative, actual estimates should be adjusted by the confidence percentage. When participants' estimates have also been collected, the decision of which estimate to use becomes an issue. If a compelling reason makes one estimate more credible than the other, then the more credible estimate should be used. If they are equally credible, the lowest value should be used with an appropriate explanation. This is one of the Guiding Principles.

In some cases, upper management may estimate the percent of improvement attributed to a program. After considering additional factors that could contribute to an improvement, such as technology, procedures, and process changes, management applies a subjective factor to represent the portion of the results that should be attributed to the program. While this is subjective, the input is usually accepted by the individuals who provide or approve funding for the program. Sometimes, their comfort level with the processes is most important.

Customer Input on Program Impact

Another helpful approach in some narrowly focused programs is to solicit input on the impact of programs directly from customers. In these situations, customers are asked why they chose a particular product or service or to explain how their reactions to the product or service have been influenced by individuals or systems involved in the program. This technique often focuses directly on what the program is designed to improve. For example, after implementing an LD program involving customer response in an electric utility, market research data showed that the percentage of customers who were dissatisfied with response time was reduced by 5 percent when compared to market survey data before the program. Since response time was reduced by the program, and because no other factor contributed to the reduction, the 5 percent reduction in dissatisfied customers was directly attributed to the program.

Routine customer surveys provide an excellent opportunity to collect input directly from customers concerning their reactions to an assessment of new or improved products, services, processes, or procedures. Pre- and postdata can pinpoint changes related to an improvement driven by a new program. When customer input is collected, linking it with the current data collection methods and avoiding the creation of surveys or feedback mechanisms is important. This measurement process should not add to the data collection systems. Customer input can, perhaps, be the most powerful and convincing data if it is complete, accurate, and valid.

Internal or External Expert Estimates

External or internal experts can sometimes estimate the portion of results that can be attributed to a program. Here, experts must be carefully selected based on their knowledge of the process, program, and situation. For example, a supplier for a specific LD program might be able to provide estimates of how much change in a specific measure can be attributed to the program and how much can be attributed to other factors. Obviously, the basis for the estimate must be credibility. Sometimes the expert is not a participant but an individual who is knowledgeable about the different factors that influence the impact measures.

Collecting the Estimates

Whether the estimates come from participants, managers, customers, or experts, they must be collected from those individuals in a nonthreatening, unbiased way. Several approaches are available to collect the data, ranging from a very structured, credible process of using focus groups, to interviews, action plans, and questionnaires. These data are often collected in conjunction with other data sets. For example, if a questionnaire is used to collect the data to isolate the effects of the program, that same respondent will usually provide a lot of data about the program for Levels 3 and 4. In essence, the impact is that the results are reported on the questionnaire, and the isolation technique follows with a series of questions. The following are the different ways to collect this important data.

Using Focus Group for Estimates

The focus group works extremely well for this challenge if the group size is relatively small—in the range of 8 to 12 people. If the group is much larger than that, it should be divided into multiple units. Focus groups provide the opportunity for members to share information equally, avoiding domination by any one individual. The process taps the input, creativity, and reactions of the entire group.

The meeting should last about one hour (or slightly longer, if multiple factors affect the results or if multiple business measures need to be discussed). The facilitator should be neutral to the process; that is, the program leader should not conduct this focus group. Focus group facilitation and input must be objective. The task is to link the results of the program to business performance. Group members are presented with the improvement, and they provide input to isolate the effects of the program. The following steps are recommended to obtain the most credible value for program impact:

1. **Explain the task.** The task of the focus group meeting is outlined. Participants should understand that performance has improved. While many factors could have contributed to the improvement, this group must determine how much of the improvement has been related to the program.

2. **Discuss the rules.** Each participant should be encouraged to provide input, and his or her comments should be limited to two minutes or less for any specific issue. Comments are to be confidential and must not be linked to a specific individual.

3. **Explain the importance of the process.** The participants' role in the process is critical. Because it is their performance that has improved, participants are in the best position to indicate what has caused this improvement; they are the experts in this determination. Without quality input, the contribution of this program (or any other processes) may never be known.

4. **Select the first measure and show the improvement.** Using actual data, the facilitator should show the level of performance prior to and following program implementation; in essence, the change in business results is reported.

5. **Identify the different factors that have contributed to the performance.** Using input from experts—others who are knowledgeable about the improvements—the facilitator should identify the factors that have influenced the improvement (e.g., the volume of work has changed, a new system has been implemented, or technology has been enhanced). If these factors are known, they are listed as ones that may have contributed to the performance improvement.

6. **Ask the group to identify other factors that have contributed to the performance.** In some situations, only the participants know

other influencing factors, and those factors should be identified at this time.

7. **Discuss the link.** Taking each factor one at a time, the participants individually describe the link between that factor and the business results. For example, for the program influence, the participants would describe how the program has driven the actual improvement by providing examples, anecdotes, and other supporting evidence. Participants may need to be prompted to provide comments. If they cannot provide feedback regarding this issue, chances are good that the factor had no influence. Each person is allocated the same amount of time, usually one or two minutes.

8. **Repeat the process for each factor.** Each factor is explored until all the participants have discussed the link between all the factors and the business performance improvement. After these links have been discussed, the participants should have a much better understanding of the cause-and-effect relationship between the various factors and the business improvement.

9. **Allocate the improvement.** Participants are asked to allocate the percent of improvement to each of the factors discussed. Typically, they are given a pie chart, which represents a total amount of improvement for the measure in question, and they are asked to carve up the pie, allocating the percentages to different improvements, with a total of 100 percent. Or participants can be provided with a table to complete instead of a pie chart. Some participants may feel uncertain with this process, but they should be encouraged to complete this step using their best estimates. Uncertainty will be addressed next.

10. **Provide a confidence estimate.** The participants are then asked to review the allocation percentages and estimate their level of confidence for each allocation. Using a scale of 0 to 100 percent, participants express their levels of certainty with their estimates in the previous step. A participant may be more comfortable with some factors than others, so the confidence estimates may vary. These confidence estimates are used to adjust the results.

11. **Ask participants to multiply the two percentages.** For example, if an individual has allocated 35 percent of the improvement to the program and is 80 percent confident, he or she would multiply the percentages (35 × 80), which gives 28 percent. In essence, the participant is suggesting that at least 28 percent of the business improvement is linked to the program. The confidence estimate serves as a con-

servative discount factor, adjusting for the possible error of the estimate. The pie charts with the calculations are collected without names and the calculations are verified. Another option is to collect pie charts and make the calculations for the participants.

12. **Report results.** If possible, the average of the adjusted values for the group is developed and communicated to group members. Also, the summary of all the information should be communicated to the participants as soon as possible. Participants who do not provide information are excluded from the analysis.

This approach provides a credible way to isolate the effects of a program when other methods will not work. It is often regarded as the low-cost solution to the issue because it takes only a few focus groups and little time to arrive at this conclusion. In most of these settings, the actual conversion to monetary value is not conducted by the group but is developed in another way. (Converting data to monetary values is detailed in Chapter 7.) However, if participants must provide input on the value of the data, it can be approached as another phase of the same focus group meeting. The steps used to reach an accepted value are very similar to those used for isolation.

Using Interviews

Sometimes, focus groups are unavailable or are considered unacceptable for the use of data collection. Participants may be unavailable for a group meeting or the focus groups may become too expensive. In these situations, collecting similar information with an interview can be beneficial. Participants must address the same elements as those addressed in the focus group, but with a series of probing questions in a face-to-face interview. The interview may focus solely on isolating the effects of the program or serve as a part of collecting other data sets. A telephone or web interview (e.g., on Skype) may also be used.

Using Action Plans

As described in the previous chapter, the action planning process is an important way for participants to drive improvements desired either by them or the organization. The action plan provides a way to indicate what specific steps are taken and when they are taken, and the impact that the actions are having on the organization. When the planning process is complete and the impact has occurred, there is improvement. This improvement is reported on the action plan itself. With this in mind, three questions are needed in the action plan to isolate the effects of the program on that data:

1. What other factors could have caused this improvement?
2. What percent of this improvement is directly related to this program?
3. What is your confidence in this allocation, on a scale of zero to 100 percent, where zero is no confidence and 100 percent is complete confidence?

Isolation is usually an easy task for these types of programs, because participants have taken a variety of steps to cause the business impact. Thus, they have a good understanding of how they influenced this particular project. When these three questions are followed, accuracy can be very credible.

Some leadership consultants suggest that if an action plan is developed for a particular program, all the improvement should go to the program with no steps needed for the isolation process. Not so!

Some of these projects or actions would be initiated anyway. Also, other factors often cause the measures to change. Take, for example, an LD process for sales managers who are focused on very ambitious goals. Part of that process involves a variety of tactics, techniques, or processes suggested by the vice president of sales to achieve success. The target business measure is an increase in sales with existing customers. Action plans are developed by each participating sales manager. When an increase occurs in six months, it could have been triggered by many underlying factors. Isolation is absolutely critical to make sure that only the amount of increase driven by the action plans is reported.

Using Questionnaires

Sometimes improvement in a particular project or program is collected by questionnaire, where success with application and impact is detailed in literally dozens of questions. When this is achieved, the results need to be isolated to the program. To do this, ask the same three questions as were asked about action plans (see the previous section).

This is still very credible, because the results as reported in the questionnaire have been achieved by the responding participant, who will usually have some appropriate level of understanding of the connection. The error adjustments can often take care of the uncertainties in this process. This approach does have the inherent weaknesses that parallel the use of the questionnaire when compared to other methods. Individuals can ignore it or provide inaccurate or perhaps even biased data. To ensure that this does not happen, apply the techniques described in Chapter 5 to assure a great response rate.

Calculating the Impact of Other Factors

Although not appropriate in all cases, calculation of the impact of factors (other than the program) that influence part of the improvement is possible. In this approach, the program takes credit for improvement that cannot be attributed to other factors.

An example will help explain the approach. In an LD program for a large bank, a significant increase in consumer loan volume was generated after the program was implemented. Part of the increase in volume was attributed to the program, and the remaining increase was due to the influence of other factors in place during the same time period. Also identified: an increase in marketing and sales promotion and falling interest rates, which caused an increase in consumer volume.

With regard to the first factor, as marketing and sales promotion increased so did consumer loan volume. The amount of this factor was estimated using input from several internal experts in the marketing department. For the second factor, industry sources were used to estimate the relationship between increased consumer loan volume and falling interest rates. These two estimates together accounted for a modest percentage of increased consumer loan volume. The remaining improvement was attributed to the program.

This method is appropriate when the other factors are easily identified and the appropriate mechanisms are in place to calculate their impact on improvement. In some cases, estimating the impact of other factors is just as difficult as estimating the impact of the program, making this approach less advantageous. It can be very credible if the method used to isolate the impact of other factors is also credible.

Use of the Techniques

With all these techniques available to isolate the impact of a program, selecting the most appropriate techniques for a specific program can be difficult. Some techniques are simple and inexpensive, while others are more time-consuming and costly. When attempting to decide, these factors should be considered:

- Feasibility of the technique
- Accuracy provided with the technique
- Credibility of the technique with the target audience
- Specific cost to implement the technique
- Amount of disruption in normal work activities as the technique is implemented
- Participant, staff, and management time needed for the particular technique

Multiple techniques or multiple sources for data input should be considered, since two sources are usually better than one. When multiple sources are used, a conservative method is recommended for combining the inputs, as the conservative approach builds acceptance. The target audience should always be provided with explanations of the process and the subjective factors involved. Multiple sources allow LD team members to experiment with different strategies and build confidence with a particular technique. For example, if management is concerned about the accuracy of participants' estimates, a combination of a control group arrangement and participants' estimates could be attempted to verify the accuracy of the estimates.

Final Thoughts

Taking credit when credit is due is the most critical step in the analysis. This chapter has presented a variety of techniques for isolating the effects of a program. The techniques represent the most effective approaches available to address this issue and are used by some of the most progressive organizations. The use of control groups, trend-line analysis, and estimates from credible sources will be the dominant approaches in leadership development. Too often, results are reported and linked with the program without any attempt to isolate the exact portion that can be attributed to it. If professionals are committed to improving the images of their functions, as well as meeting their responsibilities for obtaining results, this issue must be addressed early in the process for all major programs. The next chapter focuses on converting data to money.

CHAPTER

7

Converting Data to Money

"SHOW ME THE money" is an increasingly common request from executives.

While results at lower levels are important, converting positive business impact into monetary figures is more valuable from an executive viewpoint. This chapter explains how LD professionals are moving beyond simply tabulating business results to developing monetary values. For the return on investment, calculating monetary benefits by converting data to monetary values is necessary. A variety of methods are available to convert impact data to money and are presented in this chapter.

Why Calculate Monetary Benefits?

The answer to this question is not always clearly understood. Without data being converted to monetary values, a leadership program could be labeled a success just by using business impact data to show the amount of change directly attributed to the program. For example, a change in quality, cycle time, market share, or customer satisfaction could represent significant improvements linked directly to a new program. For some programs this information may be sufficient. However, many sponsors need the actual monetary value, and more evaluators take this extra step of converting data to monetary values. Some are responding to requests. Others are anticipating the request. Still others are proactive with this issue and are preventing the request from being made.

Value Equals Money

For some stakeholders, the most important value is money. As described in Chapter 3, there are many different types of value. However, money is becoming one of the most important values, as the economic benefits of programs are desired. This is particularly true for executives, sponsors, clients, administrators, and top leaders. They are concerned about the allocation of funds and want to see the contribution of a program in monetary values. Anything short of this value for these key stakeholders would be unsatisfactory.

Impact Is More Understandable

For some programs, the impact is more understandable when the monetary value is developed. For example, consider the impact of a leadership development program aimed at all the middle managers in an organization. As part of the program, the managers were asked to identify at least two measures that need to improve using the leadership competencies with their teams. This request could yield dozens of different measures. When the program impact is captured and these measures have changed, a myriad of improvements are developed. These results are difficult to appreciate without a conversion to monetary value. When the first-year monetary value is developed for each of the measures, the results provide sponsors with a sense of the impact of the program. Without converting to monetary values, understanding the contribution is difficult.

Money Is Necessary for Return on Investment

Monetary value is required to develop return on investment. As described in Chapter 3, a monetary value is needed to compare to costs to develop the benefit/cost ratio, the return on investment (as a percentage), and the payback period. The monetary benefits become the other half of the equation; they are absolutely essential.

Monetary Value Is Needed to Understand Problems

In all businesses, costs are necessary for understanding the magnitude of any problem. Consider, for example, the cost of employee turnover. The traditional records and even those available through an analysis of cost statements will not show the full value or cost of the problem. A variety of estimates and expert input may be needed to supplement cost statements to arrive at a particular value. That's the monetary value needed in a fully loaded format to understand the problem.

The good news is that many organizations have developed a number of standard cost items that represent issues that are undesired. For example, an insurance company was experiencing a 35 percent annual turnover of financial analysts. When the cost of turnover was developed with comparable external studies, the total annual cost was over $3 million. This amount shocked the executives and sparked the creation of a retention solution. The monetary value made the difference.

Key Steps to Convert Data to Money

In order to convert both hard and soft data to monetary values, five general steps should be completed for each data item:

1. **Focus on a unit of measure.** First, define a unit of measure. For output data, the unit of measure is the item produced (one item assembled), service provided (one package shipped), or sale completed. Time measures might include the time to complete a program, process cycle time, or customer-response time, and the unit is usually expressed in minutes, hours, or days. Quality is a common measure, with a unit being defined as one error, reject, defect, or reworked item. Soft-data measures vary, with a unit of improvement representing such things as an employee complaint, a conflict, or a one-point change in the customer satisfaction index. Table 7-1 provides examples of units of measure.

2. **Determine the value of each unit.** Now comes the challenge. Place a value (V) on the unit identified in the first step. For measures of production, quality, cost, and time, the process is relatively easy. Most organizations maintain records or reports that can pinpoint the cost of one unit of production or one defect. Soft data are more difficult to convert to money. For example, the monetary value of one customer complaint or a 1-point change in an employee attitude is often difficult to determine. The techniques described in this chapter provide an array of approaches for making this conversion. When more than one value is available, usually the most credible or the lowest value is used in the calculation.

3. **Calculate the change in performance data.** Calculate the change in output data after the effects of the program have been isolated from

Table 7-1   Breaking Down the Units of Measure

• One unit produced	• One hour of downtime
• One student enrolled	• One minute of wait time
• One package delivered	• One day of delay
• One patient served	• One hour of cycle time
• One sale made	• One hour of employee time
• One loan approved	• One hour of overtime
• One project completed	• One customer complaint
• One call escalated	• One person removed from welfare
• One FTE employee	• One less day of incarceration (prison)
• One reject	• One unit of rework
• One error	• One lost time accident
• One grievance	• One unplanned absence
• One voluntary turnover	• One lost accident

other influences. The change (Δ) is the performance improvement, measured as hard or soft data, that is directly attributed to the program. The value may represent the performance improvement for an individual, a team, a group of participants, or several groups of participants.

4. **Determine an annual amount for the change.** Annualize the change value to develop a total change in the performance data for at least one year (ΔP). Use of annual values has become a standard approach for organizations that want to capture the benefits of a particular program, although the benefits may not remain constant throughout the entire year. First-year benefits are used if the solution is short term. This approach is considered to be conservative.

5. **Calculate the annual value of the improvement.** Arrive at the total value of improvement by multiplying the annual performance change (ΔP) by the unit value (V) for the complete group in question. For example, if a group of participants is involved in the program being evaluated, the total value will include total improvement for all participants in the group. This value for annual program benefits is then compared to the costs of the program, usually with the ROI formula presented in this chapter.

Table 7-2 presents an example of an LD program for new employees that illustrates the five-step procedure for converting data to money. A restaurant

Table 7-2   Converting Early Turnover Data to Monetary Values

Setting: Leadership Development Program for New Team Leaders	
Step 1:	**Define the unit of measure.**
	One early turnover in the first 60 days.
Step 2:	**Determine the value of each unit.**
	When internal experts and external studies were used, the cost of an average early turnover was estimated to be \$1,960, when time and direct costs were considered. (V = \$1,960).
Step 3:	**Calculate the change in performance data.**
	Six months after the program was completed, the early turnover in the first 60 days improved from 28% to 15%. It was estimated that 72% was related to the new selection program (Isolating the Effects of the Program). This provided an improvement of 9.4% turnover prevented because of this change.
Step 4:	**Determine an annual amount for the change.**
	An improvement of 9.4% represents 2.8 turnovers every two months, or 2.8 × 6 = 16.8 for one year. This is rounded off to be 16.
Step 5:	**Calculate the annual value of the improvement.**
	Annual value = $\Delta P \times V$
	= 16 × \$1,960
	= \$31,360

chain implemented this program to drive a variety of measures that need to improve. One team leader had experienced very high turnover in the first 60 days of employment (28 percent). An examination of why the employees were leaving revealed that they did not feel welcomed into the organization. The team leader used a variety of approaches to help new employees feel wanted, needed, and engaged. Turnover was dramatically reduced, with a total savings of \$31,360.

Standard Monetary Values

Most hard-data items are converted to monetary values and have standard values. By definition, a standard value is a monetary value on a unit of measurement that is accepted by key stakeholders and known to participants. These standards have been developed because these are often the measures that matter in the organization. They are critical. They reflect problems and opportunities, and actions have been taken to convert them to monetary values to show their impact on the operational and financial well-being of the organization. The best way to understand the magnitude of any problem is to put a monetary value on it.

A variety of quality programs spanning the past two decades have focused on the cost of quality. Organizations have been obsessed with placing a value on mistakes or the payoff of avoiding these mistakes. This is one of the most important outgrowths of quality management systems: the standard cost of quality. In addition, a variety of process improvement programs—such as reengineering, reinventing the corporation, transformation, and continuous process improvement—have had a measurement component in which the cost of a particular measure has been developed. Finally, a variety of cost controls, cost containment, and cost management systems have been developed, such as activity-based costing. These have forced organizations, departments, and divisions to place costs on activities and, in some cases, relate those costs directly to the revenue or profits of the organization.

Standard values are usually available for the hard-data categories of output, quality, and time. Table 7-3 shows how they have been converted to costs or profits. Output is converted to either profits or cost savings. Output in the form of sales, new customers, market share, and customer loyalty add value through additional profits obtained from additional sales. Outputs where profits are not directly connected, such as the output of an individual work group, can be converted to cost savings. For example, if the outputs of a work group can be increased as a result of a particular program with no additional resources needed to drive the output, then the corresponding value is in the cost savings. That is, additional output drives the cost per unit down, resulting in a cost savings. When quality is improved, the result is either cost savings when quality is an issue or cost avoidance when the program is preventive (it avoids a mistake or substandard quality).

Table 7-3 Converting Hard Data to Money

Hard-data category	Conversion to money	ROI component
Output →	Profit	Profit
→	Cost savings	Cost savings
Quality →	Cost savings	Cost savings
→	Cost avoidance	Cost avoidance
Time →	Cost savings	Cost savings
→	Cost avoidance	Cost avoidance
Cost	Already converted	Cost savings
		Cost avoidance

Time is converted in the same way. If time is reduced, it is converted to a cost savings. If the time does not increase when normally it should, it represents cost avoidance. Therefore, the ultimate payoff of typical hard-data items is profit, cost savings, or cost avoidance. This logic also explains why most ROI studies pay off with cost savings or cost avoidance instead of profits. Those programs directly related to customers and sales are normally converted to profits. Others are converted to cost savings or cost avoidance. The additional details on how these conversions are made are presented next. However, many hard-data items have been converted to monetary values as standard values.

Converting Output Data to Money

When a program produces a change in output, the value of the increased output can usually be determined from the organization's accounting or operating records. For organizations operating on a profit basis, this value is typically the marginal profit contribution of an additional unit of production or service provided. For example, a team within a major appliance manufacturer was able to boost the production of small refrigerators after a comprehensive work cell leadership program. The unit of improvement was the profit margin of one refrigerator.

For organizations that are performance driven rather than profit driven, this value is usually reflected in the savings accumulated when an additional unit of output is realized for the same input. For example, in the visa section of a government office, an additional visa application was processed at no additional cost. Thus, an increase in output translated into a cost savings equal to the unit cost of processing a visa application.

The formulas and calculations used to measure this contribution depend on the type of organization and the status of its recordkeeping. Most organizations have standard values readily available for performance monitoring and setting goals. Managers often use marginal cost statements and sensitivity analyses to pinpoint values associated with changes in output. If the data are not available, the HR team must initiate or coordinate the development of appropriate values.

One of the more important outcomes is productivity, particularly in a competitive organization. Today, most organizations competing in a global economy do an excellent job of monitoring productivity and placing value on it. For example, consider the Snapper, Inc., lawnmower manufacturer. Robots do the welding, lasers cut parts, and computers control the steel stamping processes. At Snapper, each factory worker is measured every hour, every day, every month, and every year. And everyone's performance is posted publicly for all to see. Production at the Snapper plant is rescheduled every week according to the pace at which stores sell across the nation. A computer juggles work assignments and balances the various parts of the assembly process. Not only is productivity important, it is measured and valued. Snapper knows the value of improving productivity by an infinitesimal amount because the president knows that the factory must be efficient to compete in a global market with low-cost products. This requires that every factory worker be measured every hour of every day.

The benefit of converting output data to money with this approach is that these calculations are already completed for the most important data items and are reported as standard values. Perhaps no area is more dramatic with the standard values than those in the sales and marketing area. Table 7-4 shows a sampling of measures in the sales and marketing area that are routinely calculated and are considered to be standard values.[30] For example, the first two entries go together. The sales cannot be used in an ROI value until they have been converted to profit. Sales are usually affected by the profit percentage to generate the actual value of the improvement. Other profit margins can be developed for a particular unit, a product line, or even a customer. Retention rates, return rates, and the lifetime value of a customer are routinely developed. Even these days, the market share and loyalty are developed because they all translate directly into additional sales. For the most part—with the exception of workload and inventories—the monetary value is developed through profits. Even market share and customer loyalty are usually valued based on profit from sales or additional sales obtained from the customer.

Calculating the Cost of Quality

Quality and the cost of quality are important issues in most manufacturing and service firms. In recent years, quality processes have moved to the public sector and nonprofits. Because some leadership programs may influence quality measures, the program team or participants may have to place a value on the improvement of certain quality measures. With some quality measures, the task is easy. For example, if quality is measured with the defect rate, the value of the improvement is the cost to repair or replace the product. The most obvious cost of unacceptable quality is the scrap or waste generated by mistakes. Defective products, spoiled raw materials, and discarded parts

Table 7-4 Standard Values from Sales and Marketing

Metric	Definition	Converting issues
Sales	The sale of the product or service recorded in a variety of different ways: by product, by time period, by customer	This data must be converted to monetary value by applying the profit margin for a particular sales category.
Profit margin, %	(Price – cost)/cost for the product, customer, or time period	This is the most common way factored to convert sales to data.
Unit margin	Unit price less the unit cost	This shows the value of incremental sales.
Channel margin	Channel profits as a percentage of channel selling price	This is used to show the value of sales through a particular marketing channel.
Retention rate	The ratio of customers retained to the number of customers at risk of leaving	The value is the money saved to retain a new replacement customer.
Churn rate	The complement of the retention rate. It is the percentage of customers leaving compared to the number who are at risk of leaving.	The value is the money saved for acquiring a new customer.
Customer profit	The difference between the revenues earned from and the cost associated with the customer relationship during the specified period	The monetary value added is the additional profit obtained from customers. It all goes to the bottom line.
Customer value lifetime	The present value of the future cash flows attributed to the customer relationship	This is the bottom line: as customer value increases, it adds directly to the profits. Also, as a new customer is added, the incremental value is the customer lifetime average.
Cannibalization rate	The percentage of the new product sales taken from existing product lines	This needs to be minimized, because it is an adverse effect on existing product, with the value added being the loss of profits from the sales loss.

(continued on next page)

Table 7-4 Standard Values from Sales and Marketing *(continued)*

Metric	Definition	Converting issues
Workload	Hours required to service clients and prospects	This involves the salaries, commissions, and benefits for the sales staff for the time they spend on the workloads.
Inventories	The total amount of product or brand available for sale in a particular channel	The inventories are valued at the cost of carrying the goods, space, handling, and the time value of money. Insufficient inventories is the cost of expediting the new inventory or loss of sales because of the inventory outage.
Market share	The sales revenue as a percentage of total market sales	The actual sales are converted to money through the profit margins. This is a measure of competitiveness.
Loyalty	The length of time the customer stays with the organization, the willingness to pay a premium, the willingness to search, etc.	The value added is from the sale or the profit on the premium.

are all the result of unacceptable quality. Scrap and waste translate directly into a monetary value. In a production environment, for example, the cost of a defective product is the total cost incurred up to the point at which the mistake is identified, minus the salvage value. In the service environment, a defective service is the cost incurred up to the point that the deficiency is identified, plus the cost to correct the problem, plus the cost to make the customer happy, plus the loss of customer loyalty.

Employee mistakes and errors can be expensive. The most costly rework occurs when a product or service is delivered to a customer and must be returned for correction or replacement. The cost of rework includes both labor and direct costs. In some organizations, rework costs can be as much as 35 percent of operating expenses.

In one leadership program, a measure focused on customer service provided by dispatchers in an oil company. The dispatchers processed orders and scheduled deliveries of fuel to service stations. A measure of quality that was considered excessive was the number of pullouts experienced. A pullout occurs when a delivery truck cannot fill an order for fuel at a service station. The truck must then return to the terminal for an adjustment to the order. This is essentially a rework item. The average cost of a pullout is developed by tabulating the cost from a sampling of actual pullouts. The elements in the tabulation included driver time, the cost of the truck while adjusting the load, the cost of terminal use, and extra administrative expenses. This value was developed and became the accepted standard following completion of the program. Organizations have made great progress in developing standard values for the cost of quality. Quality costs can be grouped into six major categories:

- *Internal failure* represents costs associated with problems detected prior to product shipment or service delivery.
- *Penalty costs* are fines or penalties received as a result of unacceptable quality.
- *External failure* refers to problems detected after product shipment or service delivery. Costs include product support, complaint investigation, and remedial fixes.
- *Appraisal costs* are the expenses involved in determining the condition of a particular product or service.
- *Prevention costs* include efforts undertaken to avoid unacceptable product or service quality. These efforts include quality management, audits, and process improvements.
- *Customer dissatisfaction* is perhaps the costliest element of inadequate quality. In some cases, serious mistakes result in lost business.

As with output data, the good news is that a tremendous number of quality measures have been converted to standard values. Table 7-5 shows a sampling of the quality measures that are typically converted to actual monetary value.

The definition of these measures can vary slightly with the organization, and the magnitude and the costs can vary significantly. The most common method for converting cost is to use internal failure, external failure, appraisal costs, or penalty costs. Some larger organizations literally track thousands of quality measures, as standard values have been developed for many of them.

Converting Employee Time by Using Compensation

Saving employee time is a common impact for leadership development programs. The ultimate goal is for the team to be able to complete tasks in less

Table 7-5 Standard Quality Measures

Defects	Failure
Rework	Customer complaints
Variances	Delay
Waste	Missing data
Processing errors	Fines
Date errors	Penalties
Incidents	Inventory shortages
Accidents	Unplanned absenteeism
Grievances	Involuntary employee turnover
Downtime—equipment	Risk
Downtime—system	Days sales uncollected
Repair costs	Queues

time or with fewer people. For example, a team project in senior executive leadership development focuses on reorganization of a function; this results in fewer people needed and saves the company having to pay 11 salaries. A major team project could drive a reduction of several hundred employees. On an individual basis, a time management component of a leadership program is implemented to help managerial employees save time with daily tasks. The value of the time saved is an important measure, and determining the monetary value for it is relatively easy.

The most obvious time savings are from reduced labor costs for performing the same amount of work. The monetary savings are found by multiplying the hours saved by the labor cost per hour. For example, in the time management module, participants estimated that they saved an average of 74 minutes per day, worth $31.25 per day, or $7,500 per year. The time savings were based on the average salary plus benefits for the typical participant.

For most calculations, the average wage, with a percent added for employee benefits, will suffice. However, employee time may be worth more. For example, additional costs in maintaining an employee (office space, furniture, telephones, utilities, computers, secretarial support, and other overhead expenses) could be included in calculating the average labor cost. Thus, the average wage rate may escalate quickly. In a large-scale employee reduction effort, calculating additional employee costs may be more appropriate for showing the value. However, for most programs the conservative approach of using salary plus employee benefits is recommended.

When time savings are being developed, caution is needed. Savings are realized only when the amount of time saved translates into a cost reduction or a profit contribution. If a team-based program sparks a new process that eliminates several hours of work each day, the actual savings will be based on a reduction in staff or overtime pay. Even if a program produces savings in manager time, a monetary value is not realized unless the manager puts the additional time saved to productive use. Having managers estimate the percentage of saved time that is used on productive work may be helpful, if followed up by a request for examples of how the time was used. Therefore, a necessary preliminary step in developing time savings is determining whether the expected savings will be genuine—that is, if the time saved is put to productive use. The examples add credibility to the results.

Finding Standard Values

Standard values are available for all types of hard data and are available in all types of functions and departments. A standard value is defined as monetary value for a unit of measure. This value is usually known to the individuals who work with the data. Essentially, every major department will develop standard values that are tracked and monitored in that area. Table 7-6 shows the common functions in a major organization where standard values are tracked. Sometimes, the value is in the departments that monitor, collect, and publish the data. Thanks to enterprisewide systems software, these functions, including the standard values in some cases, are integrated and available for

Table 7-6   Examples of Standard Values, Which Are Everywhere

• Finance and accounting	• Customer service and support
• Audit/controls	• Organizational effectiveness
• Production/production controls	• Quality standards/processes
• Operations	• Procurement
• Engineering	• Logistics/delivery
• Methods/processes	• Compliance
• Information technology	• Research and development
• Administration	• HR systems
• Sales and marketing	• Legal and risk management
• Library/information services	• Call centers

access to a variety of people. Access may be an issue that needs to be addressed or changed to ensure that the data can be obtained.

Some HR team members, using the ROI Methodology, have taken the extra step of collecting the standard values from the various systems and developing a handbook of values. This involves tapping into the databases or departmental files of these functions and others. The result is an interesting list of what things are worth. When this list has been compiled beforehand, it becomes a much-sought-after document for others examining cross-functional processes who also need the value of the measures. This would be an excellent program for wide-scale implementations.

Data Conversion When Standard Values Are Not Available

When standard values are not available, several strategies for converting data to monetary values are available. Some are appropriate for a specific type of data or data category; others may be used with virtually any type of data. The challenge is to select the strategy that best fits the situation. These strategies are presented next, beginning with the most credible approach.

Using Historical Costs from Records

Sometimes, historical records contain the value of a measure and reflect the cost (or value) of a unit of improvement. This strategy relies on identifying the appropriate records and tabulating the actual cost components for the item in question (for example, an LD program in a large construction firm focused on safety improvement). The program improved several safety-related performance measures, ranging from government fines to total workers' compensation costs. After examination of the company's records using one year of data, the average cost for each safety measure was developed. This involved the direct costs of medical payments, insurance payments, insurance premiums, investigation services, and lost-time payments to employees, as well as payments for legal expenses, fines, and other direct services. Also, the amount of time used to investigate, resolve, and correct any of the issues had to be included. This time involved not only the health and safety staff but also other staff members. In addition, the cost of lost productivity, the disruption of services, morale, and dissatisfaction were also estimated to obtain a fully loaded cost. Corresponding costs for each item were then developed. This brief example shows how difficult it is to keep systems and databases for use in finding values for particular data items.

Sorting through databases, cost statements, financial records, and a variety of activity reports takes a tremendous amount of time, which may not be readily available. It helps to keep in perspective the amount of time required to go through this process. This step (converting data to monetary value) is only one in the ROI Methodology, and it is only one measure among many that may need to be converted to monetary value. Resources need to be conserved.

In some cases, data are not available to show all the costs for a particular item. While some direct costs are associated with a measure, often the same numbers of indirect or invisible costs, or costs that cannot be obtained easily, are associated with the program. Calculating the cost of voluntary turnover is one example.

Figure 7-1 shows the fully loaded costs of turnover and can be compared to the "Iceberg principle."[31] The visible part of the scope of the issue, or the "iceberg," is the "green money," or visible turnover costs; these are the costs that are in the records, reports, and cost statements. Although capturing them all would be a difficult undertaking, it would be still more difficult to do so for the "blue money" items—the invisible costs, the part of the "iceberg" that cannot be seen from a surface observation. Often labeled "hidden costs" or "indirect costs," they can be significant and make converting data to monetary values not only a time-consuming process but also one that will involve estimates and expert input.

In some cases, the effort just to secure data from databases becomes difficult. With the proliferation of data warehousing and data capturing systems, combined with existing legacy systems that may not talk to each other, finding the values for a particular cost item sometimes becomes an insurmountable task.

Compounding the problems of time and availability is access. Occasionally, monetary values may be needed from a system or record set that is under someone else's control. Cost data are more sensitive than other types of data and are often protected for many reasons, including the competitive advantage. Therefore, easy access becomes difficult and is sometimes even prohibited unless an absolute need to know exists.

Finally, an acceptable level of accuracy is needed in this analysis. While a measure calculated in the current records may give the impression that it is based on accurate data, this may be an illusion. When data are calculated, estimations are involved, access to certain systems is denied, and different assumptions are necessary (which can be compounded by different interpretations of *systems*, *data*, and *measures*). Because of these limitations, the calculated values may be suspect unless care is taken to ensure that they are accurate.

Figure 7-1 Fully Loaded Turnover Costs

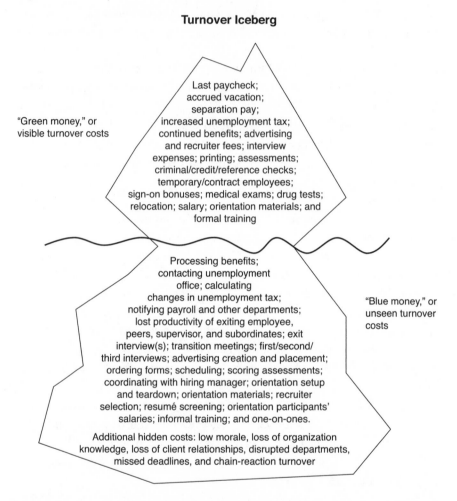

Turnover Iceberg

"Green money," or visible turnover costs

Last paycheck; accrued vacation; separation pay; increased unemployment tax; continued benefits; advertising and recruiter fees; interview expenses; printing; assessments; criminal/credit/reference checks; temporary/contract employees; sign-on bonuses; medical exams; drug tests; relocation; salary; orientation materials; and formal training

Processing benefits; contacting unemployment office; calculating changes in unemployment tax; notifying payroll and other departments; lost productivity of exiting employee, peers, supervisor, and subordinates; exit interview(s); transition meetings; first/second/third interviews; advertising creation and placement; ordering forms; scheduling; scoring assessments; coordinating with hiring manager; orientation setup and teardown; orientation materials; recruiter selection; resumé screening; orientation participants' salaries; informal training; and one-on-ones.

"Blue money," or unseen turnover costs

Additional hidden costs: low morale, loss of organization knowledge, loss of client relationships, disrupted departments, missed deadlines, and chain-reaction turnover

Calculating the monetary value of data using records should be done with caution and only when these two conditions exist:

1. The sponsor approves spending additional time, effort, and money to develop a monetary value from the current records and reports.
2. The measure is simple and available in a few records.

Otherwise, moving to another method is preferred. Other methods may be just as accurate and certainly less time-consuming than this particular approach.

Using Input from Experts

When one is faced with the prospect of converting data items for which historical cost data are not available, using input from experts might be an option. Internal experts provide the cost (or value) of one unit of improvement. Individuals with knowledge of the situation and the respect of management must be willing to provide estimates, as well as the assumptions made in arriving at the estimates. Most experts have their own methodology for developing these values. So when their input is requested, explaining the full scope of what is needed and providing as many specifics as possible is critical.

Internally, experts are not difficult to find. Obviously, they can sometimes be found in the department where the data originated or the department that collected the data. For example, the quality department generates quality measures, the payroll department generates payroll measures, the IT department generates IT data, and the marketing department generates sales and marketing data.

In some cases, the expert is the individual or individuals who sent the report. The report is either sent electronically or entered into a database, and the origins are usually known. If the report is sent on a routine basis, the person sending it may be the expert or at least can direct program leaders to the expert. Sometimes, an individual's job title can indicate whether he or she might be an expert. For example, in one insurance firm, when a claim was turned down, the customer had the ability to appeal the process. In an LD program, a measure was selected to lower the number of customer appeals, and the ROI analysis of the program had to be developed based on the reduction of appeals. The cost of an appeal was needed. To find the cost, the program leader contacted the individuals whose title was "customer appeals coordinator," and in a focus group they developed the data directly from their input.

When identification of the expert is not as easy as looking up a job title, asking is also helpful. A few questions asked may lead to the person who knows. Internally, for almost every data item generated, someone is considered an expert about that data.

Externally, the experts—consultants, professionals, or suppliers in a particular area—can be found in some obvious places. For example, the costs of accidents could be estimated by the workers' compensation insurance carrier, or the cost of a grievance could be estimated by the labor attorney providing legal services to defend the company in grievance transactions.

The credibility of the expert is the critical issue when using this method. Foremost among credibility measures is the individual's experience with the process or the measure. This individual must be knowledgeable of the processes for this measure; ideally, he or she should work with it routinely. Also, experts must be neutral in terms of the measure's value. Bias can be difficult to detect. It can be very subtle. For example, an internal labor relations expert (who coordinates grievances for the company) may exaggerate the cost of a grievance to show the importance of his or her particular job. However, since the expert works with these types of situations, he or she may have the most knowledge, so the bias may have to be filtered in some way. In a case like this, going to an external expert who is not connected with the issue may be more appropriate. Externally, part of the expertise may be based on the credentials of the person, such as degrees or certifications in a related area. Publications, degrees, and other honors or awards are important for validating and supporting the expertise of these outside people. For professionals who routinely provide information, their track records of estimations are important. If the values they estimate have been substantiated in more detailed studies and found to be consistent, this track record could be the most credible confirmation of their expertise to provide this type of data.

External experts must be selected based on their experience with the unit of measure. Fortunately, many experts are available who work directly with important measures such as employee attitudes, customer satisfaction, turnover, absenteeism, and complaints. They are often willing to provide estimates of the cost (or value) of these intangibles. The expert's reputation is critical, because the accuracy and credibility of the estimates are directly related to it.

Using Values from External Databases

For some soft data, using cost (or added monetary value) estimates based on the work and research of others may be appropriate. This technique taps external databases that contain studies and research programs that focus on the cost of data items. Fortunately, many databases include cost studies of data items related to programs, and most are accessible through the Internet. Data are available about the cost of turnover, absenteeism, incidents, accidents, complaints, and even customer satisfaction. The difficulty lies in finding a database with studies or research appropriate to the current program. Ideally, the data should come from a similar setting in the same industry, but that is not always possible. Sometimes, data on all industries or organizations are sufficient, perhaps with some adjustments to suit the program at hand.

For some, the web holds the most promise for finding monetary values for data not readily available from standard values and experts. Tremendous progress has been made—and continues to be made—in web searches to develop monetary values. Here are a few guidelines. Although they have a lot in common with web search engines, general web directories and portals may be helpful. These databases may include less than 1 percent of what search engine databases cover, but they still serve unique research purposes and in many cases may be the best starting point.

A specialized directory is more appropriate for accessing immediate expertise in online resources on a specific topic. A specialized database such as ERIC—the Education Resources Information Center (www.eric.ed.gov) or Ebsco (www.ebscohost.com)—may be helpful. These sites bring together well-organized collections of Internet resources on specific topics and provide an important starting point. For example, Table 7-7 shows selected turnover cost data captured from dozens of impact studies on ERIC. The data are arranged by job category, ranging from entry-level, nonskilled jobs to middle managers. The ranges represent the cost of turnover as a percentage of base pay of the job group. The ranges are rounded off for ease of presentation. The costs included in these studies are fully loaded to include exit cost of departing employees, recruiting, selection, orientation, initial training, wages and salaries while in training, lost productivity, quality problems, customer dissatisfaction, loss of expertise/knowledge, supervisor's time for turnover, and temporary replacement costs. The sources for these studies on ERIC comprise these general categories:

- Industry and trade magazines where the costs have been reported for a specific job within the industry
- Practitioner publications in general management, HR management, HR development, and performance improvement
- Academic and research journals where professors, consultants, and researchers publish the results of their work on retention
- Independent studies conducted by organizations and not reported in the literature but often available on a website or through membership arrangements. These are research-based groups supported by professional and management associations.
- Cost impact studied, developed, and reported by consulting firms

This list is not intended to be all-inclusive, but it illustrates the availability of special databases.

Table 7-7 Turnover Costs Summary

Job type/category	Turnover cost ranges as a percentage of annual wage/salary
Entry level—hourly, nonskilled (e.g., fast-food worker)	30 – 50%
Service/production—hourly (e.g., courier)	40 – 70%
Skilled—hourly (e.g., machinist)	75 – 100%
Clerical/administrative (e.g., scheduler)	50 – 80%
Professional (e.g., sales representative, nurse, accountant)	75 – 125%
Technical (e.g., computer technician)	100 – 150%
Engineer (e.g., chemical engineer)	200 – 300%
Specialist (e.g., computer software designer)	200 – 400%
Supervisor/team leader (e.g., section supervisor)	100 – 150%
Middle manager (e.g., department manager)	125 – 200%

Percentages are rounded to reflect the general range of costs from studies. Costs are fully loaded to include all of the costs of replacing an employee and bringing him or her to the level of productivity and efficiency of the former employee.

The search engines hold promise because of their vast coverage. General online search engines such as Google Scholar stand in contrast to a web directory in three primary ways:

1. They are much larger, containing over a billion records instead of a few million.
2. Virtually no human selectivity is involved in determining which web pages are included in the search engine's database.
3. They are designed for searching (responding to a user's specific query), rather than browsing and therefore provide much more substantial searching capabilities than directories.

A range of news resources are also available on the Internet, including news services, news wires, newspapers, and news consolidation services. Because some studies concerning particular values are newsworthy, these may be excellent sources for capturing the values of data. Overall, Internet searches are an important tool in collecting data.

A typical concern of web searches is the quality of the content. Some people think that the Internet has low-quality content, although in reality, it is no different from other sources. Right alongside high-quality publications often available on newsstands are those with low-quality content. Here are a few guidelines:

- **Consider the source.** From what organization does the content originate? Look for the group to be identified both on the web page itself and at the web address. Is the content identified as coming from a known source, such as a news organization, the government, an academic journal, a professional association, or a major investment firm? The web address will identify the owner, and the owner may be revealing in terms of the quality.
- **Consider the motivation.** What is the purpose of this site: academic, consumer protection, sales, entertainment, or political? The motivation can be helpful in assessing the degree of objectivity.
- **Look for the quality of the writing.** If the content contains spelling and grammatical errors, those can mean that there are content quality problems as well.
- **Look at the quality of the source documentation.** First, remember that even in academic circles, the number of footnotes is not a true measure of the quality of the work. On the other hand, if facts are cited, does the page identify the origin of that information? Check out some of the cited sources to see if the facts have actually been quoted.
- **Are the site and its content as current as they should be?** If the site is reporting on current events, the need for currency and the answer to the question of whether the site is up to date will be apparent.
- **Verify the facts used in the data conversion using multiple sources, or choose the most authoritative source.** Unfortunately, many facts given on web pages are simply wrong as a result of carelessness, exaggeration, guessing, or other reasons. Often they are wrong because the person creating the page content did not check the facts.

These are helpful ways to help focus only on the quality content, which is critical when determining the monetary value of a particular measure.

Linking with Other Measures

When standard values, records, experts, and external studies are not available, a feasible approach might be to find a relationship between the measure in question and another measure that may be converted easily to a monetary value. This involves identifying existing relationships, if possible, that show a significant correlation between one measure and another with a standard value.

For example, a classical relationship depicted in Figure 7-2 shows a correlation between increasing job satisfaction and employee turnover. In a leadership program designed to improve job satisfaction, a value is needed for changes in the job satisfaction index. A predetermined relationship showing the correlation between improvements in job satisfaction and reductions in turnover can link the changes directly to turnover. When standard data or external studies are used, the cost of turnover can easily be developed, as described earlier. Therefore, a change in job satisfaction is converted to a monetary value or, at least, an approximate value. It is not always exact because of the potential for error and other factors, but the estimate is sufficient for converting the data to monetary values.

Sometimes it's possible to find a correlation between a customer satisfaction measure and another measure that can easily be converted to a monetary value. Usually, a significant correlation exists between customer satisfaction and revenue. Many organizations are able to show a connection between these two measures. When a relationship between the two variables is established, an estimation of the actual value of customer satisfaction can be made by linking it to other measures. Furthermore, a correlation often exists between customer loyalty—which may be defined in terms of customer retention or defection—and the actual profit per customer.

Figure 7-2 Relationship Between Job Satisfaction and Voluntary Employee Turnover

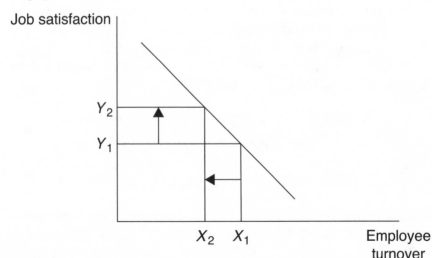

In some situations, a chain of relationships may establish a connection between two or more variables. In this approach, a measure that may be difficult to convert to a monetary value is linked to other measures that are linked in turn to measures upon which a value can be placed. Ultimately, these measures are traced to a monetary value often based on profits. A model used by Sears, one of the world's largest retail chains, connects job attitudes (collected directly from the employees) to customer service, which is directly related to revenue growth.[32] These links between measures, often called the "service-profit chain," create a promising way to place monetary values on hard-to-quantify measures. This research practice is significant, and the opportunity for customized work is tremendous.

Using Estimates from Participants

In some cases, participants in an LD program should estimate the value of improvement. This technique is appropriate when participants are capable of providing estimates of the cost (or value) of the unit of measure improved with the program. When using this approach, participants should be provided with clear instructions, along with examples of the type of information needed. The advantage of this approach is that the individuals who are closest to the improvement often are capable of providing the most reliable estimates of its value.

Using Estimates from the Management Team

Sometimes, participants in a program may be incapable of placing a value on the improvement. Their work may be removed from the value of the process and thus they cannot provide reliable estimates. In these cases, supervisors or managers of participants may be able to give estimates. Therefore, they may be asked to provide a value for a unit of improvement linked to the program.

In other situations, managers are asked to review and approve participants' estimates and confirm, adjust, or discard the values. For example, a leadership program involving customer service team members was designed to reduce customer complaints, among other measures. Although the program resulted in a reduction of complaints, the value of a single customer complaint was still needed to determine the value of the improvement. Although team leaders knew about some issues concerning customer complaints, they could not gauge the full impact, so their managers were asked to provide a value.

These managers had a broader perspective of the full impact of a customer complaint, particularly the long-term impact of a dissatisfied customer.

In some cases, senior management provides estimates of the value of data. With this approach, senior managers interested in the program are asked to place a value on the improvement based on their perception of its worth. This approach is used when it is difficult to calculate the value or when other sources of estimation are unavailable or unreliable.

Using Staff Estimates

The final strategy for converting data to monetary values is to use internal HR staff estimates. Using all the available information and experience, the staff members most familiar with the situation provide estimates of the value. For example, in a coaching program for store managers, one of the measures improved was unscheduled absenteeism, among other performance measures. Unable to identify a value using other strategies, the LD staff estimated the cost of an absence to be $200. This value was then used in calculating the savings for the reduction in absenteeism that followed the coaching project. Although the LD staff may be capable of providing accurate estimates, this approach is sometimes perceived as being biased. It should therefore be used only when other approaches are unavailable or inappropriate.

Technique Selection and Finalizing the Values

With so many techniques available, the challenge is selecting one or more strategies appropriate for the situation and available resources. Developing a table or list of values or techniques appropriate for the situation may be helpful. The guidelines that follow may help determine the proper selection and finalize the values.

Use the Technique Appropriate for the Type of Data

Some strategies are designed specifically for hard data, while others are more appropriate for soft data. The type of data often dictates the strategy. Standard values are developed for most hard-data items. Company records and cost statements are used with hard data. Soft data are often involved in external databases, linking with other measures, and using estimates. Experts are used to convert both types of data to monetary values.

Move from Most Accurate to the Least Accurate

Table 7-8 shows the techniques presented in order of accuracy, beginning with the most accurate. Working down the list, each technique should be considered for its feasibility in the situation. The technique with the most accuracy is always recommended if it is feasible for the situation.

Consider the Resources

Sometimes, the availability of a particular source of data will drive the selection. For example, experts may be readily available. Some standard values are easy to find; others are more difficult. In other situations, the convenience of a technique may be an important selection factor. The Internet is making external database searches more convenient.

As with other processes, it is important to keep the time invested in this phase to a minimum, so that the total effort for the ROI study does not become excessive. Some techniques can be implemented in much less time than others. Too much time spent on this step may dampen otherwise enthusiastic attitudes about the use of the methodology.

Table 7-8   Accuracy of the Techniques to Convert to Money

Accuracy	Technique using . . .	Comment
Most accurate	Standard values	80 percent of measures that matter have standard values, monetary values that are accepted by stakeholders.
	Organizational records and cost statements	Use only if complete and fully loaded. Unfortunately, it takes much time to complete.
	Experts	Most have a comprehensive knowledge of the issue and can be unbiased and neutral.
	External databases of other studies	The Internet has opened many opportunities. The studies must have similar settings.
	Linking with other measures	More relationships are being developed.
Least accurate	Estimates	Use the most credible source.

When Estimates Are Sought, Use the Source
with the Broadest Perspective on the Issue

According to Guiding Principle 3 (see Chapter 3), the most credible data source must be used. The individual providing estimates must be knowledgeable of the processes and the issues surrounding the value of the data. For example, consider estimating the cost of a grievance in a manufacturing plant. Although a supervisor may have insight into what has caused a particular grievance, he or she may be limited in terms of a broad perspective. A high-level manager may be able to understand the total impact of the grievances and how that will affect other areas; thus, that manager would be a more credible source than a supervisor because of the broader perspective.

Use Multiple Techniques When Feasible

Sometimes, having more than one technique for obtaining values for the data is beneficial. When multiple sources are feasible, they should be used to serve as comparisons or to provide additional perspectives. The data must be integrated using a convenient decision rule, such as the lowest value. A conservative approach of using the lowest value is recommended as Guiding Principle 4, but only if the sources have equal or similar credibility.

Converting data to monetary value does have its challenges. As the particular method is selected and used, several adjustments or issues need to be considered to make it the most credible and applicable value with the least amount of resources.

Apply the Credibility Test

The techniques presented in this chapter assume that each data item collected and linked to a program can be converted to a monetary value. Although estimates can be developed using one or more strategies, the process of converting data to monetary values may lose credibility with the target audience, which may question its use in analysis. Highly subjective data, such as changes in employee attitudes or a reduction in the number of employee conflicts, are difficult to convert. The key question when making this determination is: Could these results be presented to senior management with confidence? If the process does not meet this credibility test, the data should not be converted to monetary values but listed as intangibles. Other data, particularly hard-data items, would normally be used in the ROI calculation, leaving the highly subjective data expressed in intangible terms.

This issue of credibility when combined with resources is illustrated clearly in Figure 7-3. This is a logical way to either convert data to a monetary value or leave it as an intangible, and it addresses both the minimum resources. Essentially, if no standard value exists, many other methods are available to capture or convert the data to monetary value. However, there is a question of resources: Can it be done with minimum resources? Some of the techniques mentioned in this chapter, such as searching records, perhaps even searching the Internet, cannot be used with minimum resources. However, an estimate obtained from a group or a few individuals would use minimum resources.

Figure 7-3 Data Conversion Four-part Test

To Convert or Not to Convert?

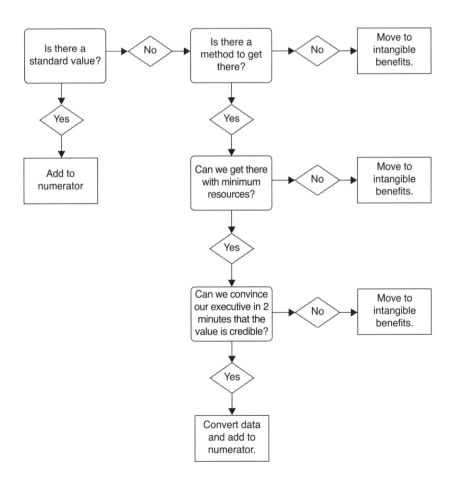

Then we move to the next challenge: credibility. Our standard credibility test is simple: If an executive who is interested in the program will buy into the monetary value for the measure in two minutes, then it is credible enough to be included in the analysis; if not, then move it to the intangibles. Incidentally, the intangibles are very important and are covered in much more detail in Chapter 9.

Review the Client's Needs

The accuracy of data and the credibility of the conversion process are important concerns. Program managers sometimes avoid converting data because of these issues. They are more comfortable reporting that a program reduced talent turnover from, say, 26 to 18 percent, without attempting to place a value on the improvement. They may assume that the sponsor will place a value on the reduction. Unfortunately, the target audience for the program may know little about the cost of unemployment and will usually underestimate the actual value of the improvement. Consequently, some attempt should be made to include this conversion in the ROI analysis.

Is This Another Project?

Because the efforts involved in developing a credible monetary value may be extensive and yet desired by the sponsor, an appropriate response to this question of whether this is another project is: Yes, it can be done; no, it cannot be done using minimum resources; and yes, it will be another program.

Essentially, bringing up the issue of converting data to monetary value in terms of the resources required is appropriate. Although it is part of the planning for a study, the resources required can be discussed. If the sponsor is interested in converting data to money when it hasn't been done before, then this realistically should be considered a separate program. This keeps it from bogging down the ROI study and places the proper emphasis and resources on the process to do a credible job on the conversion.

Consider a Potential Management Adjustment

In organizations in which soft data are used and values are derived with imprecise methods, senior managers and administrators are sometimes offered the opportunity to review and approve the data. Because of the subjective nature of this process, management may factor (reduce) the data so that the final results are more credible. In one example, senior managers at Litton Industries adjusted the value for the benefits derived from implementing self-directed teams.

Consider the Short-Term/Long-Term Issue

When data are converted to monetary values, usually one year of data are included in the analysis. This is Guiding Principle 9, which states that only the first-year benefits are used for short-term solutions. They would be considered long-term for some programs, and the issue of short-term or long-term is defined in the context of the time it takes to complete or implement the program. If one individual participating in the program and working through the process takes months to complete it, then it is probably not short-term. Some programs literally take years to implement with even one particular group. It is generally appropriate to consider a program short-term when the time is a month or less for the individual to learn what needs to be done to make the program successful. When the lag between implementing the program and the subsequent consequences is relatively short, a short-term solution is appropriate. No set time is used when a program is long-term, but the time value should be set before the program evaluation.

Input should be secured from all stakeholders, including the sponsor, champion, implementer, designer, and evaluator. After some discussion, the estimates of the time factor should be very conservative and should perhaps be reviewed by finance and accounting. When it is a long-term solution, the concept of forecasting will need to be used to estimate multiple years of value. No sponsor will wait several years to see how a program turns out. Some assumptions have to be made, and forecasting must be used.

Consider an Adjustment for the Time Value of Money

Since a program investment is made in one time period and the return is realized at a later time, some organizations adjust program benefits to reflect the time value of money using discounted cash-flow techniques. The actual monetary benefits of the program are adjusted for this time period. The amount of adjustment, however, is usually small when compared with the typical benefits of programs.

Although this may not be an issue for every program, it should be considered for each program, and some type of standard discount rate should be used. Here is an example of how this is calculated: Assume that a program costs $100,000, and a two-year period will be observed before the full value of the estimate will be covered. In other words this is a long-term solution spanning two years. Using a discount rate of 6 percent, the amount of cost for the program for the first year would be $100,000 × 106 percent = $106,000. For the second year it is $106,000 × 106 percent, or $112,360. Thus, the program cost has been adjusted for a two-year value with a 6 percent discount rate. This assumes that the program sponsor could have invested the money in another program and obtained at least a 6 percent return on that investment; hence, another cost is added.

Final Thoughts

With some programs, money is an important value. Evaluators strive to be more aggressive in defining the monetary benefits of an LD program. Leadership managers are no longer satisfied to simply report the business performance results. Instead, they take additional steps to convert impact data to monetary values and weigh them against the program costs. In doing so, they achieve the ultimate level of evaluation: the return on investment. This chapter presented several strategies used to convert business results to monetary values, offering an array of techniques to fit any situation or program. The costs are presented in the next chapter.

Leadership Development Costs and Return on Investment

T HE COST OF providing leadership development is on the rise, increasing the pressure for LD directors to know how and why money is spent. Sometimes executives need to know the total cost of a program, pushing the cost profile beyond direct costs to include indirect costs as well. Also, the costs represent the bottom part of the ROI formula. When program costs are used in the ROI formula, the appropriate costs must be actuated routinely, efficiently, and sensibly. Finally, the actual ROI calculation must be consistent with accepted financial practices and be based on conservative assumptions. Its meaning should be clearly communicated. This chapter explores all the important issues for costs and return on investment for leadership development.

Cost Issues

Tabulating program costs is an essential step in developing the ROI calculation. Fully-loaded cost information is needed to manage resources, develop standards, measure efficiencies, explore alternative delivery processes, and, of course, calculate return on investment. Here's a recap of why it is necessary to measure program costs and the important issues about capturing cost data.

Why Measure Leadership Development Costs?

Several influences have increased the need to monitor costs accurately and thoroughly. LD directors should know how much money is spent on programs—or at least be aware of the direct expenditures. Some LD directors calculate this expenditure and compare it to similar expenditures at other organizations, although these comparisons are often unreliable because of the different bases for cost calculations. Determination of LD costs as a percentage of learning and development costs is a standard calculation.

The LD team should know the relative cost of programs and their components. Monitoring costs by program allows the team to determine how costs are changing. If a program's cost rises, reevaluation of the program's impact and overall success may be appropriate. The LD team may also compare specific components of costs with those of other programs or organizations. Significant differences may signal a problem. Also, costs associated with analysis, design, development, implementation, or operation can be compared with those of other programs within the organization and used to develop cost standards.

Accurate direct costs are necessary to predict future direct costs. Historical costs for a program serve as a basis for predicting future costs of a similar program or for budgeting for a program. Sophisticated cost models make it possible to estimate or predict costs with reasonable accuracy.

When an analysis of return on investment or benefit/cost is needed for a specific program, direct and indirect cost data need to be developed. For these analyses, the total cost data is just as important as the program's economic benefits. To develop a realistic ROI determination, costs must be accurate and credible. Otherwise, the painstaking attention given to the monetary benefits is wasted because of inadequate or inaccurate costs.

Fully-Loaded Costs

Establishing direct costs is easy; determining indirect costs related to a program is more difficult. With the fully loaded costs approach, all costs that can be identified and linked to a particular program are included. A fully loaded cost profile includes such items as those in Table 8-1 (see page 178). When return on investment is calculated and reported to target audiences, the methodology should withstand even the closest scrutiny in terms of its accuracy and credibility. The only way to meet this test is to ensure that all costs are included. Of course, from a realistic viewpoint, if the controller or CFO insists on not using certain costs, then it is best to leave them out.

The Danger of Reporting Costs Without Benefits

Communicating the total costs of a leadership program without presenting benefits is risky. Unfortunately, some LD managers have fallen into this trap. They present costs to management in different ways (e.g., the cost of the program or the cost per participant). Although these costs may be helpful for efficiency comparisons, they can be troublesome without benefits. When most executives see the costs of a program, a logical question follows: What benefit has been received from the program? This is a typical management reaction, particularly when costs are perceived to be high. To avoid this situation, some organizations have developed a policy of not communicating cost data for a specific program unless the monetary benefits can be demonstrated or there is a strategy in place to develop the monetary benefits. This approach helps to keep a balance between the two issues.

Cost Guidelines

For some organizations, it may be helpful to detail the philosophy and policy on costs in guidelines for the LD team or for others who monitor and report costs. Cost guidelines detail specifically what costs are included with a program and how cost data are collected, analyzed, and reported. Cost guidelines can range from a one-page job aid to a 50-page document in a large, complex organization where there is a culture of cost control. The simpler approach is better. When developed, the guidelines should be reviewed by the finance and accounting staff. When return on investment is calculated and reported, costs are included in a summary form and the cost guidelines are referenced in a footnote or attached as an appendix.

Cost Monitoring Issues

Several issues will surface when costs associated with LD programs are monitored. Accuracy, coverage, and feasibility will play into the accumulation and monitoring approach.

Prorated Versus Direct Costs

Usually, all cost data related to an LD program are collected and expensed to that program. However, some cost categories should be prorated. For example, initial analysis, design and development, and acquisition are significant costs that should be prorated over the life of the program. With a conservative approach, the life of an LD program is usually considered to be medium-term. Skills, behavior, and competencies don't change quality for a particular job group. Some organizations consider three to five years of operation for the program; others may consider more than five years. If the specific time period to be used in the prorating formula is disputed, the shorter period should be used. If possible, finance and accounting staff should be consulted.

Consider, for example, an LD program for high-performance teams that is developed for a multinational chemical company. When planning the evaluation, the team agrees to a five-year life cycle (i.e., the content will not change significantly in that period). During the five years, roughly 1,500 participants should attend. The cost for development is estimated to be about $58,000. The cost per participant is $39 ($58,000 divided by 1,500). An evaluation is planned for two groups of 30 each. The charge for development for this study is $2,340 (39 × 60).

Accounting for People's Time

One of the most significant cost categories is the expense of taking people away from their normal work. While this can involve any number of different stakeholders, the most important category is usually the time of the participants.

There are three ways to account for this time, one of which is a standard in the ROI Methodology. Often the easiest and most credible approach is the first one: to hire replacements for participants while they attend training. For example, in a job rotation for management development, if a person is actually replaced while on assignment, that replacement cost is what is lost by taking the participant away from the job. This cost is the value used in the calculation. For most leadership development, replacements are not a factor. This leads to the second approach.

When someone is off the job, value is lost. If this value could be calculated, it would be included as the cost of taking the person away from work. If a manager is absent for a week and there is some way to know what is lost as a result, this would figure into the calculation. Obviously, this loss is difficult to quantify. A sales manager who is involved in a leadership program wouldn't necessarily lose sales unless she or he has direct sales responsibilities; however, if a sales professional participates in an LD program, a loss of direct sales could result. It's not the sales that were lost, but the profit of the sales was. So many factors can affect loss of a sale; for example, if a person is selling a product that represents a loss to the company, in essence it is helping the company to be off the job from a profit perspective. The company benefits from lack of a sale during that week. Thus, analysis becomes a little tricky.

The third approach, which is the standard one, calls for using fully loaded compensation costs for the hours, days, and weeks in training. These costs include all direct and indirect compensation, including the employee benefits factor. The salaries themselves may not necessarily be needed. Estimates from subject matter experts or even human resources will suffice. The average salary for a particular job could be appropriate. This estimate is only for the time away from normal work, not time spent on efforts such as after-hours programs or weekend managerial retreats.

Employee Benefits Factor

The costs should include salaries for the time spent by stakeholders involved with the program, as well as the cost of their benefits for that time period. The time of participants will usually be the largest item in this category. Employee benefits are expressed as a percentage of payroll (salaries). Organizations usually have this figure readily available for use in a variety of cost applications. It represents the cost of all employee benefits expressed as a percentage of base salaries. In some organizations this value can be as high as 60 percent. In others, it may be as low as 25 or 30 percent. The average in the United States is approximately 38 percent.

Estimates Are Okay

Although the direct costs are easily retrieved from the cost tracking system, the indirect costs are not always readily available. Estimates are appropriate. For example, for an evaluation of a program initiated two years ago, an estimate of the costs of the initial analysis, design, and development would be appropriate. These costs are then prorated across the life cycle of the program. When conference or meeting rooms are used to conduct the program, the cost of those facilities would be allocated to the program if a significant amount of time was involved (usually more than a couple of hours). The cost of renting a facility on a daily basis, for example, would be estimated and prorated to the duration of the session. Tracking down the detail on these types of costs is unnecessary. Just remember: The indirect costs are probably debatable. Some people would argue that these costs should not be included. We are including them to be conservative, so a great deal of precision is not necessary.

Be Sensible

A reasonable amount of caution must be exercised to avoid too much precision when costs are estimated or included. ROI Guiding Principle 10 (see Chapter 3) will serve you well, as it suggests that all costs categories be included. While all costs should be represented when they are significant, they can be omitted when they are not. For example, a virtual LD program is implemented to improve leadership skills for team leaders and help them meet certain goals. The total costs of the program would include all of the categories listed in Table 8-1. An issue surfaces in terms of including participants' time for the session. The team leader participates in a one-hour module every two weeks, usually after regular work hours. Including the cost of time for this session may be inappropriate, as it may be too conservative. Obviously, if the session lasted a full day and took place during the normal workday, the costs of that time should be used; otherwise, they should not be used.

Major Cost Categories

One way to consider program costs is within the framework of how the program unfolds. Figure 8-1 shows the LD program implementation cycle, beginning with initial analysis and progressing to evaluation and reporting of results. These functional process steps represent the typical flow of work.

Needs assessment yields a need, and then the organization designs, develops, or acquires a solution and implements it. The LD team routinely reports to the client or sponsor throughout the process and then undertakes an evaluation to show the project's success. A group of costs also supports the process (e.g., administrative support and overhead costs). For costs to be fully understood, the project needs to be analyzed in these different categories.

Defining which specific costs to include in a tabulation of program costs is the most important step. This step involves decisions that will be made by the LD team and, in most cases, approved by management. If appropriate, finance and accounting staff may need to approve the list. Table 8-1 shows the recommended cost categories for a fully loaded, conservative approach to estimating costs. Each category is described next.

Initial Assessment and Analysis

One of the most overlooked cost items is the cost of conducting the initial assessment of the need for the LD program. In some programs this cost is zero

Figure 8-1 Typical LD Program Cycle

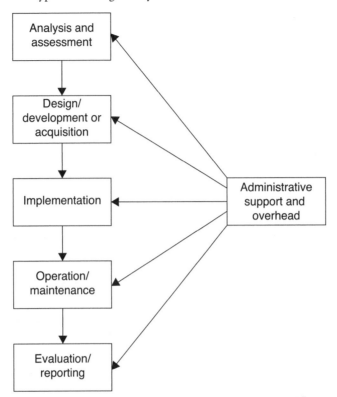

because the program is implemented without an initial assessment of need. However, as organizations focus increased attention on needs assessment, this item will become a more significant cost in the future.

While it's best to collect data on all costs associated with the assessment and analysis to the fullest extent possible, estimates are appropriate. These costs include the time of LD team members to conduct the assessment, direct fees, expenses for external consultants who conduct the needs assessment, and internal services and supplies used in the analysis. The total costs are usually prorated over the life of the program. Depending on the type and nature of the program, the life cycle should be kept to a reasonable number in the one- to two-year time frame. The exception would be for expensive programs for which the needs are not expected to change significantly for several years.

Table 8-1   Leadership Program Cost Categories

Cost item	Prorated	Expensed
Initial assessment and analysis	✓	
Design and development	✓	
Acquisition	✓	
Implementation		✓
• Salaries and benefits—coordination time		✓
• Materials and supplies		✓
• Travel		✓
• Facilities		✓
• Participants' salaries and benefits for the time involved in the program		✓
Operation and maintenance		✓
Evaluation		✓
Overhead/leadership development function	✓	

Design and Development Costs

One of the most significant items is the cost of designing and developing the program. This cost item includes internal staff and consultant time for both design and development of software, podcasts, job aids, and other support material directly related to the program. As with needs assessment costs, design and development costs are usually prorated, perhaps by using the same time frame. Three to five years is recommended unless the program is expected to remain unchanged for many years and the design and development costs are significant.

Acquisition Costs

In lieu of development costs, many organizations purchase programs to use off-the-shelf or in a modified format. The acquisition costs for these programs include the purchase price and other costs associated with the rights to implement the program. These acquisition costs should be prorated typically over three or five years using the same rationale described above. If the organization needs to modify or further develop the program, those costs should be included as development costs. In practice, many programs have both acquisition costs and development costs.

Implementation Costs

Perhaps the most important segment of LD costs is implementation. Five major categories are included:

1. **Salaries of coordinators and organizers.** The salaries of all individuals involved in coordination and direct support should be included. If a coordinator is involved in more than one program, the time should be allocated to the specific program under review. The key point is to account for all the direct time of internal employees or external consultants who work with the program. Include the employee benefits factor each time direct labor costs are involved.
2. **Materials and supplies.** Specific program materials such as workbooks, handouts, brochures, guides, job aids, and podcasts should be included in the delivery costs, along with license fees, user fees, and royalty payments.
3. **Travel expenses.** Include direct costs of travel, if required, for participants, facilitators, and coordinators. Lodging, meals, and other expenses should also be included in this category.
4. **Facilities for sessions.** Take into account the direct cost of the meeting facilities. When external meetings are held, this item represents the direct charge from the conference center or hotel. If meetings are held internally, use of the meeting room represents a cost to the organization and should be included, even if it is not the practice to include facility costs in other cost reporting.
5. **Participants' salaries and benefits.** The salaries plus employee benefits of participants for their time away from work represent an expense that should be included. Estimates are appropriate in the analysis.

Operation and Maintenance

This item includes all costs related to routine operation of the program. The category encompasses all costs in the same categories listed under implementation, plus perhaps equipment and services.

Evaluation

The evaluation cost is included in the program costs to compute the fully loaded cost. For an ROI evaluation, the costs include developing the evaluation strategy and plans, designing instruments, collecting data, analyzing data, and preparing and presenting results. Cost categories include time, purchased services, materials, purchased instruments, and surveys.

Overhead

A final charge is the cost of overhead: the additional costs of the LD function not directly charged to a particular program. The overhead category represents any LD function cost not considered in the previous calculations. Typical items include the cost of administrative support, administrative expenses, salaries of LD managers, and other fixed costs. A rough estimate developed through some type of allocation plan is usually sufficient.

Cost Reporting

Here is an actual case study that demonstrates how to present total costs. Table 8-2 shows the cost for a major executive leadership program. This was an extensive leadership program involving four off-site, week-long training sessions with personal coaches and learning coaches assigned to the participants. Working in teams, participants tackled a project that was important to top executives. Each team reported the results to management. The project teams could hire consultants as well. These costs are listed as project costs. The costs for the first group of 22 participants are detailed in the table.

The evaluation costs were unusually high due to extensive use of interviews and focus groups. Prorating costs was a consideration. In this case, organizers felt relatively certain that a second group would be conducted. The analysis, design, and development expenses of $580,657 could therefore be prorated over two sessions. Consequently, in the actual ROI calculation, half of this number was used to arrive at the total value ($290,328). This left a total program cost of $2,019,598 to include in the analysis ($2,309,926 − $290,328). On a participant basis, this amount totaled $91,800, or $22,950 for each week of formal sessions. Although this program was expensive, it was still close to benchmark data of weekly costs for senior executive leadership programs involving the same time commitments.

Return on Investment: Basic Issues

With fully-loaded costs and benefits, it is now possible to calculate the return on investment. The calculation is presented in two different but related ways.

Table 8-2 Leadership Development Program Costs

Program Costs	
Analysis/design/development:	
External consultants	$ 525,330
Leadership center	28,785
Management committee	26,542
Implementation and operation:	
Conference facilities (hotel)	142,554
Consultants/external	812,110
Leadership center salaries and benefits (for direct work with the program)	15,283
Leadership center travel expenses	37,500
Management committee (time)	75,470
Project costs ($25,000 × 4)	100,000
Participants' salaries and benefits (class sessions)	84,564
(Average daily salary × benefits factor × number of program days)	
Participants' salaries and benefits (project work)	117,353
Travel and lodging for participants	100,938
Cost of materials (e.g., handouts, purchased materials)	6,872
Research and evaluation:	
Research	110,750
Evaluation	125,875
Total costs	$2,309,926

This section reviews some fundamental terminology, use of annualized values, and methods for calculating the benefit/cost ratio (BCR) and the return on investment (ROI).

Definition

The term *return on investment* is often misused. Sometimes it is used in a broad sense to include any benefit from the LD program, a vague concept in which even subjective data linked to a program are included in the concept of the return. In this book, return on investment has a precise meaning; it represents a number developed by comparing program benefits to costs. The two most common measures are the BCR and the ROI formulas. Both are presented, along with other approaches that calculate the return.

Annualized Values

The formulas presented in this chapter use annualized values so that the first-year impact of the program investment is developed for short-term programs. Use of annual values is a generally accepted practice for developing the return on investment. This approach is a conservative way to develop the return on investment because many short-term programs have added value in the second or third year of operation. For long-term LD programs, longer time frames are used. For example, in an ROI analysis of a development program for employees with high potential in the National Security Agency, a four-year time frame was used. In an executive development program for a major oil company, with four weeks off the job spread over one year, a five-year time frame was used. When forecasting was used, combined with actual impact data, the results were present at the end of the program, not five years later. However, for many leadership programs with a duration of 3 to 10 days, first-year values are appropriate.

Benefit/Cost Ratio

One of the first methods used for evaluating investments is the benefit/cost ratio. As described in Chapter 3, this method compares the benefits of the program to the costs in a ratio. In formula form, the ratio is:

$$\text{Benefit/Cost Ratio (BCR)} = \frac{\text{Program Monetary Benefits}}{\text{Program Costs}}$$

In simple terms, the benefit/cost ratio compares the annual economic benefits of the program to the cost of the program. A benefit/cost ratio of 1, usually written as 1:1, means that the benefits equal the costs. A benefit/cost ratio of 2, usually written as 2:1, indicates that for $1 spent on the program, $2 in monetary benefits had been generated. Some LD executives prefer to use the benefit/cost ratio instead of return on investment.

Return on Investment Formula

Perhaps the most appropriate formula for evaluating investments is net program benefits divided by costs. The ratio is usually expressed as a percentage. In formula form, the return on investment becomes:

$$ROI\ (\%) = \frac{\text{Program Monetary Benefits} - \text{Program Costs}}{\text{Program Costs}} \times 100$$

or

$$ROI\ (\%) = \frac{\text{Net Program Benefits}}{\text{Program Costs}} \times 100$$

You can derive the ROI value from the benefit/cost ratio by subtracting 1 and then multiplying by 100. For example, a benefit/cost ratio of 2.45 is the same as an ROI value of 145 percent:

$$2.45 - 1 = 1.45 \times 100 = 145\%\ ROI$$

This formula is essentially the same as return on investment in other types of investments. For example, when a firm builds a new plant, the return on investment is calculated by dividing annual earnings by the investment. The annual earnings figure is comparable to net benefits (annual benefits minus the cost). The investment is comparable to program costs, which represent the investment in the program.

Using the ROI formula essentially places leadership investments on a level playing field with other investments by use of the same formula and similar concepts. The ROI calculation is easily understood by key management and financial executives who regularly use return on investment with other investments.

The following example illustrates the use of the benefit/cost ratio and return on investment. An international car rental system introduced a new LD program for first-level managers. Each manager brought two business measures in the work unit that needed to improve. These measures could have been improved using the LD competencies. A total of 36 managers were evaluated, representing two groups of 18. Three months later, 29 participants reported the improvement, along with their monetary values. These first-year monetary benefits were totaled, reflecting $329,000. The fully-loaded costs were $161,000.

The benefit/cost ratio can be calculated as follows:

$$BCR = \frac{\$329,000}{\$161,000} = 2.04$$

Therefore, for every dollar invested in this program, almost $2 in benefits was returned. The return on investment was:

$$ROI = \frac{\$329,000 - 161,000}{\$161,000} \times 100 = 104\%$$

For every dollar invested in the program, the costs (investment) were recovered, and an additional $1.04 was "returned" as earnings.

Return on Investment Interpretation

The concept of return on investment for leadership development is intriguing. Of all the six data sets elected or generated in the ROI Methodology, only the return on investment generates a range of reactions among program sponsors. LD managers may be concerned that executives will respond unfavorably to an ROI calculation unless it is very low and reasonable. If it is too high, executives may not believe the data; if it is negative, they may want to end the program. Because of these concerns, the concept of the return on investment must be clearly understood, and it should be developed very credibly following the processes and guidelines in this book. Also, an examination at this level should be undertaken on the basis of process improvement: if it's not working, adjustments will need to be made. This section focuses on those issues that are critical to the use, understanding, and interpretation of return on investment.

Choosing the Right Formula

Which quantitative measure best represents top management goals? Many managers are preoccupied with the measures of sales, profits (i.e., net income), and profit percentages (i.e., the ratio of profits to dollar sales). However, the ultimate test of profitability is not the absolute amount of profit or the relationship of profit to sales. The critical test is the relationship of profit (or cost avoidance) to invested capital, and the most popular way of expressing this relationship is by means of return on investment.

The concept of profit for LD programs is usually replaced with monetary benefits. Profits are only generated when LD programs directly affect the sales scenario with designs to build skills to develop high performance or to motivate individuals to high levels of achievement. When these programs work and sales are increased, the profit of the sales is used in the ROI calculation.

For most LD programs, the monetary benefits will be based, not on profits, but on cost reductions, savings, or cost avoidance. In practice, there are more opportunities for cost savings than for profit making. Cost savings can be generated when improvement in productivity, quality, efficiency, cycle time, or actual cost reduction occurs. A review of almost 1,000 studies in which the authors have been involved showed that cost savings was the basis for profits in the vast majority. Approximately 85 percent of the studies had payoffs based on output, quality, efficiency, or a reduction in time or cost. The others had payoffs based on sales increases, in which earnings were derived from the profit margin. This issue is relevant for nonprofit and public sector organizations where the profit opportunity is often unavailable. Because most LD initiatives are connected directly to cost savings or cost avoidance, ROI calculations can still be developed in those settings.

The finance and accounting literature define *return on investment* as net income (earnings) divided by investment. In the context of LD programs, net income is equivalent to net monetary benefits (program benefits minus program costs). Investment is equivalent to program costs. The term *investment* is used in three different senses in financial analysis, thus giving three different ROI ratios: return on assets (ROA), return on owners' equity (ROE), and return on capital employed (ROCE).

Financial executives have used the ROI approach for centuries. Still, this technique did not become widespread in industry for evaluating operating performance until the early twentieth century. Conceptually, return on investment has innate appeal because it blends all the major ingredients of profitability in one number; the ROI statistic by itself can be compared with opportunities elsewhere, both inside and outside. Practically, however, according to its developers return on investment is an imperfect measurement that should be used in conjunction with other performance measurements.[33]

The formula for return on investment defined above should be used. Deviations from the formula can create confusion not only among users but also among the finance and accounting staff. Ideally, the chief financial officer (CFO) and the finance and accounting staff should be partners in the implementation of the ROI Methodology. Without their support, involvement, and commitment, it is difficult to use return on investment on a wide-scale basis. The LD team should use the same financial terms and in the same way as do the chief financial officer and finance and accounting staff.

Table 8-3 shows how some have misused financial terms in the literature. Terms such as "return on intelligence" (or *information* or *inspiration*), abbreviated as ROI, confuse the chief financial officer, who may think ROI is the actual return on investment. Sometimes "return on expectations" (ROE),

Table 8-3 Misuse of Financial Terms

Term	Misuse	CFO definition
ROI	Return information *or* return on intelligence *or* return on inspiration	Return on investment
ROE	Return on expectations *or* return on event	Return on equity
ROA	Return on anticipation	Return on assets
ROCE	Return on client expectations	Return on capital employed
ROP	Return on people	?
ROR	Return on resources	?
ROV	Return on value	?
HCV	Human capital value	?
ROT	Return on training	?

"return on anticipation" (ROA), or "return on client expectations" (ROCE) are used, again confusing the chief financial officer, who may think they mean return on equity, return on assets, and return on capital employed, respectively. Use of such terms in the calculation of a payoff of LD investment does nothing except perhaps confuse and diminish the support of the finance and accounting staff.

Other terms, such as "return on people," "return on resources," "return on value," "human capital value," and "return on training," are used with almost no consistent and accepted financial calculations. The bottom line: Don't confuse the chief financial officer. Consider him or her to be your ally, and use the same terminology, processes, and concepts when applying financial returns for programs.

Return on Investment Objectives: The Ultimate Challenge

When reviewing the specific ROI calculation and formula, it is helpful to position the ROI calculation in the context of all the data. The ROI calculation is only one measure generated with the ROI Methodology. Six types of data are developed, five of which are the five levels of evaluation. A specific objective drives the data collection for each level of evaluation, as described earlier. In terms of return on investment, specific objectives are often set, creating the expectations of a minimal acceptable ROI calculation.

Four strategies have been used to establish a minimum expected requirement, or objective, for return on investment in an LD program. The first approach is to set the return on investment using the same values used to invest in capital expenditures, such as equipment, facilities, and new companies. For North America, Western Europe, and most of the Asian Pacific area, including Australia and New Zealand, the cost of capital has been reasonable, and this internal target for return on investment is usually in the range of 15 to 20 percent. By using this strategy, LD executives would set the ROI target the same as the value expected from other investments.

A second strategy is to use an ROI target that represents a higher standard than the value required for other investments. This target value is above the percentage required for other types of investments. The rationale: ROI application in leadership development is still relatively new and often involves subjective input, including estimates. Thus, applying a higher standard is appropriate. For most organizations in North America, Western Europe, and the Asian Pacific area, this value is usually set at 25 percent.

A third strategy is to set the ROI target at the breakeven point (0 percent return on investment), which is equivalent to a benefit/cost ratio of 1. The rationale for this approach is an eagerness to recapture the cost of the LD program only. Many public sector organizations have this ROI objective. If the funds expended for programs can be captured, there is still value and benefit from the program through the intangible measures, which are not converted to monetary values. Also, behavior change is evident in the application and implementation data.

Finally, a fourth and sometimes recommended strategy is to let the client or program sponsor set the ROI target. In this scenario, the individual who initiates, approves, sponsors, or supports the program establishes the ROI objective. Almost every program has a major sponsor who may be willing to offer the acceptable value. If so, this input links the expectations of financial return directly to the expectations of the individual sponsoring the LD program.

Return on Investment Can Be Very High

As some of the examples in this book have demonstrated, the actual ROI value can be quite high—far exceeding what might be expected from other types of investments in plant equipment and other companies. LD programs may generate returns on investment in the 100 to 700 percent range. Not all ROI studies are positive, however; many are, in fact, negative. Nevertheless, the impact of some LD programs can be quite impressive when the following situations exist: a specific need has been identified, a business performance gap exists related to the LD solution, the program is implemented at the right time to the right participants at a reasonable cost, the program is implemented and supported in the work setting, and the program is linked to one or more business measures. When these conditions are met, it is possible to achieve high ROI values.

It's beneficial to remember what drives the ROI value. Consider, for example, the investment in team leaders to reduce turnover. If a leader's behavior changes as he or she works directly with the team, a chain of impact can produce a measurable change in performance from the team. This measure now represents the team's measure of turnover. That behavior change, translated into a measured improvement for the entire year, can be quite significant. When the monetary value of the improvement in the team's turnover is considered for an entire year and compared to the relatively small amount of investment in one team leader, it is easy to see why this number can be quite large.

What Happens When the Return on Investment Is Negative?

Perhaps one of the greatest fears of those involved in the design, development, and implementation of the program is the possibility of having a negative ROI value. Few individuals want to be involved in a process that exposes a failure, especially their own. They may be concerned that the failure reflects unfavorably on them.

Ironically, a negative ROI study provides the best opportunity to learn and improve processes. The principal focus of the use of return on investment is process improvement. The methodology reveals problems and barriers. As data are collected through the chain of impact, the reasons for failure become clear. Data on barriers and enablers generated during application and implementation usually reveal why a program has been unsuccessful. Although a negative ROI study is the ultimate learning opportunity, no one wants to invite the opportunity to his or her back door. The preference would be to learn from others.

Sometimes the damage created by a negative return on investment stems from expectations that are not managed properly up-front and the fear of the consequences of a negative return on investment. The following strategies help minimize the unfavorable and sometimes disastrous perceptions of a negative return on investment:

1. **Raise questions about the feasibility of the impact study.** Is it appropriate to use the ROI Methodology for this particular program? Sometimes, a program, by its very nature, may appear to be a failure, at least in terms of return on investment, but it succeeds in some other important way.

2. **Make sure there is a clear understanding of the consequences of a negative return on investment.** This issue should be addressed early and often. The ROI Methodology is a process improvement tool and not a performance evaluation tool for the LD team. The individuals involved should not be penalized or have their performance evaluated unfavorably because of the negative return on investment.

3. **Look for warning signs early in the process.** Warning signs are usually everywhere. Reaction data can often send strong signals that an evaluation may result in a negative return on investment. Perhaps the participants see no relevance of the program or decline the opportunity to implement it.

4. **Manage expectations.** It is best to lower expectations around return on investment. Anticipating a high ROI value and communicating it to the client or other stakeholders can create an expectation that will not materialize. Keep the expectations low and the delivery high.

5. **Reposition the story using the negative data.** Instead of communicating that great results have been achieved with this effective program, the story now becomes: We have excellent information that tells how to change the program to improve results. This is more than a play on words; it underscores the importance of understanding what has gone wrong and what can be done in the future.

6. **Use the information to drive change.** Sometimes a negative return on investment can be transformed into a positive one with some minor alterations of the program. You may need to address implementation issues in terms of support, responsibility, and involvement. In other situations, a complete redesign of the program may be necessary. In a few isolated cases, discontinuing the program may be the only alternative. Whatever the option, use the data to drive action so that the maximum value of conducting the study can be realized.

Consequences of Not Developing Leaders

For some organizations, the consequences of not providing an LD program can be quite serious. An organization's inability to perform adequately might mean that it is unable to take on additional projects or that it may lose existing projects because of major problems. Leadership development can also help avoid serious operational problems, noncompliance issues, or retention problems. In these situations, the method of calculating the return on investment is the same and involves these steps:

- Recognize that there is a potential problem, loss, or negative consequence if the status quo is maintained.
- Identify the specific measure that reflects the potential problem.
- Isolate the potential problem linked to lack of leadership behavior.
- Pinpoint the anticipated "problem" level of the measure if no program is implemented (e.g., industry average or benchmarking data).
- Calculate the difference in the measure from current levels desired and the potential "problem" level of the measure. This becomes the change that can occur if the program is not implemented.
- Develop the unit value of the measure using standard values, expert input, or external databases.
- Develop an estimate of the total potential value. This becomes the total expected value of benefits derived from implementing the program.
- Estimate the total cost of the proposed program using the techniques outlined earlier in this chapter.
- Compare projected benefits with costs.

This approach has some advantages. It provides a vehicle to use the ROI Methodology in situations where the status quo is acceptable. The approach can show the value of investing in new programs to maintain a current favorable position. Essentially, the steps are the same in each situation. The challenge is to determine where the measure would be positioned if no program were implemented.

Cautions When Using Return on Investment

Because of the sensitivity of the ROI Methodology, caution is needed when developing, calculating, and communicating return on investment. The implementation of return on investment is an important issue and a goal of many HR departments. A few issues should be addressed to keep the process from going astray:

- **Remember to take a conservative approach when developing both benefits and costs.** Conservatism in ROI analysis builds accuracy and credibility. What matters most is how the target audience perceives the value of the data. A conservative approach is always recommended for both the numerator of the ROI formula (i.e., net benefits) and the denominator (i.e., program costs). The conservative approach is the basis for the Guiding Principles.

- **Be careful when comparing the return on investment in leadership development with other financial returns.** Several methods can be used to calculate the return on funds invested or assets employed. Return on investment is just one of them. Although the calculation for return on investment in leadership development uses the same basic formula as in other investment evaluations, it may not be fully understood by the audience. Its calculation method and its meaning should be clearly communicated. More important, it should be an item accepted by management as an appropriate measure for LD program evaluation.

- **Involve management in developing the return.** Management ultimately makes the decision if an ROI value is acceptable. To the extent possible, management should be involved in setting the parameters for calculations and establishing targets by which programs are considered to be acceptable within the organization.

- **Fully disclose assumptions and methodology.** When discussing the ROI Methodology and communicating data, you need to be straightforward about the process steps and assumptions used in the process. Communicate clearly the strengths, weaknesses, confidence levels, and shortcomings of the ROI evaluation.

- **Approach sensitive and controversial issues with caution.** Occasionally, sensitive and controversial issues will be generated when an ROI value is discussed. During the presentation of a study it is best to avoid debates over what is measurable and what is not. Debates should occur early in the process. Some programs may involve politically sensitive issues that must be considered early and often in the analysis and reporting. Also, some programs are so fundamental to the survival of the organization that any attempt to measure them is unnecessary. For example, a program designed for top leaders may escape the scrutiny of an ROI evaluation on the assumption that if the program is well designed, it will improve organizational performance.

- **Teach others the methods for calculating return on investment.** Each time a return on investment is calculated, the LD director should use the opportunity to educate other managers, colleagues, and the LD team. Although measurement may not be in these individuals' area of responsibility, they will be able to see the value of this approach to evaluation. Also, when possible, each project should serve as a case study to educate the HR staff on specific techniques and methods.

- **Recognize that not everyone will buy into return on investment.** Not every audience member will understand, appreciate, or accept the ROI calculation. For a variety of reasons, one or more individuals may not agree with the input values. These people may be highly emotional about the concept of showing accountability for human resources. Attempts to persuade them may be beyond the scope of the task at hand.

- **Don't boast about a high return.** Generating what appears to be a very high return on investment for a program is not unusual. Several examples in this book have illustrated the possibilities. LD directors who boast about a high rate of return open themselves to potential criticism from others unless the calculation is grounded in indisputable facts. In addition, future programs may not generate the same high returns on investment, possibly leaving managers with a sense of failure and the target audience with feelings of unmet expectations.

- **Choose the time and place for the debates.** The time to debate the ROI Methodology is not during a presentation (unless it cannot be avoided). There are constructive times to debate the ROI process: in a special forum, in an educational session, in professional literature, on panel discussions, or even during the development of an ROI impact study. Select the setting and timing for debates with care so as not to detract from the quality and quantity of information presented.

- **Do not attempt to use return on investment on all programs.** As discussed earlier, the value of some programs is difficult to quantify, and an ROI calculation may not be feasible. Other methods of presenting the benefits may be more appropriate.

Final Thoughts

Costs are important for a variety of uses and applications. They help the LD team manage the resources carefully, consistently, and efficiently. They also allow for comparisons between different elements and cost categories. Cost categorization can take several different forms; the most common ones are presented in this chapter. Costs should be fully loaded for a return on investment calculation. From a practical standpoint, including certain cost items may be optional, based on the organization's guidelines and philosophy. Nevertheless, because of the scrutiny involved in ROI calculations, it is recommended that all costs be included, even if they go beyond the requirements of the company policy.

When impact data are converted to monetary values and a fully loaded cost profile is developed, the ROI calculation becomes an easy next step. It is just a matter of plugging the values into the formula. This chapter has presented the two basic approaches for calculating the return—benefit/cost ratio and the ROI formulas. This chapter has also given several examples and highlighted issues and cautions to keep in mind when performing ROI calculations. The next chapter focuses on intangibles.

CHAPTER

9

Measuring Intangibles

INTANGIBLE MEASURES—that is, the nonmonetary benefits or detriments directly linked to leadership development that cannot or should not be converted to monetary values—are often monitored after a program has been implemented. Although they are not converted to monetary values, they are still important in the evaluation process and important to sponsors and clients. The range of intangible measures is almost limitless; this chapter describes a few common measures often linked with leadership development (see Table 9-1).

Key Concepts About Intangibles

By design, some measures are captured and reported as intangibles. Although they may not be perceived to be as valuable as the measures converted to monetary values, intangible measures are critical to the overall success of the organization.

In management development, executive education, and leadership development, intangible (nonmonetary) benefits can be more important than tangible (monetary) measures. Consequently, intangible measures should be monitored and reported as part of the overall evaluation. In practice, every project or program, regardless of its nature, scope, and content, has intangible measures associated with it; the challenge is to identify and report them efficiently.

Table 9-1 Common Intangible Measures Linked with Leadership Development Programs

• Accountability	• Employee engagement
• Alliances	• Employee satisfaction
• Attention	• Employee transfers
• Awards	• Ethics
• Branding	• Human life
• Climate	• Image
• Communication	• Innovation and creativity
• Conflict	• Leadership effectiveness
• Cooperation	• Networking
• Corporate social responsibility	• Organizational commitment
• Culture	• Reputation
• Customer complaints	• Stress
• Customer loyalty	• Sustainability
• Customer satisfaction	• Teamwork
• Decisiveness	• Timeliness
• Diversity	• Wellness/fitness
• Employee complaints	• Work/life balance

Tangibles and Intangibles: What's the Difference?

Perhaps the first step to understanding intangibles is to clearly define the difference between tangible and intangible assets in a business organization. As shown in Table 9-2, tangible assets are required for business operations; they are readily visible, rigorously quantified, and routinely represented as line items on balance sheets.[34] Intangible assets are the key to competitive advantage. They are invisible, difficult to quantify, and not tracked through traditional accounting practices. With this distinction, it is easy to understand why intangible measures are difficult to convert to monetary values.

Another basis for the distinction between tangible and intangible assets is the concept of hard data versus soft data. This concept, discussed in Chapter 4, is perhaps more familiar to LD practitioners. Table 9-3 shows the difference between hard and soft data. The most significant part of the definition of soft data lies in the difficulty in converting the data to monetary value. Intangible measures are defined as measures that are purposely not converted to monetary values. Use of this simple definition avoids confusion of whether a data item should always be classified as hard data or soft data. It is considered soft

Table 9-2 Comparison of Tangible and Intangible Assets

Tangible assets (required for business operations)	Intangible assets (key to competitive advantage in knowledge area)
• Are readily visible	• Are invisible
• Are rigorously quantified	• Are difficult to quantify
• Are part of the balance sheet	• Are not tracked through accounting practices
• Produce known returns	• Their assessment is based on assumptions
• Can be easily duplicated	• Cannot be bought or imitated
• Depreciate with use	• Appreciate with purposeful use
• Have finite application	• Can be used in multiple applications without reduction in value
• Are best managed with "scarcity" mentality	• Are best managed with "abundance" mentality
• Are best leveraged through control	• Are best leveraged through alignment
• Can be accumulated	• Are dynamic: have a short shelf life when not in use

Table 9-3 Characteristics of Data

Hard data	Soft data
• Objectively based	• Subjectively based in many cases
• Easy to measure and quantify	• Difficult to measure and quantify
• Relatively easy to assign monetary values	• Difficult to assign monetary values
• Used as common measures of organizational performance	• Less credible as performance measures
• Credible with management	• Usually behaviorally oriented

data if a credible, economically feasible process is unavailable for conversion. The ROI Methodology discussed throughout this book uses this definition of intangibles.

Identification of Measures

Data on intangible measures are available from different sources that represent different time frames, as illustrated in Figure 9-1. First, intangibles

Figure 9-1 Identifying Intangible Measures

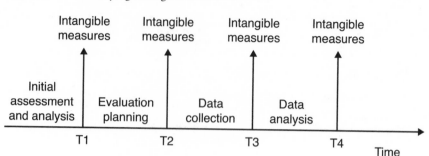

can be uncovered early in the process, during the needs assessment and initial analysis. For example, a new LD program may have several hard-data measures, such as productivity and quality, linked to the program. Employee satisfaction is an intangible measure that can be identified and monitored without any intention of converting it to a monetary value. Therefore, from the very beginning, this measure is destined to be a nonmonetary benefit reported along with the ROI results. This is T1 in Figure 9-1.

Second, intangible measures can be identified during planning discussions with clients or sponsors about the impact of a program. Clients can usually identify intangible measures that are expected to be influenced by the program. For example, a large multinational company implemented a wellness and fitness program and then planned for an ROI analysis. During the ROI planning session, program designers, the contractor, and a senior executive identified potential intangible measures that were perceived to be influenced by the program. These measures were included on the ROI analysis planning document. This is T2 in the figure.

Third, intangible measures can be collected during a follow-up evaluation. Perhaps a measure is not expected or anticipated in the initial program design, but it surfaces later on a questionnaire, in an interview, or during a focus group. These data collection methods often include questions about other improvements linked to the program. Participant responses often provide several intangible measures, and there are no planned attempts to place a value on the actual measure. This is T3 in the figure.

For example, in an innovation and creativity program, participants were asked specifically what had improved in their work as a result of the program. The participants provided several intangible measures, which managers perceived to be linked to the program.

Fourth, intangible measures are identified during an attempt to convert the data to monetary values. If the conversion process loses credibility, the measure should be reported as an intangible benefit. For example, in a customer relationship management program, customer satisfaction was identified early in the process as one of the measures of program success. A conversion of the data to monetary values was attempted. However, the process of assigning a value to the data diminished the credibility of the analysis; therefore, customer satisfaction was reported as an intangible benefit. This is T4 in the figure.

Are the Data Measurable?

Sometimes a debate erupts over whether a particular item perceived as intangible (i.e., soft) can actually be measured. In reality, any item that represents the outcome of the LD program can be measured. The measure may have to be a perception of the issue taken from a stakeholder involved in the process, but it is still a measure. The ROI Methodology rests on the assumption that anything can be measured. In the mind of the sponsor or senior executive, if an intangible (soft) item cannot be measured, why bother? The state of the situation or issue will never be known if it cannot be measured. Thus, on a practical basis, any intangible can be measured—some precisely, others not very precisely. For example, the number of team conflicts is a measure that can be assessed and categorized. Human resources staff can record all conflicts observed and place them into categories. But to place a value on a conflict may cause the data item to be labeled "intangible" if no credible, economically feasible way is available to convert it to monetary value.

Can They Be Converted?

Chapter 7 focused on various ways to convert data to monetary values. The philosophy is simple: Any data item can be converted to monetary value; there is no measure to which a monetary value cannot be assigned. The key issue is credibility of the converted value. Is it a believable value? Is a credible process used to convert data to monetary values? Does it cost too much to convert the data to monetary value? Is that value stable over time? Senior executives weigh these critical issues as they examine the conversion of data to monetary value. For tangible data conversion, the issue is of little concern. Tangible data items, such as increased output, reduction in rejects, and time savings,

Table 9-4 Test for Converting Intangibles to Monetary Value

Four-Part Test

1. Does an acceptable, standard monetary value exist for the measure? If yes, use it; if no, go to step 2.

2. Is there a method you can use to convert the measure to money? If no, list it as an intangible; if yes, go to step 3.

3. Can you accomplish the conversion with minimum resources? If no, list it as an intangible; if yes, go to step 4.

4. Can you describe the conversion process to an executive audience and secure buy-in in two minutes? If yes, use it in the ROI calculation; if no, list it as an intangible.

---

are easily converted. But soft measures (stress, complaints, attitudes, etc.) tend to lose credibility in the conversion process.

Table 9-4 shows a four-part test for converting intangibles to monetary values, presented in Chapter 7. This is the test that often leads to the classification of data as intangible. The ultimate question is posted in step 4, which is a practical issue that protects the credibility of the impact study and also allows for consistency from one study to another. The methodology would be unreliable if one evaluator converted a particular data item to monetary value whereas another evaluator did not. Maintaining this consistency is an important part of building the standards necessary for the ROI Methodology.

Analysis

For most intangible data, no specific analysis is planned for intangibles. Any previous attempts to convert intangible data to monetary units would have been unsuccessful. In some cases, you may attempt to isolate the effects of the program using one or more of the methods outlined in Chapter 6. This step is necessary when there is a need to know the specific amount of change in the intangible measure that is linked to the program. In many cases, however, intangible data reflect evidence of improvement. You do not need either the precise amount of the improvement or the amount of improvement related directly to the leadership program. Because the value of the intangible data is not plugged into the ROI calculation, intangible measures normally are not used to justify addition of programs or continuation of existing programs.

Consequently, a detailed analysis is unnecessary. Intangible benefits provide supporting evidence of the program success and can be presented as qualitative data.

Typical Intangible Measures

Most of the remainder of the chapter focuses on a few typical intangible measures. These measures are often presented as intangibles in impact studies. In some cases, organizations do convert intangible data to monetary values. The following are a few examples.

Employee Satisfaction

Employee satisfaction is perhaps one of the most important intangible measures. Improving job satisfaction is the goal of a variety of LD programs. Organizations carry out attitude surveys to measure the extent to which employees are satisfied with the organization, their jobs, their supervisor, coworkers, and a host of other job-related factors. For example, in a vision and values program implemented for all employees at one organization, the annual attitude survey contained five questions directly tied to perceptions and attitudes influenced by the program.

Because attitude surveys are usually taken annually, survey results may not be in sync with the timing of a specific LD program. When employee satisfaction is one of the program objectives and is a critical outcome, some organizations conduct surveys at a prescribed time frame after the program is implemented and design the survey instrument around issues related to the program. This approach, however, is expensive.

Although employee satisfaction has always been an important issue in employee relations, in recent years it has taken on increased importance because of the correlation between job satisfaction and other key measures. A classic relationship with employee satisfaction is in the area of employee recruitment and retention. Firms with excellent employee satisfaction ratings are often attractive to potential employees. The high ratings become a subtle but important recruiting tool. "Employers of Choice" and "Best Places to Work," for example, often have high levels of employee satisfaction ratings, which attract employees.

The significance of the relationship between employee satisfaction and employee turnover has grown as turnover and retention have become critical issues in the last decade and are likely to remain so in the future. The relationship is easily developed with current human capital management systems, which have modules to calculate the correlation between the turnover rates and the employee satisfaction scores for the various job groups, divisions, departments, and so forth.

Employee satisfaction has an important connection to customer service. Hundreds of applied research projects are beginning to show a very high correlation between employee satisfaction scores and customer satisfaction scores. These links, often referred to as service-profit chain, create a promising way to identify important relationships between attitudes and profits in an organization.

Even with these developments, most organizations do not or cannot place credible values on employee satisfaction data. The trend is moving in the right direction, but, for now, job satisfaction is usually listed as an intangible benefit in impact studies.

Organizational Commitment/Employee Engagement

In recent years, organizational commitment (OC) measures have complemented or replaced job satisfaction measures. Organizational commitment measures go beyond employee satisfaction and include the extent to which the employees identify with organizational goals, mission, philosophy, value, policies, and practices. In recent years, the concept of involvement and engagement with the organization has become a key issue. Employee engagement (EE) is now the preferred measure. Employee engagement measures the extent to which employees are actively engaged in decisions and issues on the job. Organizational commitment and employee engagement measures closely correlate with productivity and other performance improvement measures, in contrast to employee satisfaction, which does not always correlate with improvements in productivity. As OC/EE scores improve (according to a standard index), a corresponding improvement in productivity should develop. The organizational commitment/employee engagement is often measured the same way that attitude surveys are, with a 5- or 7-point scale taken directly from employees or groups of employees. Productivity is usually measured by revenue per employee.

Organizational commitment/employee engagement is rarely converted to monetary value. Although some relationships have been developed to link it to more tangible data, this research is still in development. For most studies, they would be listed as intangibles.

Culture/Climate

In recent years, much attention has been focused on the culture of the organization. Culture is a function of the organization's practices, beliefs, opinions, behaviors, policies, vision, and values. Various LD culture change projects attempt to strengthen, solidify, or adjust the culture. The culture in some organizations is distinct and defined, but it is always difficult to measure precisely.

Some organizations use culture instruments to collect data on this measure before and after a program to measure improvement. The scores on these instruments represent important data that may be connected directly to the program. In practice, it is difficult to convert culture data to monetary value in a credible way; therefore, culture change is usually listed as an intangible measure.

Some organizations conduct climate surveys, which reflect work climate changes such as communication, openness, trust, and quality of feedback. Closely related to organizational commitment and culture, climate surveys are very general and often focus on a range of workplace issues and environmental enablers and inhibitors. Climate surveys conducted before and after an LD program is implemented may reflect the extent to which the program has changed these intangible measures.

Diversity

Diversity continues to be important as organizations strive to develop and nurture a diverse workforce. Leadership development programs influence the diversity mix of the organization, and various data are available to measure the impact of focusing on diversity. The diversity mix is a measure showing employee categories along diversity definitions such as race, creed, color, national origin, age, religion, and sex. This diversity mix shows the makeup of the team at any given time and is not a measure that can be converted to monetary value credibly.

The payoff of having a diverse group influences several other measures, including absenteeism, turnover, discrimination complaints, morale, and sometimes productivity and quality. Also, a variety of diversity perception instruments are available to measure the attitudes of employees toward diversity issues; they are often administered before and after diversity projects. In addition, some organizations collect input on diversity issues in an annual feedback survey. All of these measures are important and reveal progress on an important issue, but they are difficult to convert directly to monetary value and are usually listed as intangibles.

Employee Complaints

Some organizations record and report specific employee complaints. These feedback mechanisms are usually highly visible and have catchy names such as Speak Out, Talk Back, or Hey, Mike (in an organization where the CEO's first name is Mike). A reduction in the number of employee complaints is sometimes directly related to an HR program, such as a team-building program. Consequently, the level of complaints is used as a measure of the program's success and is usually reported as an intangible measure. Because of the difficulty in converting a complaint to a monetary value, this measure is almost always listed as an intangible benefit.

Stress Reduction

Leadership development programs can reduce work-related stress by preparing employees to identify and confront stress factors to improve job performance, accomplish more in a workday, and relieve tension and anxiety. The subsequent reduction in stress may be directly linked to the program. Although excessive stress may be directly linked to other, easy-to-convert data, such as productivity, absenteeism, and medical claims, it is usually listed as an intangible benefit.

Employee Tardiness

Some organizations actually monitor tardiness, especially in highly focused work and tightly contained work environments such as call centers. Tardiness is an irritating work habit that can cause inefficiencies and delays. Organizations can use electronic and computerized time reporting to identify problem areas. Some LD programs are designed to reduce or prevent it. Tardiness is very difficult to convert to a monetary value because of the many aspects of the impact of the unacceptable work habit. Consequently, when tardiness is presented as an improvement from an HR program, it is usually listed as an intangible benefit.

Employee Transfers

Another way for employees to withdraw is to request a transfer to another section, department, or division of the organization. Requests for transfers often reflect dissatisfaction with a variety of issues, including management, policies, and practices in the organization. Transfers are essentially internal turnover. Some LD programs aim to reduce or remove these unpleasant environmental influences. In these situations, requests for transfers are monitored and reported as an intangible benefit of the program. Although it is possible to place a value on this internal turnover, usually no attempt is made to assign a monetary value to a transfer.

Innovation and Creativity

For many progressive organizations, innovation is important to success. To improve this critical area, innovation and creativity programs are implemented. Innovation is a paradox in that it is both easy and difficult to measure. It is easy to measure outcomes in areas such as copyrights, patents, inventions, new projects, and employee suggestions. It is more difficult to measure the creative spirit and behavior of employees.

An employee suggestion system, a longtime measure of the innovative and creative processes of an organization, still flourishes today in many companies. Employees are rewarded for their suggestions if those ideas are approved and implemented. Tracking the suggestion rates and comparing them with those of other organizations is an important benchmarking item for innovation and creative capability. Other measures, such as the number of new projects, products, processes, and strategies, can be monitored and measured in some way.

Some organizations actually measure the creative spirit of employees with inventories and instruments. Comparison of scores of groups of employees over time reflects the degree to which employees are improving innovation and creativity in the workplace. Subjectivity often enters the measurement process with these issues. Having consistent and comparable measures is still a challenge. Because of the difficulty of converting data to monetary values, these measures are usually listed as intangibles.

Ethics

In the wake of a variety of business scandals in recent years, the issue of ethics has gained a higher level of interest and priority in organizations. Some LD programs focus on shaping the desired ethical behavior and conduct. The menu of available programs ranges from briefings to policies to role modeling to training. Also, these programs often provide an opportunity for employees to use hotlines or special contacts to expose unethical practices. While measures are available to show improvements in ethical behavior (or the perception of improvement), these measures are often not converted to monetary value but left as intangibles.

Customer Satisfaction

Because of the importance of building and improving customer service, several measures are often monitored and reported as a payoff of a leadership development program. One of the most important measures is survey data showing the degree to which customers are pleased with the products and services. These survey values, reported as absolute data or as an index, represent important data from which to compare the success of a customer service program.

As described earlier, customer satisfaction data are attracting much interest. The data's value is often linked to other measures such as revenue growth, market share, and profits. Several models are available to show what happens when customers are dissatisfied, along with the economic impact of those decisions. Even in the healthcare area, researchers are showing linkages between patient satisfaction and customer retention. Still others are demonstrating relationships between customer satisfaction and such measures as innovation, product development, and some tangibles. Techniques are available to convert survey data to monetary values, but, in most situations, the conversion is rarely attempted. Consequently, customer satisfaction improvements at the present time are usually reported as intangible benefits.

Customer Complaints

Most organizations monitor customer complaints. Each complaint is recorded with the disposition and the time required to resolve the complaint, as well as specific costs associated with the complaint resolution. Organizations sometimes design LD programs to reduce the number of customer complaints. The total cost and impact of a complaint has three components:

- The time it takes to resolve the complaint
- The cost of making restitution to the customer
- The ultimate cost of ill will generated by the dissatisfaction (lost future business)

Because of the difficulty of assigning an accurate monetary value to a customer complaint, the measure usually becomes a very important intangible benefit.

Customer Loyalty

Customer retention is a critical measure that is sometimes linked to sales, marketing, and customer service programs. Long-term, efficient, and productive customer relationships are important to the success of an organization. Although the importance of customer retention is understood, it is not always converted to monetary value. Specific models can show the value of a customer and the value of keeping customers over a period of time. For example, the average tenure of a customer can translate directly into bottom-line profits.

Tied closely to customer loyalty is the rate at which customers leave the organization. This churn rate is a critical measure that can be costly not only in lost business (e.g., forgone profits from lost customers) but also in the expenditure necessary to generate a new customer. Because of the difficulty of converting it directly to a specific monetary value, customer loyalty usually is listed as an intangible benefit.

Teamwork

Various measures that reflect how well teams are working can be monitored. Although the output of teams and the quality of their work are often measured as hard data and converted to monetary values, other interpersonal measures can be reported also. Sometimes organizations survey team members before and after an LD program to determine if the level of teamwork has increased. Using a variable scale, team members provide a perception of improvement. The monetary value of increased teamwork is rarely developed, and, consequently, it is reported as an intangible benefit.

Cooperation

The success of a team often depends on the cooperative spirit of team members. Through use of a perception scale, some instruments measure the level of cooperation before and after the implementation of a leadership program.

Because of the difficulty of converting this measure to a monetary value, it is almost always reported as an intangible benefit.

Conflict

In team environments, the level of conflict is sometimes measured. A reduction in conflict may reflect the success of an LD initiative. Although conflict reduction can be measured by perception or numbers of conflicts, the monetary value is an elusive figure. Consequently, in most situations, a monetary value is not placed on conflict reduction, and it is reported as an intangible benefit.

Final Thoughts

Dozens of intangible measures are available to reflect the success of leadership development programs. Although they may not be perceived as useful as specific monetary measures, they are, nevertheless, an important part of an overall evaluation. Intangible measures should be identified, explored, examined, monitored, and analyzed for changes when they are linked to the program. Collectively, intangibles add a unique dimension to the overall program results because most, if not all, programs have intangible measures associated with them. Some of the most common intangible measures were covered in this chapter. The next chapter discusses the importance of properly communicating results.

10

Communicating and Using Evaluation Data

Y OU HAVE YOUR data in hand, so what's next? Should the data be used to modify the program, change the process, show the contribution, justify new programs, gain additional support, or build goodwill? How should they be presented? Who should present them? Where and when should the data be communicated? This chapter delves into these and other questions, but most importantly, it tells you how evaluation data, properly communicated to the right audiences, can drive improvement in your organization.

Principles of Communicating Results

The skills required to effectively communicate results are almost as delicate and sophisticated as those needed to obtain results. Style is as important as the substance. Regardless of the message, audience, or medium, a few general principles apply. Because they are important to the overall success of the communication effort, these principles should serve as a checklist for the leadership development team when they are disseminating program results.

Communication Must Be Timely

In general, results should be communicated as soon as they are known. From a practical standpoint, communication is delayed until a convenient time, such as the next management meeting, regional managers meeting, or annual leadership development conference. Address issues of timing: Is the audience ready for the results, considering other things that may have happened? Is the audience expecting results? When is the best time for having the maximum effect on the audience? Are there circumstances that dictate a change in the timing of the communication?

Communication Should Be Targeted to Specific Audiences

Communication is more effective if it is designed for a particular group. The message should be specifically tailored to the interests, needs, and expectations of the target audience. The results described in this chapter reflect outcomes at all levels of evaluation. When to communicate results depends in part on when the data are developed. The data developed early in the project can be communicated during the project. Data collected after implementation can be communicated in a follow-up study. Therefore, the results, in their broadest sense, range from early feedback with qualitative data to ROI values in various quantitative terms.

Media Should Be Carefully Selected

For particular groups, some media are more effective than others. Face-to-face meetings may be better than special bulletins. A memo distributed exclusively to top management may be more effective than the company's newsletter. Choosing the most appropriate method of communication can help improve the effectiveness of the process.

Communication Should Be Unbiased and Humble

Facts must be separated from fiction, and accurate statements must be separated from opinions. Some audiences are likely to be skeptical about accepting communication from the LD team because they anticipate receiving biased opinions. Boastful statements sometimes turn off recipients, and then most—if not all—of the content's significance is lost. Observable, credible facts carry far more weight than extreme or sensational claims. Although such claims may get audience attention, they often detract from the importance of the results.

Communication Must Be Consistent

The timing and content of the communication should be consistent with past practices. Unexpected communication at an unusual time during the program may provoke suspicion. Also, if a particular group, such as top management, regularly receives communication about outcomes, it should continue receiving communication—even if the results are not positive. If some results are omitted, it might leave the impression that only positive results are reported.

Confidentiality and Privacy Are Paramount

The reputation of the LD team is an important consideration. Negative comments or sensitive feedback may be detrimental to the source, if not protected properly. Data should be treated confidentially to guard the privacy of individuals. Data should be combined in such a way that an individual's responses cannot be identified. The LD team must strive to maintain a high level of credibility and respect when communicating results. Credibility should never be jeopardized by compromising people's privacy.

Planning the Communication Is Critical

Carefully plan communication to produce maximum results. Planning ensures that each audience receives the proper information at the right time and that appropriate actions are taken. Table 10-1 shows the questions that need to be asked in order to zero in on the essential areas of focus in the communication plan as it is being developed.

These general questions are important to the overall success of the communication effort. They should serve as a checklist for the LD team when program results are disseminated.

Table 10-1   Communication Planning Questions

Who are the target audiences?

What will actually be communicated?

When will the data be communicated?

How will the information be communicated?

Where will the communication take place?

Who will communicate the information?

What specific actions are required or desired?

Selecting the Audience for Communication

To the greatest extent possible, the LD team should know and understand the target audience. The staff should find out what information must be obtained and why it is needed. Each group has its own needs relative to the information desired. Some seek information that is detailed, and others want it brief. Input from others may be needed to determine audience needs. The staff should attempt to understand audience bias. LD team members should be empathetic and try to appreciate differing views. When they do, communications can be tailored to each group. This is especially critical when the potential exists for the audience to react negatively to the results. The questions in Table 10-2 should be addressed when an audience is selected.

Potential target audiences who are to receive information about results have different job levels and responsibilities. One way to select audiences is to analyze the reason behind the communication. Table 10-3 shows common target audiences and the basis for selecting them.

Perhaps the most important audience is the sponsor—the individual or team supporting the evaluation. This audience initiates the program, reviews data, and weighs the final assessment of the effectiveness of the program. Another important target audience is the top management group. This group is responsible for allocating resources for the LD program and needs information to help justify expenditures and gauge the effectiveness of the efforts.

Selected groups of managers (or all managers) are also important target audiences. Management's support and involvement in the process and the LD department's credibility help ensure success. Effectively communicating program results to management can increase both support and credibility.

Table I0-2   Key Questions for Selecting Audiences

Are they interested in the program?

Do they really want to receive the information?

Has someone already made a commitment to them regarding communication?

Is the timing right for this audience?

Are they familiar with the program?

How do they prefer to have results communicated?

Do they know the team members?

Are they likely to find the results threatening?

Which medium will be most convincing to this group?

Table 10-3 Rationale for Specific Target Audiences

Reason for communication	Primary target audiences
To secure approval for the program	Sponsor, top executives
To gain support for the program	Managers, team leaders
To secure agreement with the issues	Participants, team leaders
To build credibility for the leadership development team	Top executives, managers
To enhance reinforcement of the processes	Immediate managers
To drive action for improvement	Sponsor, LD team
To prepare participants for the program	Team leaders, participants
To enhance results and quality of future feedback	Participants
To show the complete results of the program	Sponsor, LD team
To underscore the importance of measuring results	Sponsor, LD team
To explain techniques used to results	Sponsor, LD team
To create desire for a participant to be involved	Team leaders, participants
To stimulate interest in leadership development	Top executives, managers
To demonstrate accountability for expenditures	All employees
To market future programs	Prospective sponsors, managers, team leaders

Communicating with the participants' team leaders (or immediate managers) is essential. In many cases, team leaders must encourage participants to implement the program. Also, they often support and reinforce the objectives of the program. Positive results enhance the commitment to leadership development and improve credibility for the LD team.

Occasionally, results may be communicated to encourage participation in the program. This approach is especially effective for programs that employees attend on a voluntary basis. The potential participants are important targets for communicating results.

Participants (stakeholders) need feedback on the overall success of the effort. Some individuals may not have been as successful as others in achieving the desired results. Communicating the results adds additional pressure to effectively implement the program and improve results for the future. For those achieving excellent results, communication serves as a reinforcement of what is expected. Communication of results to participants is often overlooked because it is assumed that because the program is complete, participants do not need to be informed of its success.

The support team needs communication about program results. Those who designed, developed, and implemented the program should receive detailed information about the process so they can make adjustments and measure results.

All employees and stockholders are less likely recipients. General interest news stories may increase employee respect for leadership development. Goodwill and positive attitudes toward the organization may also be byproducts of communicating results. Stockholders, on the other hand, are more interested in the return on their investment.

Table 10-3 shows the most common target audiences, although organizations may have others. For example, management or employees could be divided into different departments, divisions, or even subsidiaries of the organization. The number of audiences can be large in a complex organization. Four target audiences should receive communication:

- A senior management group
- The participants' immediate manager or team leader
- Participants
- The LD team

Developing the Information: The Impact Study

When an impact study is conducted, all of the data will be collected into an impact and ROI study report. This report describes the program, the methodology, and the results achieved. This is the beginning point for any communication. How formal this report will be will depend on whether the report is actually distributed. In some cases, it may only serve as a resource for other types of communication. However, early in the use of the ROI process, it is recommended that a complete evaluation study be conducted and printed in a readable, descriptive manner. When the dialogue and some detailed background are removed, it is essentially the impact study conducted for this particular project.

The impact study report contains the detailed information needed for the various target audiences. Brief summaries of results with appropriate charts may be sufficient for some communication efforts. In other situations, particularly with a significant program requiring extensive funding, a detailed evaluation report may be necessary. This report provides the base of information for specific audiences and various media. The report may contain the following sections:

The **executive summary** is a brief overview of the entire report, which explains the basis for the evaluation and the significant conclusions and recommendations. It is designed for individuals who are too busy to read a detailed report. It is usually written last but appears first in the report for easy access.

Background information provides a general description of the program. If applicable, the analysis that led to the implementation of the program is summarized, including the events that resulted in the evaluation. Other items are included as necessary so that a full description of the program is provided.

The **objectives** for both the impact study and the program are outlined. The report details the particular objectives of the study itself so that the reader clearly understands the rationale for the study and how the data are to be used. In addition, this section highlights the specific objectives of the program, as these are the ones from which the different types or levels of data will be collected.

The **evaluation strategy** outlines all of the components that make up the total evaluation process. The specific purposes of evaluation are outlined, and the evaluation design and methodology are explained. Any unusual issues in the evaluation design are discussed. Finally, other useful information related to the design, timing, and execution of the evaluation is included.

The **data collection and analysis** section explains the methods used to collect data. Here, the instruments used in data collection are described and presented as exhibits. The methods used to analyze data are given, including ways to isolate the effects of the program and convert data to monetary values.

The **reaction** section delineates the data collected from key stakeholders (i.e., the participants involved in the process) to measure their reactions to the program and levels of satisfaction with various issues and parts of the process. Also included may be other input from the sponsor or managers to show the levels of satisfaction.

The **learning** section consists of a brief summary of the formal and informal methods for measuring learning. It explains how participants have learned new processes, skills, tasks, procedures, and practices.

The **application and implementation** section shows how the program has actually been implemented and describes the success with the application of new skills and knowledge. This section also addresses implementation issues, including any major success and/or lack of success.

The section on **barriers and enablers** reveals the various problems and obstacles that inhibit the success of the program; it presents them as barriers to implementation. Also included as enablers are factors and/or influences that have had a positive effect on the program. Together, they provide insight into what can hinder or enhance programs in the future.

Business impact (if applicable) shows the actual business impact measures that reflect the business needs that have provided the basis for the program. This data summary shows the extent to which business performance has changed because of the program implementation.

Program costs include a summary of the costs by category. For example, analysis, development, implementation, and evaluation costs are recommended categories for cost presentation. A brief explanation of the assumptions made in developing and classifying costs needs to be made.

Return on investment (if applicable) shows the ROI calculation along with the benefit/cost ratio. It compares the ROI value to what was expected and provides an interpretation of the ROI calculation.

The **intangible measures** section shows the various intangible measures directly linked to the program. Intangibles are those measures purposely not converted to monetary values.

Conclusions and recommendations are based on all the results. If appropriate, a brief explanation can be made as to how each conclusion was reached. Also, a list of recommendations or changes in the program can be provided, if appropriate, along with a short explanation of each recommendation.

These components make up the major parts of a complete evaluation report. Figure 10-1 shows the table of contents from a typical evaluation report.

This report is an effective, professional way to present data. The methodology needs to be explained along with assumptions made in the analysis.

Figure 10-1 Table of Contents for an Impact Study Report

- Executive Summary
- General Information
  - Background
  - Objectives of Study
- Methodology for Impact Study
  - Levels of Evaluation
  - Collecting Data
  - Isolating the Effects of the Program
  - Converting Data to Monetary Values
  - Assumptions
- Data Analysis Issues
- Results: General Information
  - Response Profile
  - Success with Objectives
- Results: Reaction and Satisfaction
  - Data Sources
  - Data Summary
  - Key Issues
- Results: Learning
  - Data Sources
  - Data Summary
- Results: Application and Implementation
  - Data Sources
  - Data Summary
  - Key Issues
- Barriers and Enablers
  - Barriers
  - Enablers
- Results: Business Impact
  - Linkage with Business Measures
  - Methods of Isolating
  - Converting Data to Money
- Results: Return on Investment and Its Meaning
  - Costs
  - Return on Investment
- Results: Intangible Measures
- Conclusions and Recommendations
  - Conclusions
  - Recommendations
- Exhibits
  - Key Issues

The reader should readily see how the data have been developed and how the specific steps have been followed to make the process more conservative, credible, and accurate. Detailed statistical analyses should be placed in an appendix.

Because this document reports the success of a group of employees, complete credit for the success must go to the stakeholders involved. Their performance generated the success. Boasting about results should be avoided. Although the evaluation may be accurate and credible, it still may have some subjective issues.

Selecting Communication Media

Many options are available to communicate program results. In addition to the impact study report, the most frequently used media are meetings, reports, the organization's publications, e-mail, brochures, websites, and case studies. The following sections describe the use of these media for communicating evaluation results. Table 10-4 shows the variety of possibilities for reporting results.

Meetings

In addition to meetings with the senior executives to discuss results, other meetings are excellent opportunities for communicating program results. Various meetings may be organized to communicate the results to those who are involved in the study. This could include the managers of the participants involved, the project team that conducted the study, and various stakeholders

Table 10-4 A Variety of Options for Communicating Results

Meetings	Detailed reports	Brief reports	Electronic reporting	Mass publications
Executive briefings	Impact study	Executive summary	Website	Announcements
Manager meetings	Case study (internal)	Slide overview	E-mail	Bulletins
Project team meetings	Case study (external)	One-page Summary	Blogs	Newsletters
Stakeholder meetings	Major articles	Brochure	Video	Brief articles

who have a strong interest because of their involvement or support for the program. All organizations discuss results in meetings such as the following:

- Staff meetings designed to review progress, discuss current problems, and distribute information
- Manager meetings
- Best-practices meetings
- Business-update meetings to review progress and plans

A few highlights of major program results can be integrated into these meetings to build interest, commitment, and support for leadership development initiatives. Along with the selected results, operating issues, plans, and forecasts should be mentioned.

Interim and Progress Reports

Although usually limited to large evaluation projects, a highly visible way to communicate results is through interim and routine memos and reports. Published or disseminated via an intranet on a periodic basis, these reports inform management about the status of the program, to communicate the interim results achieved in the program, and activate needed changes and improvements. A more subtle reason for the report is to gain additional support and commitment from the management group.

Organizational Communication Tools

To reach a wide audience, the LD team can use in-house publications. Whether a newsletter, magazine, newspaper, or website file, these types of media usually reach all employees. The information can be quite effective, if it is communicated appropriately. The scope should be limited to general-interest articles, announcements, and interviews.

E-mail and Websites

Internal and external online sites, companywide intranets, and e-mail are excellent vehicles for releasing results, promoting ideas, and informing employees and other target groups about leadership development results. E-mail, in particular, provides a virtually instantaneous means with which to communicate and solicit responses from large numbers of people.

Brochures and Pamphlets

A brochure might be appropriate for voluntary LD programs conducted on a continuing basis. A brochure should be attractive, present a complete description of the program, and include a major section devoted to the results achieved. Measurable results and reactions from participants, or even direct quotes from individuals, could add interest to an otherwise dull brochure. Also, the results may provide convincing data that the program has been successful.

Case Studies

Case studies are an effective way to communicate program results. They should be developed for major evaluation projects. A typical case study describes the situation, provides appropriate background information (including the events that led to the implementation of the program), presents the techniques and strategies used to develop the study, and highlights the key issues in the program. Case studies tell an interesting story of how the evaluation has been developed and the problems and concerns identified along the way.

Case studies have value for both internal use and external use. As shown in Table 10-5, the internal use is to build understanding, capability, and support internally. Case studies are impressive to hand to a potential client and somewhat convincing for others seeking data about the success of LD programs. Externally, case studies can be used to bring exposure and recognition to the LD team and help the organization brand its overall leadership development function and, in some cases, itself. A variety of publication outlets are available for case studies—not only in the HR print space but also in general publications. A few published ROI case studies on leadership development are presented in Chapters 12 through 14.

Table 10-5 Internal and External Use of Case Studies

Internal use	External publication
Communicate results	Provide recognition to participants
Teach others	Improve image of function
Build a history	Enhance brand of department
Serve as a template	Enhance image of organization
Make an impression	

Communicating the Information

Perhaps the greatest challenge of communication is the actual delivery of the message. This can be accomplished in a variety of ways and settings based on the target audience and the media selected for the message. Three particular approaches deserve additional coverage. Each approach is explored in more detail in the following sections.

Providing Feedback During Program Implementation

One of the most important reasons for collecting reaction, satisfaction, and learning data is to provide feedback quickly so adjustments or changes can be made in the program. In most programs, data are routinely collected and quickly communicated to a variety of groups. Some of these feedback sessions result in identification of specific actions that need to be taken. This process becomes comprehensive and needs to be managed in a proactive way. Table 10-6 presents the steps for providing feedback and managing the feedback process.

Following these steps will help move the project forward and provide important feedback, which often will ensure that adjustments are supported and made.

Table 10-6   Steps to Provide Feedback During Program Implementation

- Communicate quickly.
- Simplify the data.
- Explain the role of the LD team and the program's sponsor in the feedback.
- Use negative data in a constructive way.
- Use positive data in a cautious way.
- Choose the language of the meeting and communication very carefully.
- Ask the sponsor for reactions to the data.
- Ask the sponsor for recommendations.'
- Use support and confrontation carefully.
- React and act on the data.
- Secure agreement from all key stakeholders.
- Keep the feedback process short.

Presenting Impact Study Data to Senior Management

Perhaps one of the most challenging and stressful communications is presenting impact data to the senior management team, which also serves as the client for the evaluation study. The challenges are threefold: (1) convincing this highly skeptical and critical group that outstanding results have been achieved (assuming that they have) in a very reasonable time frame, (2) addressing the salient points, and (3) making sure the managers understand the process.

Two particular issues can create challenges. First, if the results are impressive, LD leaders must assure the managers that the data are reliable. On the other extreme, if the data are negative, LD leaders must ensure that managers don't overreact to the negative results and look for someone to blame. Several guidelines help make sure this process is planned and executed properly.

A face-to-face meeting with senior team members needs to be planned for the first one or two major impact studies. If they are unfamiliar with the ROI Methodology, an in-person meeting ensures that they understand the process. The good news is that they will probably attend the meeting because they have not seen ROI data developed for this type of program. The bad news is that this presentation takes a lot of time, usually one hour. After a group has had a face-to-face meeting with a couple of presentations, an executive summary may suffice. At this point, the team understands the process, so a shortened version may be appropriate. After the target audience is familiar with the process, a brief version may be required, which will involve a one- to two-page summary with charts and graphs showing the six types of measures.

When the initial presentation is made, the results should not be distributed beforehand or even during the session; instead, they should be saved until the end of the session. Doing so will allow enough presentation and reaction time before the target audience sees the ROI calculation. The ROI Methodology should be presented step by step, showing how the data were collected, when data were collected, who provided the data, how the effect of the program was isolated from other influences, and how data were converted to monetary value. The various assumptions, adjustments, and conservative approaches should be shown along with the total cost of the program, so that the target audience will begin to buy into the process of developing the return on investment.

Results are presented one level at a time, starting with Level 1 and moving through Level 5 and ending with the intangibles. Doing so allows the audience to see the reaction, learning, application and implementation, business impact, and return on investment.

After some discussion on the meaning of the return on investment, the intangible measures should be shared. Time should be allocated for each level as appropriate for the audience. This provides an opportunity for the potentially emotional reactions to a very positive or negative return on investment to be overcome.

The consequences of additional accuracy should be shown, if that is an issue. The trade-off for more accuracy and validity is often more expense. In this case, additional data may be required. Concerns, reactions, and issues about the process should be monitored, and adjustments should be made accordingly, for the next presentation. Figure 10-2 illustrates the approach. Improving communications with this group of sponsors requires developing an overall strategy and a defined purpose.

Figure 10-2 Communicating Impact Studies to Senior Management

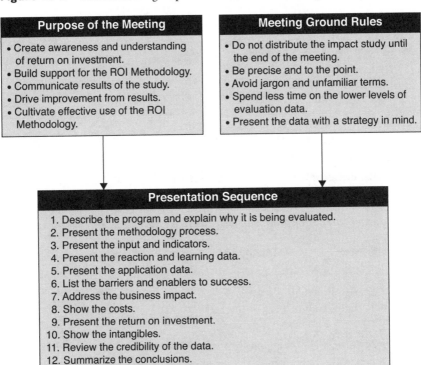

Purpose of the Meeting

- Create awareness and understanding of return on investment.
- Build support for the ROI Methodology.
- Communicate results of the study.
- Drive improvement from results.
- Cultivate effective use of the ROI Methodology.

Meeting Ground Rules

- Do not distribute the impact study until the end of the meeting.
- Be precise and to the point.
- Avoid jargon and unfamiliar terms.
- Spend less time on the lower levels of evaluation data.
- Present the data with a strategy in mind.

Presentation Sequence

1. Describe the program and explain why it is being evaluated.
2. Present the methodology process.
3. Present the input and indicators.
4. Present the reaction and learning data.
5. Present the application data.
6. List the barriers and enablers to success.
7. Address the business impact.
8. Show the costs.
9. Present the return on investment.
10. Show the intangibles.
11. Review the credibility of the data.
12. Summarize the conclusions.
13. Present the recommendations.

Figure 10-3   One-page Summary of Impact Study

ROI IMPACT STUDY					
Program Title: Coaching for New Professionals					
Target Audience: New candidates for employment in professional function					
Description: Managers volunteered to coach new employees to fit into the culture and values of this software company.					
Results					
Level 1: Reaction	**Level 2: Learning**	**Level 3: Application**	**Level 4: Impact**	**Level 5: ROI**	**Intangible Benefits**
• 95% of participants see this as necessary and helpful • Managers see this as important	• 100% of managers certified on coaching • Successful skill practice demonstration on coaching skills • Participants and coaches followed the process	• Program administered properly • Coaches were available • Peer group interviewers were consistent and thorough • Candidates used the coaches	• Early turnover reduction: 21% to 9% • Cost per early turnover: $29,000 • Total improvement: $638,000 • Number of turnovers prevented = 22	83%	• Job satisfaction • Stress reduction • Improved recruiting image
Technique to Isolate Effects of Program: Trend analysis					
Technique to Convert Data to Monetary Value: External studies for cost of early turnover, validated by the LD team					
Fully-Loaded Program Costs: $348,000					

Figure 10-3 is an example of a one-page summary that can be sent to the management team if they understand the process. Collectively, the steps shown in this example can help with preparation for and presentation of one of the most critical meetings with the management team.

Routine Communication with Executive Management and Sponsors

No group is more important than top executives when it comes to routine communication of results. In many situations, this group is also the sponsor. Improving communications with this group requires an overall strategy, which may include all or part of the following actions.

- **Strengthen the relationship with executives.** An informal and productive relationship should be established between the LD director and the top executive at the location where the program is being implemented. Each person should feel comfortable discussing needs and results. One approach is to establish frequent, informal meetings with the executive to review problems with current projects and discuss other performance problems and/or opportunities in the organization. Frank and open discussions can provide the executive with insight that is not possible from any other source.

- **Show how LD programs have helped solve major problems.** Although hard results from recent programs are comforting to an executive, solutions to immediate problems may be more convincing. This is an excellent opportunity to discuss future programs for impact analysis or ROI evaluation.
- **Distribute program results.** When a program has achieved significant results, appropriate top executives need to be made aware of them by being provided with a one-page summary (see Figure 10-3) or a summary outlining what the program was intended to accomplish, when it was implemented, who was involved, and the results achieved. This summary should be presented in a for-your-information format that consists of facts rather than opinions. A full report or meeting may be presented later. All significant communications on evaluation projects, plans, activities, and results should include the executive group. Routine information on major evaluation projects, as long as it is not boastful, can reinforce credibility and accomplishments.
- **Ask executives to be involved in a review of leadership development programs.** An effective way to enhance commitment from top executives is to ask them to serve on an LD review committee that provides input and advice to the LD team on a variety of issues, including needs, problems with existing programs, and evaluation issues.
- **Use the CEO's/CFO's preferred communication methods.** It is very important to speak the same language as the CEO/CFO and use the same channels and methods.

Analyzing Reactions to Communication

Commitment and support from the management group indicates that effective communication about the evaluation of an LD program has taken place. The allocation of requested resources and strong commitment from top management are tangible evidence of management's perception of the results of programs. In addition to this top-level reaction, there are a few techniques the LD team can use to measure the effectiveness of their communication efforts.

Whenever results are communicated, the reaction of the target audiences can be monitored. These reactions include nonverbal gestures, oral remarks, written comments, or indirect actions that reveal how the communication has been received. During the presentation, the audience may ask questions or challenge some of the information. These challenges and questions are helpful to determine the type of information to include in future communications. Positive comments about the results, whether offered formally or informally, should also be noted.

A human resources staff meeting is an excellent arena for a discussion of the reaction to results. Comments may come from many sources, depending on the particular target audiences. Input from different members of the staff can be summarized to help judge the overall effectiveness of the communication.

The purpose of analyzing reactions is to make adjustments in the communication process—if adjustments are necessary. Although the reactions may involve intuitive assessments, a more sophisticated analysis can provide more accurate information to make these adjustments. The net result should be a more effective communication process.

Using Evaluation Data to Drive Improvement

Evaluation is a process improvement tool. Evaluation data should drive changes to overcome lack of success or to enhance current success. In addition, evaluation data can provide useful information to enhance the image, credibility, and success of leadership development and provide recognition to all the stakeholders involved. This section explores the strategies for using evaluation data properly and describes how to monitor improvements generated from the evaluation data.

Adjust Program Design

Perhaps one of the most important reasons for evaluation is to make changes in the design of the program. This strategy is particularly appropriate in the early stages of the launch of a new program. Reaction and learning data can indicate problems with content, design, and sequencing. This information can be quickly provided to designers to make adjustments as needed. Even follow-up application and impact data may reveal design flaws or situations where design features need to be adjusted to enhance success.

Influence Application and Impact

Sometimes a measurement is taken to reinforce to participants what they should accomplish during implementation. In effect, the measurement is actually reminding them of what they should do and the success they should achieve. This use of data is particularly appropriate with follow-up questionnaires provided before the time the questionnaires are due. Participants are made aware of expectations that influence the success of the program. Some LD managers may argue that this use of data is unfairly biasing the evaluation and measurements that influence success. Nevertheless, if the designers are convinced that this measurement adds value, then including it every time may ensure success. It becomes built into the process.

Improve Management Support for Leadership Development

Managers at the middle and top levels in the organization often do not support leadership development for a variety of reasons. The value of LD programs must be expressed in terms they understand and appreciate. Evaluation data, particularly showing the application, impact, and even return on investment, can provide convincing evidence for these managers so they will increase future support. Nevertheless, this approach works only if the data provided are understandable to and valued by managers. The items they are interested in are typically application, impact, and ROI data.

Improve Satisfaction with Stakeholders

A variety of stakeholders are involved in the implementation of LD programs. Evaluation data give stakeholders a sense of the success of the program. In essence, they become more satisfied with a program when they see the value it adds. Application and impact data are particularly helpful for these stakeholders so that they can see that their actions are really making a difference in the organization.

Recognize and Reward Stakeholders

The most critical stakeholder in leadership development is the actual participant who must learn, apply, and achieve results if the program is to add value. When participants excel in terms of their application and desired impact of leadership development on the job, they should be rewarded. Evaluation data provide this important clarification of the role of the participant, giving credit to group members who actually achieved the success: the participants involved in the learning and development processes.

Justify or Enhance Leadership Development Budget

In today's economic environment, one of the most important reasons for developing evaluation data is to show the value of leadership development. In tough economic times, the LD team uses evaluation to justify an existing budget or enhance the current budget. This use of data can only be accomplished if the evaluation is pushed to the levels of business impact and return on investment. This way, executives approving budgets can clearly see the connection between leadership development and value added to the organization. Conversely, many LD budgets are being cut because data are unavailable to prove the actual value of leadership development.

Reduce Costs

Evaluation data can show efficiencies generated with adjustments in the design, development, and implementation of an LD program. For example, asking participants how the implementation could succeed with an alternative process often gives important insights into ways to save money. Questioning how the particular program could be improved or how success could be enhanced provides useful information for making cost-effective adjustments. In many situations, evaluation data are used to drive changes that usually result in conserving budgets or reducing expenditures.

Entice Prospective Participants to Get Involved in the Program

When participants have an option of being involved, such as in a wellness and fitness program, evaluation data can provide a convincing case for their involvement. Evaluation data can show how others have reacted to and used the knowledge and skills from the program and achieved success at the impact level. In essence, the participants, through evaluation data, show the advantages of being involved in the program. This information proves to be effective in brochures, documents, and other promotional materials to show others why they should be involved.

Market LD Programs

Closely tied with the previous use of the data is the development of marketing material designed to let others know about the particular program. Included in the marketing material should be evaluation data that show the success of the program. The data add an extra dimension to marketing by enticing individuals to become involved themselves or to send others to the program based on outcomes, not content. You can only develop this type of marketing message if data are collected to show application, impact, and even return on investment. In essence, this dimension provides a strategic marketing focus for leadership development, moving from the position of trying to sell it to making it attractive based on its value proposition.

Expand Implementation to Other Areas

One of the most profitable ways to use evaluation data is to make a convincing case to implement a program in other areas if the same need is there. When a pilot program offered in one division is showing substantial contribution and adds tremendous value to the organization, a compelling case can be made to implement it in other areas if a needs assessment or performance analysis has indicated the same need there. Previously, this decision has been made with qualitative data, often based on reaction to the program. Evaluation data showing application, impact, and return on investment can provide a more convincing case for program implementation and moves the LD function to results-based decision making.

Strategy Uses

The uses of evaluation data are limitless, and the options for providing data to various target audiences are vast. Table 10-7 shows all the uses of data described in this chapter, linked to the various levels of evaluation. This matrix illustrates how valuable evaluation data can be in terms of driving improvement in the organization.

Table 10-7 Matching Strategies to Levels

Strategies for Using Data	Appropriate Level of Data				
	1	2	3	4	5
Adjust program design.	✓	✓			
Influence application and impact.			✓	✓	
Improve management support for LD.			✓	✓	✓
Improve satisfaction with stakeholders.			✓	✓	
Recognize and reward participants.			✓	✓	
Justify or enhance the LD budget.				✓	✓
Reduce costs.		✓	✓	✓	✓
Entice prospective participants to be involved in LD programs.	✓	✓	✓	✓	
Market LD programs.	✓		✓	✓	✓
Expand implementation to other areas.			✓	✓	✓

To ensure that data are applied as intended, it may be helpful to draft project plans or follow-up actions that track improvements. For example, if evaluation has indicated that a redesign of a program is necessary, a plan of action will ensure that the redesign actually occurs. In some cases, this type of data should be provided to various stakeholders and sometimes even to participants. They may need to understand that the evaluation is actually serving a purpose. The specific types of follow-up mechanisms may vary, and several options are available. This final step may be the most important part of the process.

Final Thoughts

This chapter presented the final part in the evaluation process—communicating results and driving improvement. If this issue is not taken seriously, the organization will not be able to capitalize on the benefits of LD programs. A full array of possibilities exists to translate communication into action. This chapter presented the tools to communicate the results of program evaluation to a variety of audiences, the first step in helping the LD function prove its value to the organization's bottom line. Special emphasis was placed on communicating with senior executives. The next chapter focuses on implementing and sustaining the use of ROI Methodology.

Taking a Sensible Approach to the ROI Methodology

T HE BEST-DESIGNED model, technique, or process is worthless unless it is effectively integrated into the organization. Even a simple, methodical process fails in the best organizations if it is not fully supported by those who should make it work. As you begin to plan for and implement the ROI Methodology, you may encounter some resistance to it. Fundamentally, resistance to evaluation is much the same as resistance to any change process, but you can minimize resistance with careful implementation of a sensible approach to return on investment.

The Basis for Resistance

Leadership development team members and others closely associated with programs usually resist the ROI evaluation because they think it will require a great deal of their time, which is already in short supply, or because they worry about the consequences of the final outcomes. These two concerns are not groundless. Implementing a comprehensive, high-level evaluation takes time, effort, and leadership. The LD team may already feel overwhelmed and be wary of having another task to do. The fear of poorly designed or implemented programs being "exposed" can cause resistance. Few people want the "world" to know that their programs are not working. Also, discovering that a particular program really did cost too much can be unsettling.

Figure 11-1 What Do You Think About ROI Evaluation?

Rate the extent to which you agree with the following statements:
A rating of 1 = strongly agree
A rating of 5 = strongly disagree

	Strongly agree 1	2	3	4	Strongly disagree 5
1. I do not have time for ROI.	☐	☐	☐	☐	☐
2. An unsuccessful ROI evaluation will reflect on my performance.	☐	☐	☐	☐	☐
3. A negative ROI will kill my program.	☐	☐	☐	☐	☐
4. My budget will not allow for ROI.	☐	☐	☐	☐	☐
5. ROI evaluation is not part of my job.	☐	☐	☐	☐	☐
6. I did not have input on this process.	☐	☐	☐	☐	☐
7. I do not understand ROI.	☐	☐	☐	☐	☐
8. Our managers will not support ROI.	☐	☐	☐	☐	☐
9. Data will be misused.	☐	☐	☐	☐	☐
10. ROI is too subjective.	☐	☐	☐	☐	☐

If you scored:
• 10 – 25 = You like new challenges and are accepting of change.

• 21– 30 = You go with the flow.

• 31– 40 = You stress out and resist change.

• 41 and above = You are a strong resistor.

The fundamental basis for resistance, then, is fear or uncertainty. The top 10 resistors to ROI evaluation, listed in the context of comments often made by stakeholders involved in evaluation implementation, are listed in Figure 11-1. You can use this instrument to assess the current level of resistance of the LD team and adjust a strategy to minimize it.

These issues can lead to resistance to any new evaluation process. The resistance is amplified when the term "ROI" is used. The remainder of this chapter focuses on specific actions that can be taken to reduce these fears, minimize the resistance to ROI evaluation, and use the process in a sensible way.

Fearless Implementation

Resistance to something new is inevitable; it is a part of human nature. Regardless of the reasons for the opposition, change causes a flurry of questions, doubts, and fears. At times the reasons for resistance are legitimate; however, the opposition often exists for the wrong reasons. An initial step in overcoming resistance to ROI evaluation is separating the myths from legitimate concerns. When legitimate barriers to implementation exist, minimizing or removing them altogether is necessary.

As additional impact studies are conducted, consistency becomes an important consideration. With consistency come accuracy and reliability. Consistency is achieved through clearly defined processes each time evaluation is pursued. Cost control and efficiency are also issues. Implementation tasks must be completed efficiently as well as effectively to keep costs to a minimum and use time efficiently.

Figure 11-2 shows actions outlined in this chapter, presented as building blocks to overcoming resistance. They are all necessary to establish the proper framework to dispel myths and remove or minimize barriers. The remainder of this chapter presents specific strategies and techniques around each of the building blocks identified in Figure 11-2.

Assess the Climate

As a first step toward implementation, some organizations assess the current climate for achieving results. One way to assess is to use a survey to determine

Figure 11-2 Building Blocks for Overcoming Resistance

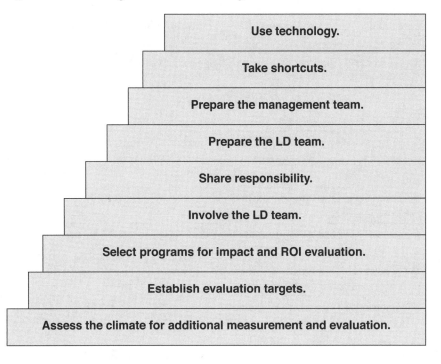

current perspectives of the management team and other stakeholders about program results. Another way is to conduct interviews with key stakeholders to determine their willingness to implement additional measurements and evaluation. With an awareness of the current status, the LD team can plan for significant changes and pinpoint issues that need support for more evaluation.

Establish Evaluation Targets

Specific targets for evaluation levels and projects are necessary to make progress with measurement and evaluation. Targets enable the LD team to focus on the improvements needed within specific evaluation categories or levels. When targets are being established, the percentage of programs planned for each level of evaluation needs to be determined.

Regardless of what type of program is planned, the first step is to assess the present situation, as shown in Table 11-1. The number of all programs is tabulated along with the corresponding level(s) of evaluation presently conducted for each program. Next, the percentage of programs that use reaction evaluation is calculated or estimated. The process is repeated for learning, application and implementation, impact, and ROI levels of evaluation.

After the current situation is detailed, the next step is to determine a realistic target for each level within a specific time frame. Many organizations set annual targets for change. This process should involve the input of the LD team to ensure that the targets are realistic and that the staff is committed to the evaluation process and targets. If the LD team does not develop

Table 11-1 Establishing Evaluation Targets

	Current situation	Target
Total number of LD programs		
Percentage of LD programs evaluated with reaction data		
Percentage of LD programs evaluated with learning data		
Percentage of LD programs evaluated with application and implementation		
Percentage of LD programs evaluated with impact data		
Percentage of LD programs evaluated with ROI data		

Table 11-2 Evaluation Targets for a Healthcare Chain

Level of evaluation	Percentage of programs evaluated at this level
Level 1—Reaction	100
Level 2—Learning	80
Level 3—Application and implementation	30
Level 4—Impact	10
Level 5—ROI	5

ownership for this process, targets will not be met. The improvement targets must be achievable and, at the same time, challenging and motivating. Table 11-2 shows the targets established for a healthcare chain with dozens of LD programs.

Using this example, 100 percent of the programs are measured at Level 1 (reaction), consistent with practices at many other organizations. Eighty percent of the LD programs are measured at Level 2, using a formal method of learning measurement. At this organization, informal learning measurement methods are counted as a learning measure. The Level 2 measure may increase significantly in groups where there is much formal testing or if informal measures (e.g., self-assessment) are included as a learning measure. Thirty percent of programs are measured at the level of application and implementation. This means that almost one-third of the programs will have some type of follow-up method, at least for a small sample of participants in those programs. Ten percent of the programs are planned for business impact evaluation (Level 4) and half of those for ROI (Level 5). These percentages are typical and often recommended. Evaluating more than 5 or 10 percent of programs at the level of ROI is rarely needed. Sometimes targets are established for gradually increasing evaluation processes—both in terms of numbers of evaluations and evaluation levels—over several years.

Target setting is a critical implementation issue. Targets should be set early and have the full support of the entire LD team. Also, when practical and feasible, the targets should have the approval of the key management staff, particularly the senior management team.

Select Programs for Impact and ROI Evaluation

Selecting a program for ROI evaluation is an important issue. Ideally, certain types of programs should be selected for comprehensive, detailed analyses.

The typical approach for identification of programs for evaluation is to select those that are expensive, strategic, and highly visible. Figure 11-3 is a tool to help select programs for ROI evaluation. It is based on six criteria often used to select programs for this level of evaluation.

These criteria are only the basic ones; the list can be extended as necessary to bring the organization's particular issues into focus. Some large organizations with hundreds of programs use as many as 12 criteria. The LD team rates programs based on these criteria, using a rating scale of 1 through 5. All programs are rated, and the program with the highest score is the best candidate for impact and ROI evaluation.

This process only identifies the best candidates. The actual number evaluated may depend on other factors such as resources and capability. The most

Figure 11-3   Selection Tool for an ROI Impact Study

Selecting Program for ROI Evaluation					
	Programs				
	1	2	3	4	5
Criteria					
1. Lifecycle of the program					
2. Linked to objectives					
3. Costs of program					
4. Audience size					
5. Visibility of program					
6. Management interest in the evaluation					
Total					

Rating Scale	
1. Lifecycle of program	5 = Long life cycle 1 = Very short life cycle
2. Linked to objectives	5 = Closely related to organizational objectives 1 = Not directly related to organizational objectives
3. Costs of program	5 = Very expensive 1 = Very inexpensive
4. Audience size	5 = Very large audience 1 = Very small audience
5. Visibility	5 = High visibility 1 = Low visibility
6. Management interest	5 = High level of interest in evaluation 1 = Low level of interest in evaluation

important issue is to select programs designed to make a difference and represent significant investments. Also, programs that command much attention from management are ideal candidates for high-level evaluation. Almost any senior management group has a perception about the effectiveness of a particular program. Some want to know its impact, but others may not be very concerned. Therefore, management interest may drive the selection of many of the impact studies.

The next step is to determine how many impact and ROI evaluation projects to undertake initially and in which particular areas. It's a good idea to start with a small number of initial projects, perhaps two or three, in order to keep the process manageable.

Additional criteria should be considered when initial programs are selected for impact evaluation. For example, the initial program should be as simple as possible. Don't tackle complex programs until skills have been mastered. Also, the initial program should be one that is considered successful now; that is, all the current feedback data suggest that the program is adding significant value. This strategy helps avoid having a negative ROI study on the first application of ROI analysis. Still another criterion is to select a program that is void of strong political issues or biases. Although such programs can be tackled effectively with the ROI analysis, it may be too much of a challenge for an early application.

Ultimately, the number of programs selected for ROI analysis depends on the resources available to conduct the studies, as well as the internal need for accountability. The percentage of programs evaluated in Table 11-2 can be accomplished for 3 to 5 percent of the total LD budget. The costs of evaluation need not drain the organization's or department's resources.

Involve the LD Team

One group that often resists implementing a comprehensive measurement and evaluation process is the LD team, who must design, develop, implement, and coordinate programs. These team members often see evaluation as an unnecessary intrusion into their responsibilities, absorbing precious time and stifling their freedom to be creative.

The LD team should be involved in key decisions in the process. Staff input is absolutely essential as policy statements are prepared and guidelines are developed. The team will find it difficult to be critical of something they've been involved with from design to implementation. Through use of workshops, brainstorming sessions, planning sessions, and task forces, they should be involved in every phase of developing the framework and supporting documents.

The team sometimes resists ROI evaluation because their programs will be fully exposed, placing their reputations on the line. They may fear failure. To overcome this source of resistance, the ROI Methodology should clearly be positioned as a tool for process improvement—not as a tool to evaluate performance, at least during its early years of implementation.

The LD team can often learn more from disappointment than from success. If the program isn't working, it is best to find out quickly and understand the issues firsthand rather than from others. If a program is ineffective and not producing the desired results, it will eventually be known to clients and the management group, if they are not aware of it already.

A lack of results can cause managers to become less supportive of leadership development functions. Dwindling support appears in many forms, ranging from budget reductions to refusal to be involved in programs. When the weaknesses of programs are identified and adjustments are made quickly, ineffective programs can be converted into effective ones, and the credibility and respect for the LD function and staff will be enhanced.

Share Responsibility

An easy way to make evaluation routine is to have others do it. In some organizations, this may mean sharing the responsibility of various parts of ROI evaluation with a variety of other stakeholders. An important part of that effort is to include evaluation responsibilities in stakeholder involvement. Involve stakeholders in collecting, analyzing, and communicating data, and reviewing and interpreting conclusions. They will take ownership in evaluation, and the burden will be lightened for staff members directly responsible for the evaluation.

Prepare the LD Team

To make the transition to higher-level evaluation, it may be necessary to enhance the LD team's skills in the areas of measurement, evaluation, and ROI so that they can support the methodology. Measurement and evaluation are not always a formal part of preparing to become an LD specialist or manager. Consequently, each staff member may need to learn how the ROI Methodology is implemented, step by step.

In addition, LD team members must know how to develop plans to collect and analyze data as well as to interpret results from data analysis. A one- or two-day workshop can help LD team members build adequate skills and knowledge to understand the process; appreciate what that process can accomplish for the organization; see the necessity of it; and ultimately participate in a successful implementation. Make it a point for expertise not only to be an essential part of the development practice and implementation of the evaluation policy, but also a routine part of the evaluation itself.

Prepare the Management Team

Perhaps no group is more important to measurement, evaluation, and ROI efforts than the management team who must allocate resources and support programs. In addition, they often provide input and assistance in the evaluation process. It's essential to carefully plan and execute specific actions to prepare the management team and improve the relationship between the LD team and key managers. A productive partnership requires each party to understand the concerns, problems, and opportunities of the other. Developing this type of relationship is a long-term process that must be deliberately planned and initiated by key LD team members. Sometimes the decision to commit resources and support for solutions is based on this relationship.

Take Shortcuts

One of the most significant barriers to the implementation of the ROI Methodology is the potential time and cost to do so. Sometimes the perception of excessive time and cost is only imaginary; at other times it is a reality. As discussed earlier, the methodology can be implemented for 3 to 5 percent of the LD budget. However, expenses and time requirements can be significant. Cost savings approaches have commanded much attention recently and represent an important part of the implementation strategy. The following sections offer some cost savings strategies that can help offset the costs of ROI evaluation.

Take shortcuts at lower levels. When resources are a primary concern and shortcuts need to be taken, it is best to take them at lower levels in the evaluation scheme. This is a resource allocation issue. For example, when an impact evaluation (Level 4) is conducted, evaluation at Levels 1 to 3 does not have to be as comprehensive. This shift places most of the emphasis on the highest level of the evaluation so that it is credible and dependable.

Fund measurement and evaluation with savings from the use of ROI analysis. Almost every impact study generates data from which to make improvements. Results at different levels often show how the program can be altered to make it more effective and efficient. Sometimes, the data suggest that the program can be modified, adjusted, or completely redesigned. All of those actions can result in cost savings. In a few cases, the program may have to be eliminated because it is not adding value and adjustments will not necessarily improve it. In this case, tremendous cost savings are realized as the program is eliminated. A logical argument can be made to shift a portion of these savings to fund additional measurement and evaluation. Some organizations gradually migrate to an LD budget target of 5 percent for expenditures for measurement and evaluation by using the savings generated from the use of the evaluation. This transition provides a disciplined and conservative approach to additional funding.

Plan early and thoroughly. One of the most salient, cost-saving steps to evaluation is to develop program objectives and plan early for the evaluation. Impact studies are successful because of proper planning. The best way to conserve time and resources is to know what must be done at what time. This knowledge prevents unnecessary analysis, data collection at an inappropriate time, and the necessity of reconstructing events and issues because they were not planned in advance.

Integrate evaluation into the LD program. To the extent possible, evaluation should be built into the LD program. Data collection tools should be considered part of the program. If possible, these tools should be positioned as application tools and not necessarily as evaluation tools. This action enables participants or others to capture data to understand clearly the success of the program on the job. Part of this issue is to build in expectations for stakeholders to provide the appropriate data.

Provide participants with a defined role. One of the most effective cost savings approaches is to have participants conduct major steps of the process. Participants are the primary source for understanding the degree to which learning is applied and has driven success on the job. Their responsibilities should be expanded from the traditional requirement of involvement in implementing the program. Now they must be asked to show the impact of those programs and provide data about success. Consequently, the participant's role expands from learning and application to measuring the impact and communicating information.

Use quick methods. Each step of the ROI Methodology has shortcut methods that are quick but credible; for example, in data collection, the simple questionnaire is a shortcut method to generate powerful and convincing data, if it is administered properly. Other shortcut methods are available for isolating, converting, and reporting data.

Use sampling. Not all LD programs require a comprehensive evaluation, nor should all participants necessarily be evaluated in a planned follow-up. Sampling can be used in two ways. First, only a few programs should be selected for ROI evaluation using the criteria in Figure 11-3. Next, when a particular program is to be evaluated, in most cases collecting data from a sample of participants keeps costs and time to a minimum.

Use estimates. Estimates are the least expensive way to arrive at a number or value. Whether the effects of leadership development are isolated or data converted to monetary value, estimation can be a routine and credible part of the process. The important point is that the estimate must be credible and follow systematic, logical, and consistent steps. Estimation methods and assumptions need to be addressed when results of the evaluation are communicated.

Use internal resources. An organization does not necessarily have to employ consultants to work up impact studies and address other ROI issues. Internal capability can be developed, eliminating the need to depend on consultants. Several opportunities exist for the LD team to build skills and become certified in ROI evaluation. This approach is perhaps one of the most significant cost savers. With use of internal resources instead of external consultants, as much as 50 or 60 percent of the cost of a specific project can be saved.

Build on the work of LD practitioners who have implemented ROI in their organizations. You don't need to reinvent the wheel. Learn from others and build on their work. Three primary ways to accomplish this task are:

1. Use networking opportunities internally, locally, and globally.
2. Read and dissect a published case study. More than 300 cases have been published.

3. Locate a similar case study in a database of completed case studies and contact the authors for more information.

These important shortcuts can help ensure that evaluation does not drain budgets and resources unnecessarily. Other shortcuts can be developed, but a word of caution is in order: Shortcuts often compromise the process. When a comprehensive, valid, and reliable study is needed, it will be time-consuming and expensive—there's no way around it. The good news is that many shortcuts can be taken to supply the data necessary for the audience and manage the process in an efficient way.

Use Technology

A variety of software tools are available to help organizations develop consistent processes, use standard techniques, and produce consistent reports. Technology is essential for evaluation. Software not only reduces time to conduct an impact study but also helps in the development and reporting of information, often in the form of a scorecard or report.

Final Thoughts

In summary, taking a sensible approach to ROI analysis is necessary to make it successful in the organization. There will be some resistance to ROI analysis; the key to overcoming resistance is to develop a sensible implementation strategy. The actions identified in this chapter will help smooth fears and remove barriers, ensuring opportunity to successfully integrate, and more importantly, sustain ROI evaluation as a routine process.

This book clearly identifies how LD specialists, managers, and executives can show the value of the leadership development contribution. When one is considering the material covered and the progress made, perhaps it is helpful to revisit the challenge facing leadership development from two perspectives: reactive and proactive.

First is the reactive approach. Unless leadership development shows its contribution, it will continue to struggle as a reliable and thriving part of the organization. Budgets will be cut, influence will diminish, and respect will deteriorate. Many executives are now requiring this type of accountability. Sometimes justifying the budgets of particular programs and projects is necessary. From a reactive posture, this is absolutely necessary for the continued survival of the function.

On a more positive note, the proactive approach is very powerful. Some LD executives are showing the value of their contribution and convincing top management that the LD function can add tremendous value to the organization. The reality is that many LD programs contribute significantly to the organization; there is just not enough data to convince the decision makers that this is the case. As expected, there are some programs that are not adding value. Because we do not have the convincing data that identifies where they are failing, we are unable to make improvements. The proactive approach positions the LD function as an integral part of the organization. As a respectable and viable function in the organization, it earns a seat at the table for the senior LD executive.

Individuals are drawn to this methodology as a result of both proactive and reactive thinking. Whatever the rationale, the challenge is clear: Action is needed now, not later; steps need to be taken to show the contribution; we can no longer say that it cannot be done because it is being done routinely by literally hundreds of organizations. The next step is yours! Part Two presents three case studies where the ROI Methodology has been applied.

PART
TWO

Case Studies

12

Case Study: Return on Investment in Business Coaching[*]

T HE LEARNING AND development team at the Nations Hotel Corporation was challenged to identify learning needs to help executives find ways to improve efficiency, customer satisfaction, and revenue growth in the company. A key component of the program was the development of a formal, structured coaching program: Coaching for Business Impact (CBI). The corporate executives were interested in seeing the actual return on investment for the coaching project. This requirement caused the designers to alter the program to focus on results.

This case study provides critical insights into how coaching creates value, including return on investment, in an organization with a variety of measures. It is an excellent capture of application (Level 3) and impact (Level 4) data.

Background

Nations Hotel Corporation (NHC) is a large U.S.-based hotel firm with operations in 15 countries. The firm has maintained steady growth to include more than 300 hotels in cities all over the world. NHC enjoys one of the most recognized names in the global lodging industry, with 98 percent brand awareness worldwide and 72 percent overall guest satisfaction.

---

* This case study has previously been published in Phillips, Patricia Pulliam, Jack J. Phillips, and Lisa Ann Edwards, *Measuring the Success of Coaching: A Step-by-Step Guide for Measuring Impact and Calculating ROI*, Alexandria, VA: ASTD Press, 2012.

The hospitality industry is very competitive, cyclical, and subject to swings with the economy. Room rentals are price sensitive, and customer satisfaction is extremely important for NHC. Profits are squeezed if operating costs get out of hand. NHC top executives constantly seek ways to improve operational efficiency, customer satisfaction, revenue growth, and retention of high-performing employees. Executives, particularly those in charge of individual properties, are under constant pressure to show improvement in these key measures.

The learning and development function, the Nations Hotel Learning Organization (NHLO), conducted a brief survey of executives to identify learning needs to help them meet some of their particular goals. The organization was interested in developing customized learning processes including the possibility of individual coaching sessions. Most of the executives surveyed indicated that they would like to work with a qualified coach to assist them through a variety of challenges and issues. The executives believed that this would be an efficient way to learn, apply, and achieve results. Consequently, the Nations Hotel Learning Organization developed a formal, structured coaching program—Coaching for Business Impact (CBI)—and offered it to the executives at the vice president level and above.

As the project was conceived, the senior executive team became interested in showing the value of the coaching project. Although they supported coaching as a method to improve executive performance, they wanted to see the actual return on investment. The goal was to evaluate 25 executives, randomly selected (if possible) from participants in the CBI program.

The Program

Figure 12-1 shows the steps in the new coaching program from the beginning to the ultimate outcomes. This program involves 14 discrete elements and processes:

1. **Voluntary participation.** Executives had to volunteer to be part of this project. Voluntary commitment translates into a willing participant who is not only open to changing, improving, and applying what is being learned but also is also willing to provide the necessary data for evaluating the coaching process. The voluntary nature of the coaching program, however, meant that not all executives who needed coaching would be involved. When compared

Figure 12-1   Coaching for Business Impact Steps

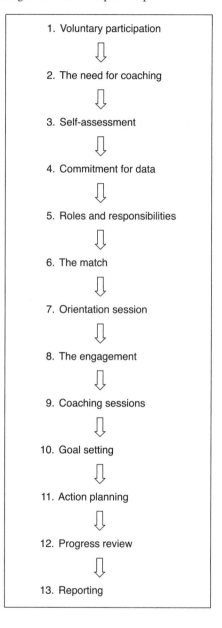

1. Voluntary participation

2. The need for coaching

3. Self-assessment

4. Commitment for data

5. Roles and responsibilities

6. The match

7. Orientation session

8. The engagement

9. Coaching sessions

10. Goal setting

11. Action planning

12. Progress review

13. Reporting

to mandatory involvement, however, the volunteer effort appeared to be an important ingredient for success. It was envisioned that as improvements were realized and executives reflected on the positive perceptions of coaching that other executives would follow suit.

2. **The need for coaching.** An important part of the process was a dialogue with the executive to determine if coaching was actually needed. In this step, NHLO staff used a checklist to review the issues, needs, and concerns about the coaching agreement. Along with establishing a need, the checklist revealed key areas where coaching could help. This step ensured that the assistance desired by the executive could actually be provided by the coach.

3. **Self-assessment.** As part of the process, a self-assessment was taken from the individual being coached, his or her immediate manager, and direct reports. This was a typical 360-degree assessment instrument that focused on areas of feedback, communication, openness, trust, and other competencies necessary for success in the competitive hospitality environment.

4. **Commitment for data.** As a precondition, executives had to agree to provide data during coaching and at appropriate times following the engagement. This upfront commitment ensured that data of sufficient quality and quantity could be obtained. The data made evaluation easier and helped executives see their progress and realize the value of coaching.

5. **Roles and responsibilities.** For both the coach and the executive, roles and responsibilities were clearly defined. It was important for the executive to understand that the coach was there to listen, provide feedback, and evaluate. The coach was not there to make decisions for the executive. This clear distinction was important for productive coaching sessions.

6. **The match.** Coaches were provided from a reputable business coaching firm where the Nations Hotel Learning Organization had developed a productive relationship. Coach profiles were presented to executives, and a tentative selection was made on a priority listing. The respective coach was provided background information on the executive, and a match was made. After this match, the coaching process began.

7. **Orientation session.** The executive and coach formally met during an orientation session. Here, the NHLO staff explained the process, requirements, timetable, and other administrative issues. This was a very brief session typically conducted in a group; however, it could also have been conducted individually.

8. **The engagement.** One of the most important aspects of the process involved making sure that the engagement was connected to a business need. Typical coaching engagements focused on behavioral

issues (e.g., an executive's inability to listen to employees). To connect to the business impact, the behavior change must link to a business consequence. In the initial engagement, the coach uncovered the business need by asking a series of questions to examine the consequences of behavior change. This process involved asking "so what?" and "what if?" as the desired behavior changes were described. As the business needs were identified, the measures needed to be categorized by productivity, sales, efficiency, direct cost savings, employee retention, and customer satisfaction. The engagement had to be connected to corresponding changes in at least three of those measures. Without elevating the engagement to a business need, it would have been difficult to evaluate coaching with this level of analysis.

9. **Coaching sessions.** Individual sessions were conducted at least once a month (usually more often) lasting a minimum of one hour (sometimes more), depending on the need and issues at hand. The coach and executive met face to face, if possible. If not, coaching was conducted in a telephone conversation. Routine meetings were necessary to keep the process on track.

10. **Goal setting.** Although individuals could set goals in any area needing improvements, the senior executives chose five priority areas for targeting: sales growth, productivity/operational efficiency, direct cost reduction, retention of key staff members, and customer satisfaction. The executives selected one measure in at least three of these areas. Essentially, they would have three specific goals that would require three action plans, described next.

11. **Action planning.** To drive the desired improvement, the action planning process was utilized. Common in coaching engagements, this process provided an opportunity for the executive to detail specific action steps planned with the team. These steps were designed to drive a particular consequence that was a business impact measure. Figure 12-2 shows a typical action planning document used in this process. The executive was to complete the action plan during the first two to three coaching sessions, detailing step by step what he or she would accomplish to drive a particular improvement. Under the analysis section, Parts A, B, and C were to have been completed in the initial development of the plan. The coaches distributed action plan packages that included instructions, blank forms, and completed examples. The coach explained the process in the second coaching session. The action plans could be revised as needed. At least three improvement measures were required out of the five areas targeted

Figure 12-2 Action Plan Form

Name: _____ Coach: _____ Date: _____

Impact objective: _____ Evaluation period: _____ to _____

Improvement measure: _____ Current performance: _____ Target performance: _____

Action steps:

1. _____

2. _____

3. _____

4. _____

5. _____

6. _____

7. _____

8. _____

Analysis is

A. What is the unit of measure? _____

B. What is the value (cost) of one unit? $ _____

C. How did you arrive at this value? _____
_____
_____
_____

D. How much did the measure change during the evaluation period? (monthly value) _____
_____

E. What other factors could have contributed to this improvement? _____
_____

F. What percentage of this change was actually caused by this program? _____ %.

G. What level of confidence do you place on the above information? (100% = Certainty and 0 percent = No Confidence) _____ %.

Intangible benefits: _____
_____

Comments: _____
_____

with the program. Consequently, at least three action plans had to be developed and implemented.

12. **Active learning.** After the executive developed the specific measures in question and the action plans, several development strategies were discussed and implemented with the help of the coach. The coach actually facilitated the efforts, utilizing any number of typical learning processes such as reading assignments, self-assessment tools, skill practices, video feedback, and journaling. Coaching is considered to be an active learning process where the executive experiments, applies, and reflects on the experience. The coach provides input, reaction, assessment, and evaluation.

13. **Progress review.** At monthly sessions, the coach and executive reviewed progress and revised the action plan, if necessary. The important issue was to continue to make adjustments to sustain the process.

14. **Reporting.** After six months in the coaching engagement, the executive reported improvement by completing other parts of the action plan. If the development efforts were quite involved and the measures driven were unlikely to change in the interim, a longer period of time was utilized. For most executives, six months was appropriate.

These elements reflected a results-based project appropriately called "coaching for business impact."

Objectives

An effective ROI study flows from the objectives of the particular project being evaluated. For coaching, it is important to clearly indicate the objectives at different levels. Figure 12-3 shows the detailed objectives associated with this project. The objectives reflect the four classic levels of evaluation plus a fifth level for ROI. Some of the levels, however, have been adjusted for the coaching environment. With these objectives in mind, it becomes a relatively easy task to measure progress on these objectives.

Planning for Evaluation

Figure 12-4 shows the completed data collection plan for this project. The plan captures the following techniques and strategies used to collect data for this project:

Figure 12-3   Objectives of Business Impact Coaching

Level 1: Reaction Objectives

The executive will:
1. Perceive coaching to be relevant to the job
2. Perceive coaching to be important to job performance at the present time
3. Perceive coaching to be value added in terms of time and funds invested
4. Rate the coach as effective
5. Recommend this program to other executives

Level 2: Learning Objectives

After completing this coaching program, the executives should improve their understanding of or skills for each of the following:
1. Uncovering individual strengths and weaknesses
2. Translating feedback into action plans
3. Involving team members in projects and goals
4. Communicating effectively
5. Collaborating with colleagues
6. Improving personal effectiveness
7. Enhancing leadership skills

Level 3: Application Objectives

Six months after completing this coaching program, executives should:
1. Finish the action plan
2. Adjust the plan accordingly for changes in the environment
3. Show improvements on the following items:
   a. Uncovering individual strengths and weaknesses
   b. Translating feedback into action plans
   c. Involving team members in projects and goals
   d. Communicating effectively
   e. Collaborating with colleagues
   f. Improving personal effectiveness
   g. Enhancing leadership skills
4. Identify barriers and enablers

Level 4: Impact Objectives

After completing this coaching program, executives should improve at least three specific measures in the following areas:
1. Sales growth
2. Productivity/operational efficiency
3. Direct cost reduction
4. Retention of key staff members
5. Customer satisfaction

Level 5: ROI Objective

The ROI value should be 25%.

Figure 12-4 Completed Data Collection Plan

Program: <u>Coaching for Business Impact</u>   Responsibility: _____   Date: _____

Level	Objective(s)	Measured data	Data collection method	Data sources	Timing	Responsibilities
1	**REACTION/SATISFACTION** • Relevance to job • Importance to job success • Value-add • Coach's effectiveness • Recommendation to others	• 4 out of 5 on a 1 to 5 rating scale	• Questionnaire	• Executives	• 6 months after engagement	• NHLO staff
2	**LEARNING** • Uncovering strengths/weaknesses • Translating feedback into action • Involving team members • Communicating effectively • Collaborating with colleagues • Improving personal effectiveness • Enhancing leadership skills	• 4 out of 5 on a 1 to 5 rating scale	• Questionnaire	• Executives • Coach	• 6 months after engagement	• NHLO staff
3	**APPLICATION/IMPLEMENTATION** • Complete and adjust action plan • Identify barriers and enablers • Show improvements in skills	• Checklist for action plan • 4 out of 5 on a 1 to 5 rating scale	• Action plan • Questionnaire	• Executives • Coach	• 6 months after engagement	• NHLO staff
4	**BUSINESS IMPACT (3 OF 5)** • Sales growth • Productivity/efficiency • Direct cost reduction • Retention of key staff members • Customer satisfaction	• Monthly revenue • Varies with location • Direct monetary savings • Voluntary turnover • Customer satisfaction index	• Action plan	• Executives	• 6 months after engagement	• NHLO staff
5	**RETURN ON INVESTMENT** • 25 percent					

Comments: Executives are committed to providing data. They fully understand all the data collection issues prior to engaging in the coaching assignment.

1. **Objectives.** The objectives are listed as defined in Figure 12-3 and are repeated only in general terms.
2. **Measures.** Additional definition is sometimes needed beyond the specific objectives. The measures used to gauge progress on the objective are defined.
3. **Methods.** This column indicates the specific method used for collecting data at different levels. In this case, action plans and questionnaires are the primary methods.
4. **Sources.** For each data group, sources are identified. For coaches, sources are usually limited to the executive, coach, manager of the executive, and the individual/team reporting to the executive. Although the actual data provided by executives will usually come from the records of the organization, the executive will include the data in the action plan document. Thus, the executive becomes a source of the data to the Nations Hotel Learning Organization.
5. **Timing.** The timing refers to the time for collecting specific data items from the beginning of the coaching engagement.
6. **Responsibility.** The responsibility refers to the individual(s) who will actually collect the data.

The data collection plan (see Figure 12-5) shows how the various types of data are collected and integrated to provide an overall evaluation of the program.

Figure 12-6 shows the completed plan for data analysis. This document addresses the key issues needed for a credible analysis of the data and includes the following:

1. **Data items.** The plan shows when business measures will be collected from one of the five priority areas.
2. **Isolating the effects of coaching.** The method of isolating the effects of coaching on the data is estimation, where the executives actually allo-

Figure 12-5   Data Integration Plan for Evaluating the Program

Data category	Executive questionnaire	Senior executive questionnaire	Action plan	Company records
Reaction	X			
Learning	X	X		
Application	X	X	X	
Impact			X	X
Costs				X

Figure 12-6 The ROI Analysis Plan for Coaching for Business Impact

Program: <u>Coaching for Business Success</u> Responsibility: _____ Date: _____

Data items (usually Level 4)	Method for isolating the effects of the program	Methods of converting data to monetary values	Cost categories	Intangible benefits	Communication targets for final report	Other influences/issues during application	Comments
Sales growth	Estimates from executive (Method is the same for all data items)	• Standard value • Expert input • Executive estimate (Method is the same for all data items)	• Needs assessment • Coaching fees • Travel costs • Executive time • Administrative support • Administrative overhead • Communication expenses • Facilities • Evaluation	• Increased commitment • Reduced stress • Increased job satisfaction • Improved customer service • Enhanced recruiting image • Improved teamwork • Improved communication	• Executives • Senior executives • Sponsors • NHLO staff • Learning and development council • Prospective participants for CBI	A variety of other initiatives will influence the impact measure, including our Six Sigma process, service excellence program, and our efforts to become a great place to work.	It is extremely important to secure commitment from executives to provide accurate data in a timely manner.
Productivity/operational efficiency							
Direct cost reduction							
Retention of key staff members							
Customer satisfaction							

cate the proportion of the improvement to the coaching process (more on the consequences of this later). There are more credible methods, such as control groups and trend analysis, but they are not appropriate for this situation. Although the estimates are subjective, they are developed by those individuals who should know them best (the executives), and the results are adjusted for the error of the estimate.

3. **Converting data to monetary values.** Data are converted by use of a variety of methods. For most data items, standard values are available. When standard values are not available, the input of an in-house expert is pursued. This expert is typically an individual who collects, assimilates, and reports the data. If neither of these approaches is feasible, the executive estimates the value.

4. **Cost categories.** The standard cost categories included are the typical costs for a coaching assignment.

5. **Communication targets.** Several audiences are included for coaching results, representing the key stakeholder groups: the executive, the executive's immediate manager, the sponsor of the program, and the NHLO staff. Other influences and issues are also detailed in this plan.

Evaluation Results

The careful data collection planning allowed the coaching program to be evaluated at all five levels.

Reaction

Reaction to the coaching program exceeded expectations of the NHLO staff. Comments received for Level 1 evaluation included these:

- "This program was very timely and practical."
- "My coach was very professional."

On a scale of 1 to 5 (1 = unacceptable and 5 = exceptional), the average rating of five items was 4.1, exceeding the objective of 4.0. Table 12-1 shows the items listed.

Learning

As with any process, the executives indicated enhancement of skills and knowledge in certain areas:

Table 12-1   Executive Reaction to Coaching

Level 1 evaluation	Rating*
Relevance of coaching	4.6
Importance of coaching	4.1
Value of coaching	3.9
Effectiveness of coach	3.9
Recommendation to others	4.2

*Scale 1 to 5, where 1 = unacceptable and 5 = exceptional

- "I gained much insight into my problems with my team."
- "This is exactly what I needed to get on track. My coach pointed out things I hadn't thought of and we came up with some terrific actions."

Table 12-2 shows seven items with inputs from both the executives and their coaches. For this level, it was considered appropriate to collect the data from both groups, indicating the degree of improvement. The most accurate, and probably most credible, is the input directly from the executive. The coach may not be fully aware of the extent of learning.

Application

For coaching to be successful, the executive had to implement the items on the action plans. The most important measure of application was the completion of the action plan steps. Eighty-three percent of the executives

Table 12-2   Learning from Coaching

Measures	Executive rating*	Coach rating*
Understanding strengths and weaknesses	3.9	4.2
Translating feedback into action plans	3.7	3.9
Involving team members in projects and goals	4.2	3.7
Communicating effectively	4.1	4.2
Collaborating with colleagues	4.0	4.1
Improving personal effectiveness	4.1	4.4
Enhancing leadership skills	4.2	4.3

*Program value scale 1 to 5

Table 12-3 Application of Coaching

Measures	Executive rating*	Coach rating*
Translating feedback into action plans	4.2	3.9
Involving team members in projects and goals	4.1	4.2
Communicating more effectively with the team	4.3	4.1
Collaborating more with the group and others	4.2	4.2
Applying effective leadership skills	4.1	3.9

*Program value scale 1 to 5, where 1 = no change in skills and 5 = exceptional increase

reported completion of all three plans. Another 11 percent completed one or two action plans.

Also, executives and the coach provided input on questions about changes in behavior from the use of skills. Here are some comments they offered on the questionnaires:

- "It was so helpful to get a fresh, unique point of view of my action plan. The coaching experience opened my eyes to significant things I was missing."
- "After spending a great deal of time trying to get my coach to understand my dilemma, I felt that more effort went into this than I expected."
- "We got stuck in a rut on one issue and I couldn't get out. My coach was somewhat distracted and I never felt we were on the same page."

The response rates for questionnaires were 92 percent and 80 percent for executives and coaches, respectively. Table 12-3 shows a listing of the skills and the rating, using a scale of 1 to 5, where 1 was "no change in the skill" and 5 was "exceptional increase."

Barriers and Enablers

With any process, there are barriers and enablers to success. The executives were asked to indicate the specific barriers (i.e., obstacles) to the use of what was learned in the coaching sessions. Overall, the barriers were weak, almost nonexistent. Also, they were asked to indicate what supported (enablers) the process. The enablers were very strong. Table 12-4 shows a list of the barriers and enablers.

Table 12-4 Barriers and Enablers of the Coaching Process

Barriers	Enablers
Not enough time	Coach
Not relevant	Action plan
Not effective when using the skill	Structure of Coaching for Business Impact
Manager didn't support it	Support of management

Impact

Specific business impact measures varied with the individual but, for the most part, were in the categories representing the five priority areas. Table 12-5 shows the listing of the actual data reported in the action plans for the first measure only. The table identifies the executive and the area of improvement, the monetary value, the basis of the improvement, the method of converting the monetary value, the contribution from coaching, the confidence estimate of the contribution, and the adjusted value. Since there are three measures, a total of all three tables are developed. The total for the three is $1,861,158.

Figure 12-7 on page 264 shows a completed action plan from one participant, whom we shall call Caroline Dobson (executive 11; name changed to protect her privacy). In this example, Caroline reduced annual turnover to 17 percent from 28 percent—an improvement of 11 percent. This represented four turnovers on an annual basis. Using a standard value of 1.3 times base salaries for the cost of one turnover and adding the total base salaries yields a total cost savings of $215,000.

As mentioned earlier, the estimates were used to isolate the benefits of coaching. After the estimates were obtained, the value was adjusted for the confidence of the estimate. Essentially, the executives were asked to list other factors that could have contributed to the improvement and allocate the amount (on a percentage basis) that was directly attributable to coaching. Then, using a scale of zero percent (no confidence) to 100 percent (total certainty), executives provided the confidence levels for their estimates.

Return on Investment

The costs were fully loaded and included both the direct and indirect costs of coaching. Estimates were used in some cases. Table 12-6 on page 265 shows the costs of coaching for all 25 executives in the study.

Only a small amount of initial assessment cost was involved, and the development cost was minor as well, because the coaching firm had developed a

Table 12-5 Business Impact from Coaching

Exec number	Measurement area	Total annual value	Basis	Method for converting data	Contribution factor	Confidence estimate	Adjusted value
1	Revenue growth	$ 11,500	Profit margin	Standard value	33%	70%	$ 2,656
2	Retention	175,000	3 turnovers	Standard value	40	70	49,000
3	Retention	190,000	2 turnovers	Standard value	60	80	91,200
4	Direct cost savings	75,000	From cost statements	Participant estimate	100	100	75,000
5	Direct cost savings	21,000	Contract services	Standard value	75	70	11,025
6	Direct cost savings	65,000	Staffing costs	Standard value	70	60	27,300
7	Retention	150,000	2 turnovers	Standard value	50	50	37,500
8	Cost savings	70,000	Security	Standard value	60	90	37,800
9	Direct cost savings	9,443	Supply costs	N/A	70	90	5,949
10	Efficiency	39,000	IT costs	Participant estimate	70	80	21,840
11	Retention	215,000	4 turnovers	Standard value	75	90	145,125
12	Productivity	13,590	Overtime	Standard value	75	80	8,154
13	Retention	73,000	1 turnover	Standard value	50	80	29,200

14	Retention	120,000	2 annual turnovers	Standard value	60	54,000
15	Retention	182,000	4 turnovers	Standard value	40	61,880
16	Cost savings	25,900	Travel	Standard value	30	6,993
17	Cost savings	12,320	Admin. support	Standard value	75	8,316
18	Direct cost savings	18,950	Labor savings	Participant estimate	55	6,253
19	Revenue growth	103,100	Profit margin	Participant estimate	75	69,592
20	Revenue	19,500	Profit	Standard value	85	12,431
21	Revenue	21,230	Profit	Standard value	80	18,889
22	Revenue	105,780	Profit margin	Standard value	70	37,023

TOTAL $1,716,313

1st measure total $817,126
2nd measure total $649,320
3rd measure total $394,712
Total benefits $1,861,158

Figure 12-7 Example of an Executive's Completed Action Plan

Name: Caroline Dobson   Coach: Pamela Mills   Follow-up date: September 1

Objective: Improve retention of staff   Evaluation period: January to July

Improvement measure: Voluntary turnover   Current performance: 28% Annual   Target performance: 15% Annual

Action Steps		Analysis
1. Meet with team to discuss reasons for turnover—using problem-solving skills.	Jan. 31	A. What is the unit of measure? One voluntary turnover
2. Review exit interview data with HR—look for trends and patterns.	Feb. 15	B. What is the value (cost) of one unit? Salary x 1.3
3. Counsel with "at-risk" employees to correct problems and explore opportunities for improvement.	Mar. 1	C. How did you arrive at this value? Standard value
4. Develop individual development plan for high-potential employees.	Mar. 5	D. How much did the measure change during the evaluation period? 11% (annual %) (4 turnovers annually)
5. Provide recognition to employees with long tenure.	Routinely	E. What other factors could have contributed to this improvement? Growth opportunities, changes in job market
6. Schedule appreciation dinner for entire team.	May 31	F. What percentage of this change was actually caused by this program? 75%
7. Encourage team leaders to delegate more responsibilities.		G. What level of confidence do you place on the above information? (100% = Certainty and 0% = No Confidence) 90%
8. Follow up with each discussion and discuss improvement or lack of improvement and plan other action.	Routinely	
9. Monitor improvement and provide recognition when appropriate.	May 11	

Intangible Benefits: Less stress on team, greater job satisfaction

Comments: Great Coach — He kept me on track with this issue.

Table 12-6 Costs of Coaching 25 Executives

Item	Cost, $
Needs assessment/development	10,000
Coaching fees	480,000
Travel costs	53,000
Executive time	9,200
Administrative support	14,000
Administrative overhead	2,000
Telecommunications expenses	1,500
Facilities (conference room)	2,100
Evaluation	8,000
Total	579,800

similar coaching arrangement previously. The costs for sessions conducted on the phone were estimated, as were the costs for occasionally using a conference room instead of the executive offices.

Using the total monetary benefits and total cost of the program, two ROI calculations can be developed. The first is the benefit/cost ratio (BCR), which is the ratio of the monetary benefits divided by the costs:

$$BCR = \frac{\$1,861,158}{\$579,800} = 3.21$$

This value suggests that for every dollar invested, $3.21 was returned. The ROI formula for investments in training, coaching, or any human performance intervention is calculated in the same way as for other types of investments: earnings divided by investment. For this coaching solution, the return on investment was calculated thus:

$$ROI\,(\%) = \frac{\$1,861,158 - \$579,800}{\$579,800} \times 100 = 221\%$$

In other words, for every dollar invested in the coaching program, the invested dollar was returned and another $2.21 was generated. In this case, the return on investment exceeded the 25 percent target.

Intangibles

As with any project, there were many intangibles revealed by this analysis. Intangibles were collected on both the follow-up questionnaire and the action plan. Two questions were included on the questionnaire: one involved other benefits from this process and the other asked for comments about the program. Some individuals indicated intangibles when they listed the comments. Also, the action plan contained a place for comments and intangibles. The intangible benefits identified through these data sources included:

- Increased commitment
- Improved teamwork
- Increased job satisfaction
- Improved customer service
- Improved communication

Note that this list includes only measures that were identified as being an intangible benefit by at least 4 of the 25 executives. In keeping with the conservative nature of the ROI Methodology, it was decided that intangibles identified by only a couple of executives would be considered extreme data items and not credible enough to list as an actual benefit of the program.

Credibility of the Return on Investment Analysis

The critical issue in this study is the credibility of the data. The data were perceived to be very credible by the executives, their immediate managers, and the coaches. Credibility rests on eight major issues:

1. The information for the analysis was provided directly by the executives. They had no reason to be biased in their input.
2. The data were taken directly from the records and could be audited.
3. The data collection process was conservative, with the assumption that an unresponsive individual had realized no improvement. This concept—no data, no improvement—is ultraconservative in regard to data collection. Three executives did not return the completed action plans.
4. The executives did not assign complete credit to this program. Executives isolated only a portion of the data that should be credited directly to this program.

5. The data were adjusted for the potential error of the above estimate.
6. Only the first year's benefits were used in the analysis. Most of the improvements should result in second-year and third-year benefits.
7. The costs of the program were fully loaded. All direct and indirect costs were included, including the time away from work for the executives.
8. The data revealed a balanced profile of success. Very favorable reaction, learning, and application data were presented along with business impact, return on investment, and intangibles.

Collectively, these issues made a convincing case for the CBI program.

Communication Strategy

To communicate appropriately with the target audiences outlined in the ROI analysis plan, three specific documents were produced. The first report was a detailed impact study that showed the approach, assumptions, methodology, and results using all the data categories. In addition, barriers and enablers were included, along with conclusions and recommendations. The second report was an eight-page executive summary of the key points, including a one-page overview of the methodology. The third report was a brief, five-page summary of the process and results. These documents were presented to the different groups according to the plan in Table 12-7.

Because this was the first ROI study conducted in this organization, face-to-face meetings were conducted with the sponsor and other interested senior executives. The purpose was to ensure that executive sponsors had a clear understanding of the methodology, the conservative assumptions, and each level of data. The barriers, enablers, conclusions, and recommendations were

Table 12-7 NHLO's Plan for Communicating Evaluation Results

Audience	Document
Executives	Brief summary
Managers of executives	Brief summary
Sponsor	Complete study, executive summary
NHLO staff	Complete study
Learning and development council	Complete study, executive summary
Prospective participants	Brief summary

an important part of the meeting. In the future, after two or three studies have been conducted, this group will receive only a one-page summary of key data items.

A similar meeting was conducted with the learning and development council. The council consisted of advisors to the Nations Hotel Learning Organization—usually middle-level executives and managers. Finally, a face-to-face meeting was held with the NHLO staff at which the complete impact study was described and used as a learning tool.

As a result of this communication, the senior executive decided to make only a few minor adjustments in the program and continued to offer Coaching for Business Impact to others on a volunteer basis. They were very pleased with the progress and were delighted to have data connecting coaching to the business impact.

Questions for Discussion

1. How did the decision to conduct an ROI study influence the design of the coaching program?
2. Critique the evaluation design and method of data collection.
3. Discuss the importance of getting participants committed to provide quality data.
4. What other strategies for isolating the impact of the coaching program could have been employed here?
5. Discuss the importance of credibility of data in an ROI study.
6. How can the outcomes of coaching be linked to your organization's business objectives?

13

Case Study: Return on Investment in Leadership Development for Cross-Functional Managers*

T HIS CASE DESCRIBES how one organization—a leading car rental corporation—implemented a program to improve profitability and efficiency by developing leadership competencies for first-level managers. The learning and development team was asked to identify measures influenced by this program and link these competencies to job performance and business impact. However, the team was faced with a difficult challenge because it was not given the time, resources, or encouragement to conduct a comprehensive analysis to link the need for leadership development to business needs. Could the participants help with this task? This is an excellent example of a low-cost study using questionnaires (a popular but sometimes weak data collection method). Compounding the challenge was the requirement to let each participant select two measures to improve using the competencies.

---

* This case study has previously been published in Phillips, Patricia Pulliam, and Jack J. Phillips, *Proving the Value of HR: ROI Case Studies*, 2nd ed., Birmingham, AL: ROI Institute Inc., 2010.

Background

Global Car Rental (GCR) operates in 27 countries with 27,000 employees. The U.S. division has 13,000 employees and operates in most major cities in the United States. The auto rental business is very competitive, and several major firms have been forced into bankruptcy in the last few years. The industry is price sensitive, and customer service is critical. Operating costs must be managed carefully to remain profitable.

Senior executives were exploring a variety of ways to improve the company, and they perceived that developing leadership competencies for first-level managers would be an excellent way to achieve profitable growth and efficiency.

The Need

A recent needs assessment for all functional areas conducted by the learning and development (L&D) staff determined that several leadership competencies were needed for first-level managers. The needs included typical competencies such as problem solving, counseling, motivation, communication, goal setting, and feedback.

Attempting to address the needs, the L&D staff developed a new program, the Leadership Challenge, designed for team leaders, supervisors, and managers who are responsible for those who actually do the work (the first level of management). Program participants were located in rental offices, service centers, call centers, regional offices, and headquarters. Most functional areas were represented, including operations, customer service, service and support, sales, administration, finance and accounting, and information technology. Essentially, this was to be a cross-functional program in the organization.

In addition to developing competencies, the L&D staff needed to link the competencies to job performance needs and business needs. The senior management team, however, did not want the L&D staff to visit all locations to discuss business needs and job performance issues. The senior executives were convinced that leadership skills were needed and that these skills should drive a variety of business measures when applied in the work units. The L&D team was challenged to identify the measures influenced by this particular program. Additionally, top executives were interested in knowing the impact and maybe even the return on investment for a group of U.S. participants in this program.

This challenge created a dilemma. L&D staff members realized that for a positive ROI study to be generated, the program should be linked to business needs. They knew, though, that they did not have the time, resources, or the encouragement to conduct a comprehensive analysis that linked the need for the leadership development to business needs. The team was faced with the challenge of connecting this program to business impact. Team members thought that perhaps the participants themselves could help with this task.

The Leadership Challenge involved four days of off-site learning with input from the immediate manager who served as a coach for some of the learning processes. Before attending, the program participants had to complete an online pretraining instrument and read a short book. Because few senior executives at Global Car Rental had challenged the L&D staff to show the business impact of a program, two groups were evaluated with a total of 36 participants (i.e., 18 in each group).

Business Alignment

Prior to attending the program, each manager was asked to identify at least two business measures in the work unit that represented an opportunity for improvement. This was done to link the program to business and job performance needs. The measures were available in operating reports, cost statements, or scorecards. A description of the program was provided in advance, including a list of objectives and skill sets. The selected measures had to meet an additional two-part test:

1. They had to be under the control of the team when improvements were to be considered.
2. They had to have the potential to be influenced by team members with the manager using the competencies in the program.

A needs assessment appeared to be appropriate for the situation, although there was some concern about whether it could be thorough. The initial needs assessment on competencies uncovered a variety of deficiencies across all the functional units; it provided the information necessary for job descriptions, assignments, and key responsibility areas. Although basic, the additional steps taken to connect the program to business impact were appropriate for a business needs analysis and a job performance needs analysis. Identification of two measures in need of improvement was a simple business needs analysis for the work unit. Selected measures were restricted to only those that could be influenced by the team with the leader using the skills from the program; doing that essentially defines a job performance need. (In essence, the individual leader is identifying something that is not currently being done in the work unit that could be done to enhance the business need.) Although more refinement and detail would be preferred, the results of this assessment process should have sufficed for this project.

Objectives

The L&D staff developed the following objectives for the program:

1. Participants will rate the program as relevant to their jobs.
2. Participants will rate the program as important to their job success.
3. Participants must demonstrate acceptable performance on each major competency.
4. Participants will use the competencies with team members on a routine basis.
5. Participants and team members will drive improvements in at least two business measures.

Appropriateness for Return on Investment Analysis

With the business and job performance needs analyses complete, this program became a good candidate for the ROI analysis. Without these two steps, it would have been difficult to conduct a successful ROI study. A consideration for conducting the ROI study was identifying the drivers for ROI analysis. In this case, the senior team was challenging the value of leadership development. An ROI study should provide convincing evidence about a major program. Also, this was a highly visible program that merited evaluation at this level because it was strategic and expensive. Consequently, the L&D staff pursued the ROI study, and an ROI objective of 20 percent was established.

Planning for Return on Investment Analysis

Because of time and cost constraints, the team developed a plan to use a follow-up questionnaire.

Data Collection Plan

Figure 13-1 shows the completed data collection plan. Although several data collection methods were possible, the team decided to use a detailed follow-up

Figure 13-1 Data Collection Plan for the Leadership Challenge Program

Purpose of this evaluation: _____

Program: _____   Responsibility: _____   Date: _____

Level	Objective(s)	Measures/data	Data collection method	Data sources	Timing	Responsibilities
1	**REACTION/SATISFACTION** • Participants rate the program as relevant to their jobs • Participants rate the program as important to their job success	• 4 out of 5 on a 5-point rating scale	• Questionnaire	• Participants	• End of program	• Facilitator
2	**LEARNING** • Participants demonstrate acceptable performance on each major competency	• 2 out of 3 on a 3-point rating scale	• Observation of skill practices • Self-assessment via questionnaire	• Facilitator • Participants	• End of program	• Facilitator
3	**APPLICATION/IMPLEMENTATION** • Participants utilize the competencies with team members routinely	• Various measures (ratings, open-ended items, and so forth)	• Questionnaire	• Participants • Participants' managers	• 3 months	• L&D staff
4	**BUSINESS IMPACT** • Participants and team members drive improvements in at least two business measures	• Various work unit measures	• Questionnaire	• Participants	• 3 months	• L&D staff
5	**RETURN ON INVESTMENT** • Achieve a 20 percent return on investment					

Comments: _____

273

questionnaire to reflect the progress made with the program. Focus groups, interviews, and observations were considered to be too expensive or inappropriate. The L&D team explored the possibility of using the 360-degree feedback process to obtain input from team members but elected to wait until the 360-degree program was fully implemented in all units in the organization. Therefore, the questionnaire was deemed the least expensive and least disruptive method.

The questionnaire was sent directly to the participant three months after program completion. At the same time, a shorter questionnaire was sent to the participant's immediate manager. Initially, a six-month follow-up was considered instead of the three-month follow-up shown on the data collection plan. However, the L&D staff thought that six months was too long to wait for results and too long for managers to make the connection between the program and the results.

Questionnaire Topics

Figure 13-2 shows the e-mail questionnaire used with this group. Important areas explored included application of skills, impact analysis, barriers to application, and enablers. A similar questionnaire that explored the role of the manager in the coaching process was sent to the next-level managers without the questions on the impact data.

To achieve a response rate of 81 percent, the L&D team used 12 different techniques:

1. Provide advance communication about the questionnaire.
2. Clearly communicate the reason for the questionnaire.
3. Indicate who will see the results of the questionnaire.
4. Show how the data will be integrated with other data.
5. Communicate the time limit for submitting responses.
6. Review the questionnaire at the end of the formal session.
7. Allow for responses to be anonymous or at least confidential.
8. Provide two follow-up reminders, using a different medium each time.
9. Have the introduction letter signed by a top executive.
10. Enclose a giveaway item with the questionnaire (e.g., a pen).
11. Send a summary of results to the target audience.
12. Have a third party collect and analyze the data.

Figure 13-2 Questionnaire for Leaders

FOLLOW-UP QUESTIONNAIRE

Program name _____ End date of program _____

Our records indicate that you participated in the above program. Your participation in this follow-up survey is important to continuously improve this program. Completion of this survey may take 45 to 60 minutes. Thank you in advance for your input.

Currency
1. This survey requires some information to be completed in monetary value. Please indicate the currency you will use to complete the questions requiring monetary value. _____

Program Completion
2. Did you: ☐ complete ☐ partially complete ☐ not complete the program? If you did not complete, go to the final question.

	Strongly disagree				Strongly agree	Not applicable
Reaction	1	2	3	4	5	
3. I recommended the program to others.	☐	☐	☐	☐	☐	☐
4. The program was a worthwhile investment for my organization.	☐	☐	☐	☐	☐	☐
5. The program was a good use of my time.	☐	☐	☐	☐	☐	☐
6. The program was relevant to my work.	☐	☐	☐	☐	☐	☐
7. The program was important to my work.	☐	☐	☐	☐	☐	☐
8. The program provided me with new information.	☐	☐	☐	☐	☐	☐

	Strongly disagree				Strongly agree	Not applicable
Learning	1	2	3	4	5	
9. I learned new knowledge/skills from this program.	☐	☐	☐	☐	☐	☐
10. I am confident in my ability to apply the knowledge/skills learned in this program.	☐	☐	☐	☐	☐	☐

11. Rate your level of improvement in skill or knowledge derived from the program content. (0% = no improvement; 100% = significant improvement. Check only one.)

0%	10%	20%	30%	40%	50%	60%	70%	80%	90%	100%
☐	☐	☐	☐	☐	☐	☐	☐	☐	☐	☐

(continued on next page)

Figure 13-2 Questionnaire for Leaders *(continued)*

Application

	None				Very much	Not applicable
	1	2	3	4	5	
12. To what extent did you apply the knowledge/skills learned during the program?	☐	☐	☐	☐	☐	☐

	Infrequently (unacceptable)				Frequently (exceptional)	Not applicable
	1	2	3	4	5	
13. How frequently did you apply the knowledge/skills learned during the program?	☐	☐	☐	☐	☐	☐

	Low				High	Not applicable
	1	2	3	4	5	
14. What is your level of effectiveness with the knowledge/skills learned during the program?	☐	☐	☐	☐	☐	☐

	Low				High	Not applicable
	1	2	3	4	5	
15. Rate the effectiveness of the coach.	☐	☐	☐	☐	☐	☐

	Not critical				Very critical	Not applicable
	1	2	3	4	5	
16. How critical is applying the content of this program to your job success?	☐	☐	☐	☐	☐	☐

	Not well				Very well	Not applicable
	1	2	3	4	5	
17. To what extent did you stay on schedule with your planned actions?	☐	☐	☐	☐	☐	☐

18. What percentage of your total work time did you spend on tasks that require the knowledge/skills presented in this program? Check only one.

0%	10%	20%	30%	40%	50%	60%	70%	80%	90%	100%
☐	☐	☐	☐	☐	☐	☐	☐	☐	☐	☐

Figure 13-2 Questionnaire for Leaders *(continued)*

Barriers/enablers to application

19. Which of the following deterred or prevented you from applying the knowledge/skills learned in the program? (Check all that apply.)
    - No opportunity to use the skills ☐
    - Lack of management support ☐
    - Lack of support from colleagues and peers ☐
    - Insufficient knowledge and understanding ☐
    - Lack of confidence to apply knowledge/skills ☐
    - Systems and processes within organization will not support ☐
      application of knowledge/skills
    - Other ☐

20. If you selected "other" above, please describe here. _____

    _____

21. Which of the following supported you in applying knowledge/skills learned in the program? (Check all that apply.)
    - Opportunity to use the skills ☐
    - Management support ☐
    - Support from colleagues and peers ☐
    - Sufficient knowledge and understanding ☐
    - Confidence to apply knowledge/skills ☐
    - Systems and processes within organization will not support ☐
      application of knowledge/skills
    - Other ☐

22. If you selected "other" above, please describe here. _____

    _____

Results–first measure

23. Please define the first measure you selected and its unit for measurement. For example, if you selected "sales," your unit of measure may be "one closed sale."

24. For this measure, what is the monetary value of improvement for one unit of this measure? For example, the value of a closed sale is value times the profit margin ($10,000 × 20% = $2,000). Although this step is difficult, please make every effort to estimate the value of a unit. Put the value in the currency you selected, round to nearest whole value, and enter numbers only (for example, $2,000.25 should be entered as $2,000).

    _____

(continued on next page)

Figure 13-2 Questionnaire for Leaders *(continued)*

---

25. Please state your basis for the value of the unit of improvement you indicated above. In the closed sale example, a standard value, profit margin, is used, so "standard value" is entered here.

_____

26. For the measure listed as most directly linked to the program, how much has this measure improved in performance? If not readily available, please estimate. If you selected "sales," show the actual increase in sales (for example, four closed sales per month, enter the number 4 here). You can input a number with up to one decimal point. Indicate the frequency base for the measure.

_____ ☐ daily   ☐ weekly   ☐ monthly   ☐ quarterly

Return on investment—first measure

27. What is the annual value of improvement in the measure you selected above? Multiply the increase (Question 26) by the frequency (Question 26) times the unit of value (Question 24). For example, if you selected "sales," multiply the sales increase by the frequency to arrive at the annum value (for example, four sales per month x 12 x $2,000 = $96,000). Although this step is difficult, please make every effort to estimate the value. Put the value in the currency you selected, round to nearest whole value, enter number only (for example, $96,000.50 should be entered as $96,000).

_____

28. List the other factors that could have influenced these results. _____

_____

29. Recognizing that the other factors could have influenced this annual value of improvement, please estimate the percentage of improvement that is attributable to the program. Express as a percentage. For example, if only 60% of the sales increase is attributable to the program, enter 60 here.
_____%

30. What confidence do you place in the estimates you have provided in the questions above? 0% means no confidence, and 100% is certainty. Round to nearest whole value, and enter a number only (for example, 37.5% should be entered as 38).
_____%

Results—second measure

31. Please define the second measure you selected and its unit for measurement. For example, if you selected "sales," your unit of measure may be "one closed sale."

_____

32. For this measure, what is the monetary value of improvement for one unit of this measure? For example, the value of a closed sale is sales value times the profit margin ($10,000 x 20% = $2,000). Although this step is difficult, please make every effort to estimate the value of a unit. Put the value in the currency you selected, round to nearest whole value, and enter numbers only (for example, $2,000.25 should be entered as $2,000).

_____

33. Please state your basis for the value of the unit of improvement you indicated above. In the closed sale example, a standard value, profit margin, is used, so "standard value" is entered here.

_____

Figure 13-2 Questionnaire for Leaders *(continued)*

---

34. For the measure listed as most directly linked to the program, how much has this measure improved in performance? If not readily available, please estimate. If you selected "sales," show the actual increase in sales (for example, four closed sales per month, enter the number 4 here). You can enter a number with up to one decimal point. Indicate the frequency base for the measure. _____

☐ daily ☐ weekly ☐ monthly ☐ quarterly

Return on investment—second measure

35. What is the annual value of improvement in the measure you selected above? Multiply the increase (Question 34) by the frequency (Question 34) times the unit of value (Question 32). For example, if you selected "sales," multiply the sales increase by the frequency to arrive at the annum value (for example, four sales per month x 12 x $2,000-$56,000). Although this step is difficult, please make every effort to estimate the value. Put the value in the currency you selected, round to nearest whole value, and enter numbers only (for example, $96,000.25 should be entered as $96,000).

36. List the other factors that could have influenced these results. _____

37. Recognizing that the other factors could have influenced this annual value of improvement, please estimate the percentage of improvement that is attributable to the program. Express as a percentage. For example, if only 60% of the sales increase is attributable to the program, enter 60 here. _____ %

38. What confidence do you place in the estimates you have provided in the questions above? 0% means no confidence, and 100% is certainty. Round to the nearest whole value, and enter a number only (for example, 37.5% should be entered as 38%). _____ %

39. What other benefits have been realized from this program? _____

40. Please estimate your direct costs of travel and lodging for your participation in this program. Put the value in the currency you selected, round to nearest whole value, and enter numbers only (for example, $10,000.49 should be entered as $10,000).

41. Please state your basis for the travel and lodging cost estimate above. _____

Feedback

42. How can we improve the training to make it more relevant to your job?

Thank you for taking the time to complete this survey!

Another important technique was to review the questionnaire with participants—question by question—at the end of the four-day workshop to clarify issues, create expectations, and gain commitment to provide data. Third-party collection was achieved by use of automated external data collection. Essentially, the data was sent by e-mail to the data collector's server.

Return on Investment Analysis Plan

The completed ROI analysis plan is shown in Figure 13-3. This plan details the specific issues that must be addressed and the particular techniques selected to complete the ROI analysis.

Method of Isolation

The method the L&D team used to isolate the effects of the program proved to be a challenge. Because the managers represented different functional areas, there was no finite set of measures that could be linked to the program for each participant. Essentially, each manager could have a different set of measures as he or she focused on specific business needs in the work unit. Consequently, the use of a control group was not feasible. In addition, the trend-line analysis and forecasting methods proved to be inappropriate for the same reason.

Therefore, the evaluation team had to collect estimations directly from participants on the questionnaire. Question 29 isolated the effects of this program using an estimate. Question 30 adjusted for the error of the estimate. The challenge was to ensure that participants understood this issue and were committed to provide data for the isolation.

Converting Data to Monetary Value

The participants provided estimates for converting their selected measures to monetary values. In the planning, the L&D team assumed that there were only a few feasible approaches for participants to place monetary value on measures. Because there was little agenda time to discuss this issue, the L&D staff had to rely on easy-to-obtain data using three options. The good news was that at Global Car Rental, as with many other organizations, standard values were developed for the measures that matter and they were the first option. If a measure is something that the company wants to increase, such

Figure 13-3 ROI Analysis Plan

Program: _____ Responsibility: _____ Date: _____

Data items (usually Level 4)	Methods for isolating the effect of the program process	Methods of converting data to monetary values	Cost categories	Intangible benefits	Communication targets for final report	Other influences/ issues during application	Comments
• Varies, depending on measures selected	• Participant estimate	• Standard value • Expert value • Participant estimate	• Needs assessment (prorated) • Program development (prorated) • Facilitation fees • Promotional materials • Facilitation and coordination • Meals and refreshments • Facilities • Participants' salaries and benefits for time away from work • Managers' salaries and benefits for time involved in program • Cost of overhead • Evaluation costs	• Job satisfaction for first-level managers • Job satisfaction for team managers • Improved teamwork • Improved communication	• Participants (first-level managers) • Participants' managers • Senior executives • L&D staff • Prospective participants • L&D council members	• Several process improvement initiatives are going on during this program implementation	• Must gain commitment to provide data • A high response rate is needed

as productivity or sales, someone already will have placed a value on that measure to show the contribution of the improvement. If it is a measure the company wants to reduce (e.g., turnover, accidents, or absenteeism), more than likely someone has placed a monetary value to show the impact of these critical measures. Consequently, the participants were asked to use standard values if they were available.

If these values were not available, as a second option participants could measure. In many cases, an individual from the department would provide the measurements; he or she would furnish a particular report in which the data came directly from the operating reports. Essentially, this was expert input.

If no standard was available or experts identified, the last option was for the participants to estimate the value. Because this was a measure that mattered to the participant, he or she should have some perception about the value of improving it. The actual amount was entered on question 24. Then, question 25 provided the basis for showing the details for how that value was developed. Question 25 is critical. If it was omitted, the business impact measure was removed from the analysis under the guiding principle of not using an unsupported claim in the analysis. Incidentally, the participants were informed about this principle as the questionnaire was reviewed with them at the end of the workshop.

Costs

The costs for the program were typical—analysis, design, development, and delivery components—and represented the fully loaded costs that contained both direct and indirect categories.

Other Issues

The L&D team anticipated some intangible benefits and, consequently, added a question to the questionnaire to identify improvements in these intangible benefits (question 39; see Figure 13-2). To ensure that all the key stakeholders were identified, the evaluation team decided which groups should receive the information in the impact study. Six specific groups were targeted for communication. The remainder of the ROI analysis plan listed other issues about the study.

Results

Twenty-nine questionnaires were returned for an 81 percent response rate. Participants provided a rich database that indicated success at each level of evaluation.

Reaction

Table 13-1 shows the reaction data obtained from the follow-up questionnaire. Although some initial reaction was collected at the end of the workshop with a standard reaction questionnaire, the team decided to collect and present to the senior team the reaction obtained in the follow-up. Each of the reaction measures exceeded the goal of a 4.0 rating, except for the issue about the amount of new information, which was slightly less than the desired level.

Learning

Although several skill practices and self-assessments were taken during the workshop to measure learning, the team decided to present the learning data directly from the follow-up questionnaire. As shown in Table 13-2,

Table 13-1   Reaction Data from Participants

Issue	Rating*
Recommended to others	4.2
Worthwhile investment	4.1
Good use of time	4.6
Relevant to my work	4.3
Important to my work	4.1
Provided me with new information	3.9

*Rating scale 1 to 5, with 1 = strongly disagree and 5 = strongly agree

Table 13-2   Learning Data from Participants

Issue	Rating*
Learned new knowledge/skills	4.3
Confident in my ability to apply new knowledge/skills	4.1

*Rating scale 1 to 5, where 1 = strongly disagree and 5 = strongly agree

the learning measures met or exceeded expectations in terms of the amount of new skills and knowledge and confidence in using them. Responses to question 11 in the questionnaire (see Figure 13-2) also revealed the average skill or knowledge improvement to be 48 percent.

Application

Table 13-3 shows application data obtained in the follow-up questionnaire. The applications exceeded expectations, and the effectiveness of the coach rating was a particular highlight. The percentage of time spent on tasks that require the use of acquired knowledge/skills (question 18; see Figure 13-2) averaged 43 percent. The participants' managers received the questionnaire primarily about the coaching component, and they reported success. They routinely coached the participants and frequently reinforced the use of the skills.

Barriers and Enablers

Much to the surprise of the staff, the barriers were minimal and the enablers were strong. The program enjoyed good management support and was tailored to the job environment. Therefore, few barriers prevented the transfer of learning, and the enablers were built into the program. Table 13-4 shows the barriers and enablers.

Business Impact

Business impact data (Level 4) are shown in Table 13-5. This table shows specific improvements identified directly from the questionnaire, by participant

Table 13-3 Application Data from Participants

Issue	Rating*
Extent of use of knowledge/skills	4.3
Frequency of application of knowledge/skills	3.8
Effectiveness with using knowledge/skills	4.3
Effectiveness of coach	4.7
Criticalness to job	4.2
Stay on schedule	4.1
*Rating scale 1 to 5, where 1 = lowest and 5 = highest	

Table 13-4 Top Five Barriers and Enablers Identified by Participants

Barriers	Frequency, %
No opportunity to use skills	14
Lack of support from colleagues and peers	14
Insufficient knowledge and understanding	10
Lack of management support	7
Lack of confidence to apply learning	3
Enablers	**Frequency, %**
Management support	55
Opportunity to use skills	52
Confidence to apply learning	38
Support from colleagues and peers	34
Sufficient knowledge and understanding	34

number, for the first 15 participants. To save space, the remaining 14 participants are included as a total. Usually, each participant provided improvements on two measures. The total for the second measure is shown at the bottom of Table 13-5. The top row of Table 13-5 reveals the linkage between the questions on the questionnaire and the columns in this table. The total annual improvement for each measure is reported first. Incidentally, the specific measure was identified and could have been reported as well, but to reduce confusion only the measure categories were reported. The heading "Converting Data to Monetary Value" shows the extent to which the three options were used to convert data to monetary value. Most participants selected "Standard" because standard values were readily available. The column of "Other Factors" indicates the number of other factors that contributed to the results. In most cases several factors were present. No more than four other factors were identified in any section. In a few cases, there were no other factors. In summary, the standard values were used 71 percent of the time, and other factors were identified 85 percent of the time.

Return on Investment Analysis

The total cost of the program, using a fully loaded analysis, is shown in Table 13-6. The needs assessment was prorated over four years, based upon the anticipated life cycle of the project. A thousand managers in the United States would attend this program in the four-year time period before another

Table 13-5 Business Impact Calculations

Participant number	Annual improvement, $ (0.27)*	Measure (0.23)*	Converting data to monetary value (0.25)*	Contribution from program, % (0.29)*	Other factors (0.28)*	Confidence estimate, % (0.30)*	Adjusted Value
1	$13,100	Sales	Standard	60	3	80	$ 6,288
3	41,200	Productivity	Expert	75	1	95	29,355
4	5,300	Sales	Standard	80	1	90	3,816
6	7,210	Cost	N/A	70	2	70	3,533
9	4,215	Efficiency	Standard	40	3	75	1,265
10	17,500	Quality	Expert	35	4	60	3,675
12	11,500	Time	Standard	60	2	80	5,520
14	3,948	Time	Standard	70	1	80	2,212
15	14,725	Sales	Standard	40	3	70	4,123
17	6,673	Efficiency	Estimate	50	3	60	2,002
18	12,140	Costs	N/A	100	0	100	12,140
19	17,850	Sales	Standard	60	2	70	7,497
21	13,980	Sales	Standard	50	3	80	5,588
22	15,362	Cost	N/A	40	4	90	5,530
23	18,923	Sales	Standard	60	1	75	8,515
					Total for the items above		$101,039
					Total for the next 14 items		$ 84,358
					Total for 2nd measure		$143,764
					Total benefits		$329,201

* Data collected from questionnaire in Figure 13-2
† Total monetary benefits = 0.27 × 0.29 × 0.30

Table 13-6 Summary of Fully-Loaded Costs

Cost of item	Cost
Needs assessment (prorated over 4 years)	$ 900
Program development (prorated over 3 years)	2,000
Program materials ($120/participant)	4,320
Travel, meals, and lodging ($1,600/participant)	57,600
Facilitation and coordination ($4,000/day)	32,000
Facilities and refreshments ($890/day)	7,120
Participants' salaries (plus benefits) for time involved	37,218
Managers' salaries (plus benefits) for time involved	12,096
Training and education overhead (allocated)	2,500
ROI evaluation costs	5,000
TOTAL for 36 participants	**$160,754**

needs assessment was conducted. Program development was prorated over three years, assuming that the delivery could change significantly in that time frame. The remainder of the costs were charged directly and included the delivery expenses, the salaries for the participants (the first-level managers), as well as their managers (at the second level). The training and education overhead was allocated using a figure of $312 per day of training.

The benefit/cost ratio is calculated as follows:

$$BCR = \frac{\text{Total Benefits}}{\text{Total Costs}} = \frac{\$329,201}{\$160,754} = 2.05$$

The return on investment is calculated as follows:

$$ROI = \frac{\text{Net Total Benefits}}{\text{Total Costs}} = \frac{\$329,201 - \$160,754}{\$160,754} \times 100 = 105\%$$

Credibility of Results

The data were perceived to be credible by both the L&D staff and senior management group. Credibility rests on seven major issues:

1. The information for the analysis was provided directly from the new managers. The managers had no reason to be biased in their input.
2. The data were provided anonymously because no one had to provide his or her name on the questionnaire. Anonymity helped eliminate the possibility of bias.
3. The data collection process was conservative; it was assumed that an unresponsive individual would realize no improvement. This concept— no data, no improvement—is an ultraconservative approach to data collection.
4. The L&D staff did not assign complete credit to this program. The participants isolated a portion of the data that should be credited directly to this program.
5. The data were adjusted for the potential error of the estimate. Estimates were used to isolate the effects of the program.
6. Only the first year's benefits were used in the analysis. Most of the improvement should result in second- and third-year benefits.
7. The costs of the program were fully loaded. All direct and indirect costs were included, including the time away from work for the participants and managers. The data represent a balanced profile of success.

Very favorable reaction, learning, and application data were presented along with business impact, return on investment, and intangibles. Collectively, these issues made a convincing case for the program.

Communication Strategy

To communicate appropriately with the target audiences outlined in the ROI analysis plan, the L&D team produced three specific documents. The first report was a detailed impact study that showed the approach, assumptions, methodology, and results and used all six data categories. In addition, barriers and enablers were included in the study, along with conclusions and recommendations. The second report was an eight-page executive summary of the key points, including a one-page overview of the methodology. The third report was a brief, five-page summary of the process and results. These documents were presented to the different groups according to the plan presented in Table 13-7.

Because this was the first ROI study conducted in this organization, face-to-face meetings were conducted with the executives. The purpose was to ensure that executives understood the methodology, the conservative

Table 13-7 Distribution Plan for Leadership Challenge Evaluation Reports

Audience	Document
Participants	Brief summary
Managers of participants	Brief summary
Senior executives	Complete study, executive summary
L&D staff	Complete study
L&D council	Complete study, executive summary
Prospective participants	Brief summary

assumptions, and each level of data. The barriers, enablers, conclusions, and recommendations were an important part of the meeting. In the future, after two or three studies have been conducted, this group will receive only a one-page summary of key data items. A similar meeting was conducted with the L&D council.

The council members were advisors to the L&D department who are usually middle- and upper-level executives and managers. Finally, a face-to-face meeting was held with the learning and development staff where the complete impact study was described and used as a learning tool.

Lessons Learned

This case study shows how the evaluation process can be accomplished with minimal resources. The approach shifted much of the responsibility for evaluation to the participants as they collected data, isolated the effects of the program, and converted the data to monetary values—the three most critical steps in the ROI process. The results were easily communicated to various target groups through three specific documents. L&D staff and senior management perceived the data to be credible. The return on investment was positive, and the program showed important connections with business results.

Discussion Questions

1. Is this approach credible? Explain.
2. Is the ROI value realistic?
3. What types of programs would be appropriate for this approach?

4. What additions or revisions could be made to the evaluation strategies provided?
5. What evaluation strategies other than the questionnaire could be used in this situation?

14

Case Study: Measuring Return on Investment in Leadership Development for Production Managers*

T HIS PROGRAM REPRESENTS a comprehensive leadership development initiative for first-level managers in a technical environment. It focuses all participants on a small group of measures. The payoffs for the program included productivity, defined as the percentage of on-time production, voluntary turnover, and unplanned absenteeism. The product is very data rich and the analysis follows all of the issues around the ROI Methodology, including forecasting.

Background

Linear Network Systems (LNS) is an important supplier to the telecommunications industry, producing a variety of network equipment. This publicly held company has been operating for more than 15 years with manufacturing and support facilities scattered throughout the United States and Canada. The organization has been very successful and stable.

---

* This case study has previously been published in Phillips, Patricia Pulliam, and Jack J. Phillips, *Proving the Value of HR: ROI Case Studies*, 2nd ed., Birmingham, AL: ROI Institute Inc., 2010.

Although the company has been very profitable, it recently experienced competitive cost and quality pressures, which caused some deterioration in sales. Several factors are related to the decline, and senior management is concerned about the ability of the first-level management team to lead today's workforce. Greg Simpson, the president of Linear Network Systems, asked the human resources development manager, Pam O'Kelly, to provide appropriate training.

For several months, the company had been attempting to develop these team leaders. Several team-building sessions had been conducted. The president felt that the leaders were experiencing difficulty in making the transition to leadership and that they needed to develop leadership skills to motivate team members to improve productivity. A leadership development program was suggested.

Situation

O'Kelly contacted a consulting firm to inquire about potential leadership training. The principal consultant suggested that a needs assessment be conducted to determine specific training needs and also to determine if other issues need to be addressed. O'Kelly reluctantly agreed to a needs assessment. Both Simpson and O'Kelly were convinced that training was needed, and they wanted the "standard leadership training" program. After some convincing, the consultant conducted the needs assessment using four methods:

1. Reviewing operational performance documents
2. Interviewing a sample of first-level managers (team leaders) and middle managers
3. Observing a small sample of first-level managers on the job
4. Administering a questionnaire to all first- and second-level managers

The assessment identified a lack of skills and a need for significant leadership training. Most of the skills focused on understanding and motivating employees, setting goals, and providing feedback.

The Program

A six-module, 24-hour training program was proposed for one plant as a pilot group. All first-level operating and support managers would be trained at the same time. The program would be conducted in six 4-hour segments scattered over a 1-month period. Between sessions, participants would be asked to apply the new skills so there would be transfer of training to the job. Initially, the program was planned to focus on the following areas:

- Understanding employee needs
- Motivating employees for improved performance
- Counseling employees
- Solving problems with employees
- Providing appropriate leadership behavior
- Inspiring teamwork

The program was labeled "Leadership for Improved Performance" and was planned for all 16 supervisors in the pilot plant. A follow-up evaluation was planned several months after the training was completed. If the program was effective, Linear Network Systems would offer it throughout its organization.

Needs Assessment

An improper or inadequate needs assessment may result in a program designed to address skills that are not needed or are already in place. The needs assessment was conducted at Level 4 (business needs), Level 3 (job performance needs), and Level 2 (skill and knowledge needs). Without a multiple-level needs assessment, it would be more difficult to evaluate the program designed to change job behavior (Level 3) and drive business impact improvement (Level 4). Thus, the needs assessment became a very critical issue for identifying performance deficiencies at all three levels and was an important component in Linear Network Systems' plan to develop first-level managers.

Business Performance Measures

The needs assessment identified several business performance measures for which improvement was needed. The job performance analysis indicates that three measures were related to inadequate leadership skills:

- Productivity (measured by the percentage of shipments met)
- Employee turnover
- Absenteeism

There was some skepticism among senior management that productivity could be enhanced through leadership training, although most of the team leaders agreed that they could boost productivity with improved teamwork. Employee turnover was high, and although there were many factors that influenced turnover, most team leaders felt that turnover was a variable under their control. Finally, absenteeism was extremely high, particularly on second shifts and on Mondays and Fridays.

Linear Network Systems had developed an adequate measurement system, which monitored, among other variables, productivity, turnover, and absenteeism measures by the production unit. Each first-level manager received absenteeism and turnover data monthly, and productivity measures were available weekly for the production departments. Support departments can significantly influence the measures by providing excellent support and assistance.

Top management approved the leadership program proposal, including the structure and timing.

Evaluation Levels

Because LNS management was interested in the accountability of training, and the consulting firm was eager to show results of training, both parties were eager to conduct an ROI evaluation for this project. ROI data can be very convincing for marketing a program to other groups. With this approach, business impact data would be collected, converted to monetary values, and compared to the program cost to develop the return on investment (Level 5). In addition, Levels 1, 2, and 3 data would be collected to measure reaction, learning, and application. Thus, all five levels of evaluation were pursued.

There was another important reason for evaluating this program at all five levels. Because this program is linked to key organizational measures, a success would show a direct linkage to the company's bottom line. A significant payoff to the company would clearly show management that leadership training is a high-impact process and that it can make a difference by improving important business performance measures.

Objectives

Because Levels 3 and 4 data must be collected, it is essential that specific objectives be measurable and directly related to the Level 3 and 4 data obtained from the needs assessment. Therefore, program objectives were revised.

It was determined that after attending this program participants should be able to:

- Describe and identify applications for two motivational models
- Describe and identify applications for two leadership models
- Set measurable performance goals each month for each employee
- Apply performance feedback skills routinely with each employee
- Reduce voluntary employee turnover from an average annual rate of 29 to 25 percent in four months
- Reduce unplanned absenteeism from a weekly average of 5 to 3 percent in four months
- Increase productivity by 2 percentage points in four months

The specific targets were difficult to develop and required the complete cooperation of the plant manager and the department heads.

Data Collection Plan

The consultant and the human resource development (HRD) manager decided that the action planning process would be utilized in the follow-up evaluation. Team leaders should know how to develop action plans, and their managers should be able to provide assistance and support with the process. The action plan would show how the newly acquired skills are applied to improve measures such as productivity, turnover, and absenteeism. A portion of the program allowed for a discussion of action plans, and the program facilitator was required to approve the action plan and verify that it has met basic requirements. A model action plan would be provided to help ensure that supervisors understand the process.

After discussions with management, it was felt that within four months supervisors should be able to apply leadership skills to achieve measurable results. Although a six-month time frame was recommended, senior management indicated that they might want to proceed with the program in other plants before six months; therefore, they preferred a three-month period. Four months was a compromise.

Because all of the action plans involved different time frames, each participant was asked to provide a progress report in four months, or in some cases the completed project would be required. This would give a "snapshot" of the performance improvement within that time frame.

Although the action plan, by design, collected Levels 3 and 4 data, a follow-up questionnaire was planned to gain more evidence of on-the-job behavior change (Level 3). Responsibilities for data collection at Levels 1 and 2 usually rest with the facilitator, and that was the case here. The area training coordinator was assigned the responsibility for collecting the questionnaire data (Level 3) and monitoring performance (Level 4). The completed data collection plan is presented in Figure 14-1.

Isolating the Effects of Training

One of the most important challenges facing program evaluators is determining the specific technique that isolates the effects of the training program, recognizing that other factors may influence outcome measures at the same time the program is being conducted.

During discussions with management and participants in the training program, two factors were identified that could have an influence on each of the business performance measures in addition to the training program. First, in this case the implementation of the Total Quality Management program placed emphasis on improving all three measures. Quality was defined in a broad sense, including being at work (measure 1: absenteeism), remaining with the company (measure 2: turnover), and ensuring that customer shipments were on time (measure 3: productivity).

The second factor was the various team-building activities that were initiated as Linear Network Systems attempted to move to a team-based structure. First-level managers were encouraged to use employee input, conduct meetings with employees, and take action to improve productivity. If team building was successful, it would increase productivity and reduce turnover and absenteeism.

Because it was important to determine the precise impact of the training program, isolation of the effects of training from the other two factors was essential. One of the most effective approaches is to use a control group arrangement in which one group receives training and another similarly situated group does not receive training. Linear Network Systems explored the control group arrangement in this setting. Initially the opportunity appeared to be an excellent one to use a particular plant location as a pilot group and select another similar plant as a control group. However, no other plant had the same product line, the same type of processes, the same workforce characteristics, and the same environmental conditions, which are all important variables to reflect performance. Thus, the control group arrangement was not considered a feasible approach.

Figure 14-1 Completed Evaluation Plan: Data Collection

Program: Leadership for Improved Performance   Responsibility: _____   Date: _____

Level	Objective(s)	Measure/data	Data collection method	Data source	Timing	Responsibilities
1	**REACTION/SATISFACTION** • Positive reaction • Identify planned actions	• Average rating of at least 4.2 on a 5.0 scale on quality, usefulness, and achievement of program objectives • 100% submit planned actions	• Standard feedback questionnaire	• Participants	• End of program	• Facilitator
2	**LEARNING/SKILLS** • Knowledge on motivational models • Knowledge on leadership models • Skills for motivating employees • Knowledge on providing counseling • Knowledge on measuring employee performance • Problem-solving skills • Knowledge/skills on teamwork • Leadership behavior skills	• Demonstrated ability to provide employee feedback/motivating/problem-solving/ leadership skills • Scale of 1 to 5 on assessment of knowledge	• Skill practice • Facilitator assessment • Participant assessment	• Participants • Facilitator • Participants	• During program	• Facilitator
3	**APPLICATION AND IMPLEMENTATION** • Extent of skill use • Frequency of skill use • Success with skill use • Setting performance goals • Complete all steps of action plan	• Scale of 1 to 5 on assessment of application • The number of steps completed on action plan	• Follow-up questionnaire • Action plan	• Participants • Participants	• 4 months after program • 4 months after program	• Area training coordinator
4	**BUSINESS IMPACT** • Reduce employee turnover • Reduce employee absenteeism • Increase productivity	• Volunteer turnover – 29% to 25% • Unplanned absenteeism – 5% to 3% • Percentage of shipments met – improve by 2%	• Action plan	• Participants	• 4 months after program	• Area training coordinator
5	**ROI** 25 percent	Comments: _____					

297

The approach utilized to isolate the effects of training was estimates from participants: the team leaders. Participants would be asked to indicate how much of their improvement was linked directly to this training. They provided the information in a portion of the action plan. Each participant was presented with a six-month average of the data prior to training to compare with posttraining data. After training, team leaders regularly would receive reports for each of the items as part of their operating data.

Converting Data to Monetary Values

The next task in setting up the ROI process is to select the techniques to convert data to monetary values. The challenge facing the evaluation team is to determine the most credible and accurate techniques for placing values for each of the business impact data items.

As part of the next step in the ROI process, Linear Network Systems' data were to be converted to monetary values. The value of improved productivity was a standard value developed by engineering and production control. Each 1 percent of improvement in productivity would save the plant $21,000 annually.

The company had no detailed historical records on turnover costs, although the company expected these costs to be significant when the costs of employment, recruiting, training, and lost productivity were considered. The consultant provided information from external studies, which showed that turnover can cost one times the annual pay of the employees (100 percent of annual direct compensation). Annual wages of nonsupervisory employees averaged $31,000. Management thought that a figure of one (1) times the annual pay would be too high for the cost of turnover since the training period was relatively short, recruiting costs were normally quite low, and exit costs were not very significant. After the matter was discussed with senior management, the compromise figure of $24,800 for the cost of turnover (80 percent of annual direct compensation) was reached. This appeared to be a very conservative estimate. Sixteen first-level managers were trained in this program, and they supervised a total of 385 employees.

The consultant located previous studies about the cost of absenteeism in a similar manufacturing sector, which showed a range of $89 to $210 per absence with an average of $180. Brief estimates taken in the training session, with input from the 16 managers, yielded an average cost of $98. This was considered the most credible value because it was developed with the focus group process using estimates from participants (supervisors) and adjusted for error. Linear Network Systems' employees worked an average of 228 days per year.

Costs

The total charge for the program from the consulting firm was $51,000, including customization time, facilitation, and needs assessment. Because the consulting firm provided standard material for the new program, development costs were insignificant. Although team leaders were not replaced while they were in training, the salaries and benefits of managers were included for the time during the training sessions. The average salary of the first-level managers was $47,500. The employee benefits factor was 39 percent of salaries. A total of three days were consumed in the program. The charge for course materials was $185 per participant. Miscellaneous refreshments and food were $195 per participant for the three days. The use of the conference room was estimated to be $200 per session, although Linear Network Systems does not routinely capture and report this as a part of training. The consultant estimated the additional cost of the evaluation to be $10,000.

Costs

The costs to train 16 supervisors were:

Needs assessment, program development, facilitation	$51,000
Supplies and materials ($185 × 16)	2,960
Food ($195 × 16)	3,120
Facilities (6 × 200)	1,200
Evaluation	10,000
Salaries and benefits, for the time away from routine work ($548 × 1.39 × 16)	12,188
Total	$ 80,468

The facilitation charge from the supplier, which totaled $51,000, included the costs for needs assessment, program development, and facilitation. If the program had been developed internally, these three charges would have to be developed separately. The daily salary was developed by dividing average salary ($47,500) by the total number of weekdays worked (52 × 5 = 260). To obtain the total salaries and benefits cost, this number is multiplied by 3, adjusted upward by the benefits factor of 39 percent. This is equivalent to multiplying the average salary by 1.39. The total for each participant is multiplied by 16 to obtain the salaries and benefits for the group.

Follow-Up

Because management was interested in knowing the results of the program as soon as possible, a four-month evaluation period was used. Data for six months prior to and four months after the program are presented in Figures 14-2, 14-3, and 14-4, which show the productivity, turnover, and absenteeism values for the plant, respectively. The training was conducted during a one-month period and no improvements were expected during that month. Consequently, the one-month training period was excluded from the analysis.

As Figure 14-2 shows, productivity was enhanced after the implementation of training. According to the records of the production control department, the average percentage of on-time production for six months prior to training was 92 percent. A value of 95 percent was used as posttraining performance, which is the average of months 3 and 4 after training. With the averaging of the two monthly values, a spike in the values is avoided. The plant's annual turnover rates averaged 29.5 percent for the six months prior to training and are presented in Figure 14-3. Turnover was calculated monthly and was reported as an annualized value for comparison (e.g., a 2 percent monthly turnover was reflected as a 24 percent annual turnover rate on the report).

Figure 14-2 Productivity

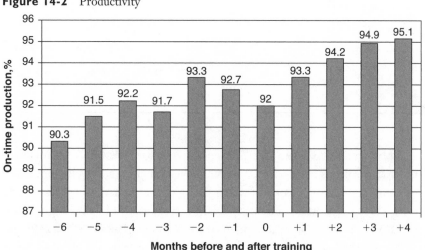

Figure 14-3 Turnover

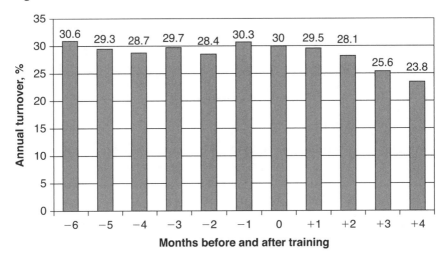

Figure 14-4 Absenteeism

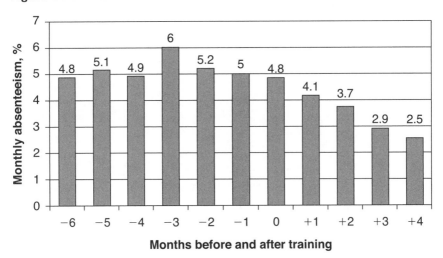

The average for months 3 and 4 after training yields a value of 24.7 percent. The monthly absenteeism rates, presented in Figure 14-4, showed the most dramatic improvement. The absenteeism rate for the six months prior to training averaged 5.2 percent and was considered much too high by management. This figure includes only unexpected and unplanned absences. The average for months 3 and 4 after training yields a value of 2.7 percent.

Table 14-1 Contribution of Various Factors

	Training program	TQM	Team building	Total
Productivity (% of schedule)	32%	49%	19%	100%
Turnover (annualized)	72	7	21	100
Absenteeism (% absence)	76	4	20	100

In addition to action plans, supervisors completed a brief questionnaire where they estimated how much of the improvement in performance was related to each of the three factors influencing the output variables. The results are presented in Table 14-1.

Four of the supervisors submitted action plans focusing on measures other than productivity, turnover, or absenteeism. Three improvement areas were identified: time savings, efficiency, and direct cost savings. Table 14-2 shows

Table 14-2 Additional Benefits

Super-visor	Annual improvement value	Basis for value	Isolation factor	Confi-dence	Adjusted value
#3	$36,000	Improvement in efficiency of group. $3,000/month × 12 (group estimate)	50%	85%	$15,300
#8	24,000	Time savings: Improvement in customer response time (8 hours to 6 hours). Estimated value: $2,000/month	55	60	7,920
#10	8,090	Time savings: Team project completed 10 days ahead of schedule. Annual salaries of $210,500 = $809/day × 10 days	45	90	3,279
#15	14,900	Direct cost savings	60	90	7,830

a summary of these additional benefits. The isolation factor is the percent of improvement directly related to the training program. The confidence estimate is level of confidence in the isolation factor.

The tabulations of the benefits for the program for the primary measures are shown in Table 14-3. Tables 14-4 and 14-5 show the total benefits of the program.

Return on Investment and Benefit/Cost Ratio Calculations

The BCR and ROI can be calculated using the following equations:

Total benefits: $513,966 + $34,329 = $548,295

$$BCR = \frac{\$548,295}{\$80,468} = 6.81$$

$$ROI\ (\%) = \frac{\$548,295 - \$80,468}{\$80,468} \times 100 = 581\%$$

Return on Investment Analysis

The values presented in this study were much higher than management anticipated, and even higher than the consulting firm envisioned. In discussions held before implementation, the senior management team (the president, the director of manufacturing, and the plant manager) agreed that for the program to be successful the payoff would have to be in productivity. This senior management group even suggested that absenteeism and turnover be considered intangible data and reported as additional improvements without a conversion to monetary values. Thus, in early discussions, absenteeism and turnover, although linked directly to the skills training, were considered to be potentially low-impact variables. If the original suggestion had been followed, the program would have generated a negative return on investment. An important lesson was learned. Behaviorally driven Level 4 data, although considered to be soft in nature, can have a tremendous impact in the organization. And in this situation, the impact would have been considerably enhanced if more appropriate values had been used for the monetary conversion of absenteeism and turnover. (Instead, lower, more conservative values were used.)

Table 14-3 Annual Values for the Primary Measures

	Pretraining, 6-month avg.	Posttraining 3- and 4-month avg.	Differences between pre-training and posttraining	Participant's estimate of impact of training	Unit value	Annual impact of training (estimates)
Productivity (% of schedule)	92%	95%	3%	.96% (3% × 32%)	$21,000 for 1%	$ 20,160
Turnover (annualized)	29.5	24.7%	4.8%	3.46% (4.9% × 72%)	$24,800 for each turnover	$330,360
Absenteeism (% absence)	5.2	2.7%	2.5%	1.9% 2.5% × 76%	$98 for each absence	$163,446

Calculations

Productivity: Savings = .96 × $21,000 $20,160

Turnover: Change in number leaving in a year = 385 × 3.46% = 13.3

Savings = 13.3 × $24,900 $331,170

Absenteeism: Change in absences (incidents) = 385 × 228 × 1.9% = 1,668

Savings = $1,668 × $98 $163,464

Table 14-4 Summary of Primary Monetary Values

Measures	Benefits
Increase in productivity	$ 20,160
Reduction in employee turnover	330,360
Reduction in absenteeism	163,446
TOTAL	$513,966

Table 14-5 Summary of Other Monetary Values

Measures	Benefits
Efficiency	$ 15,300
Time savings (participant 1)	7,920
Time savings (participant 2)	3,279
Direct cost savings	7,830
TOTAL	$34,329

An important issue evolved about the projection of output data six months to one year after the program. It was clear that the output was moving in the right direction and it appeared that further improvement was in store. While it is tempting to assume the variables will continue to improve, in reality other variables usually enter the analysis; a deterioration of the output variables may be realized unless additional training or other interventions are implemented. This is what happened in this case. Each data item continued to improve for the six months. Absenteeism tapered off and then increased slightly, turnover remained fairly constant, and productivity continued to improve, perhaps driven by the TQM and team-building sessions.

As part of the evaluation process, the evaluation team (the consultant, the facilitators, the HRD manager, and department heads) explored ways in which the process could be improved. The team discussed several issues. First, because the control group strategy most accurately isolates the effects of training, the team thought it would have been better to initiate this program in a plant that could be compared to another location in a control group arrangement. This strategy will often develop more confidence in the process and will build a more convincing case for a high-impact return on investment.

A second issue was the needs assessment. The team thought it was important to have sufficient evidence of a direct connection between the Level 4 business impact measures and the planned training program. However, some team members wanted to see more evidence of how this was accomplished so that they would be more convinced about the direct linkage.

The third issue was the early follow-up. The consultants wanted to wait six months to capture the improvement, but management insisted on making a decision in four months. Perhaps a compromising solution is to capture data at four months, make the decision based on the apparent high-impact level, and continue to capture data for another two months and develop an ROI impact study with six months of data, which would then be communicated to the decision makers.

The fourth issue involved the apparent lack of a comprehensive evaluation at Level 3. Some team members wanted a more comprehensive assessment of actual behavior changes, which would convince them that the supervisors were actually operating differently. While this is an important issue, it was a trade-off process. A comprehensive Level 3 evaluation is time-consuming and costly. When a Level 4 evaluation was planned with a specific technique to isolate the effects of training, other team members felt that a more comprehensive Level 3 was unnecessary.

Overall, the evaluation team perceived this to be an excellent ROI analysis. The process was credible with an acceptable level of accuracy.

Intangible Benefits

Other potential intangible benefits were identified, including improved job satisfaction of the team leaders, improved job satisfaction of team members, reduction in stress for the team leaders, and an increase in the bonus for supervisors (bonus pay is linked to productivity). While these items were considered to be important benefits of the program, they were not measured precisely because of the additional effort required for monitoring and analysis. Each measure became a line item on the questionnaire—to gain some insight into the issue. When intangible benefits are important and influential to the target audience, they should be monitored and analyzed in a more comprehensive way. Interestingly, the management group initially proposed absenteeism and turnover measures as intangible benefits. If this suggestion had been followed, the improvements in absenteeism and turnover would have been presented as intangible benefits, resulting in a negative return on investment. The team learned a valuable lesson. There should be an attempt to convert each intangible measure that is monitored and isolated. If the conversion process becomes unmanageable, inaccurate, or not very credible, then a data item is listed as an intangible benefit and reported without any further analysis (which is Guiding Principle 11).

Return on Investment Analysis Plan

Figure 14-5 shows the ROI analysis plan for the leadership development program. Each decision and strategy outlined in the various parts of this case is reflected on this planning document. This document is a decision-making tool for ROI analysis. It is completed before the evaluation process has begun.

Preprogram Forecast

A preprogram forecast could have been conducted, based on estimated improvements of the three business impact measures. A group of experts, most knowledgeable about these measures and the work context, would estimate the improvement that would be achieved with the implementation of the LD program. Although the numbers might not be accurate, they would provide insight into the value of the program, particularly when the ROI percentage is calculated.

Level I Return on Investment Forecast

Although it was not attempted in this case, it is possible and perhaps instructive to develop a Level 1 ROI forecast. With this process, a series of potential impact questions could be asked where participants anticipate potential changes and estimate the particular impact of changes for each of the three variables (productivity, turnover, and absenteeism). Estimates could be provided on other measures that may be driven by the program. First-year values could be developed, along with a confidence percentage obtained from participants that would reflect their level of certainty with the process. The data could be adjusted with this confidence level to provide a forecast of the benefit and the calculation of the return on investment. Although this ROI value is subjective and often inflated, the analysis would provide some insight into the relationship between the projections at the end of the program and the actual performance four months later. Also, it may actually enhance the results because participants who make projections of performance may be motivated to meet those projections.

Figure 14-5 ROI Analysis Plan

Data items (usually Level 4)	Methods for isolating the effects of the program	Methods of converting data	Cost categories	Intangible benefits	Communica-tion targets	Other influences/ issues
Productivity % of shipments met	Participant estimates	• Direct conversion • Company standard value	• Consulting fee • Program materials • Food and refreshments • Facilities • Evaluation costs • Salaries and benefits of participants	• Improved team leader job satisfaction • Improved employee job satisfaction • Stress reduction • Increase in bonus pay	• Participants • Managers of participants • Senior management • HRD and HR staff • Other plant managers • Potential clients	• Team building was in process • Total quality management program has been launched • Management support is good • Management is eager to see results
Turnover (quits and discharges)	Participant estimates	• External studies • Senior management estimate				
Absenteeism	Participant estimates	• External studies • Participant estimate				

Levels 2 and 3 Return on Investment Forecast

At Linear Network Systems, it was impossible to capture data for a Level 2 ROI forecast. For this forecast to be possible, a validated instrument must be developed to measure learning and have test scores correlated with subsequent on-the-job performance. This was not feasible in this situation.

A Level 3 ROI forecast was not considered because of the concern about the subjective assessments that must be made to convert Level 3 data to monetary values. Also, the client was very bottom-line oriented and preferred to discuss performance in terms of Level 4 measures (productivity, turnover, absenteeism, etc.). Although management recognized that skills must be acquired and behavior must be changed, they were less interested in discussing the extent to which changes have occurred and the value of the change. Thus, a Level 3 ROI forecast would have provided little value for the client.

Communication of Results

Communication of results from an ROI impact study is a very crucial step in the ROI Methodology. Three documents were created for Linear Network Systems: a detailed impact study, an executive summary, and brief summary, with a little more detail than the executive summary. Although there can be many target audiences, six audiences received the study results at Linear Network Systems:

1. The participants (i.e., team leaders) were provided a brief summary of the study results that revealed what they had accomplished collectively. The brief summary of the impact study showed how the return on investment was developed.

2. The managers of the participants (i.e., middle-level managers) received a brief summary of the study with an appropriate explanation. These department heads for the various production and support departments were aware of the ROI impact study and were anticipating the results.

3. Senior management received executive summaries and copies of the detailed study. At Linear Network Systems, this group included the president, the director of manufacturing (for all plants), and the plant manager. In addition, this group received a briefing on the study results and discussed how the study was developed along with its interpretation. This step is important to ensure that there is a complete understanding of the ROI Methodology.

4. The training and HR staff received copies of the complete study so that they could understand how the ROI Methodology is applied to this type of program. This ROI study was part of an ongoing effort to build skills and develop strategies to increase accountability of HR programs.

5. Plant managers for the other locations received copies of the executive summary to show what can be accomplished with this type of training. Essentially, this communication served as an internal marketing tool to convince others that leadership development can improve their plants.

6. Potential clients for the consulting firm received brief summary copies of the study. This target group was unique to the consulting firm. With permission of the company, the study summary was used by the consulting firm to convince other prospective clients that leadership development can have a high impact. The name of the organization was disguised and sensitive data were slightly altered to protect the identity of the company.

Collectively, these six target audiences received information on the ROI impact study, ensuring that all important audiences understood the results and the process.

Implementation Issues

A variety of implementation issues emerged at Linear Network Systems:

- The HRD staff at Linear Network Systems used the results of this study to make a request for additional funding for measurement and evaluation in the future. In essence, the plan is to use the savings generated from the studies to drive additional funding for measurement and evaluation.

- One individual was appointed as coordinator for measurement and evaluation and was asked to lead the process. Appointing this champion to implement the ROI Methodology ensures that the process works properly, is executed timely, and is supported appropriately.

- To ensure that the study can be replicated, the internal leader (champion) participated in all phases of ROI implementation. The consulting firm worked closely with this individual to ensure that each step of the ROI Methodology was understood and could be applied in other situations.

- To help accomplish the transfer of capability, the consulting firm organized additional training for the evaluation leader to develop skills in the ROI Methodology and provide additional practice with ROI calculations.
- To help improve management support, a 2½-hour briefing was scheduled with the management team (i.e., department managers and above) at the next quarterly meeting to discuss the results of this study and the potential opportunity for significant returns from training. This program also underscored the manager's responsibility to make training effective in the company.
- Specific targets were set where a few programs were identified for planned ROI calculations. This provided some guidance for the HRD director to focus on high-priority programs.
- A policy statement was developed to capture the basic requirements for measurement and evaluation. This document described the responsibilities for all stakeholders, outlined how ROI studies would be conducted, and indicated how the results would be communicated.

Collectively, these seven actions provided adequate support to implement the ROI Methodology internally and make it a routine activity at Linear Network Systems.

Discussion Questions

1. How important is the needs assessment for this situation? Is the resistance to a needs assessment typical? At what levels should the needs assessment be conducted?
2. Should more than one technique be used to isolate the effects of training? Please explain.
3. For other potential improvement measures, what range of potential techniques can be used to convert data to monetary values?
4. Would the methods used in this case study be feasible for leadership development in your organization? Why or why not?

NOTES

1. Peter Drucker, "What Makes An Effective Executive?," *Harvard Business Review*, (June 2004), accessed October 15, 2011, http://hbr.org/2004/06/what-makes-an-effective-executive/ar/1.
2. Daniel Goleman, "What Makes a Leader?," *Harvard Business Review*, November–December 1998, accessed October 15, 2011, http://hbr.org/2004/01/what-makes-a-leader/ar/1.
3. Jim Collins, "Level 5 Leadership: The Triumph of Humility and Fierce Resolve," *Harvard Business Review*, July–August 2005, accessed October 2, 2011, http://hbr.org/2005/07/level-5-leadership-the-triumph-of-humility-and-fierce-resolve/ar/1.
4. *CEO Challenge 2011: Fueling Business Growth with Innovation and Talent Development* (research report), New York: The Conference Board, 2011.
5. Norm Smallwood, "Why Leadership Development in Asia Is Better Than in Europe," HBR [*Harvard Business Review*] Blog Network (blog), March 8, 2010, accessed July 10, 2011, http://blogs.hbr.org/cs/2010/03/why_leadership_development_in_asia.html.
6. Morten T. Hansen, Herminia Ibarra, and Urs Peyer, "The Best Performing CEOs in the World," *Harvard Business Review*, January–February 2010, accessed October 1, 2011, http://hbr.org/2010/01/the-best-performing-ceos-in-the-world/ar/1.
7. *ASTD State of the Industry Report (SOIR)*, Alexandria, VA: The American Society for Training & Development, 2010.
8. Rebecca Ray, *Employee Engagement in a VUCA World* (research report), New York: The Conference Board, 2011.
9. *Employee Engagement Report 2011: Beyond the Numbers: A Practical Approach for Individuals, Managers and Executives*, Skillman, NJ: BlessingWhite Inc., January 2011.
10. Kim Lamoureaux and Karen O'Leonard, *Leadership Development Factbook 2009: Benchmarks and Analysis of Leadership Development Spending, Staffing and Programs*, Oakland, CA: Bersin & Associates, 2009.
11. Lamoureaux and O'Leonard, *Leadership Development Factbook 2009*.
12. Hay Group, *Report of the 2010 Best Companies for Leadership Study*, accessed July 10, 2011, http://www.haygroup.com/

BestCompaniesForLeadership/downloads/2010_Best_Companies_for_Leadership_Report.pdf.

13. Hay Group, "Sixth Annual Hay Group Study Identifies Best Companies for Leadership" (for 2010), news release, January 25, 2011, accessed July 10, 2011, http://www.haygroup.com/ww/Press/Details.aspx?ID=28838.

14. Marjorie Derven and Kristin Frappolli, "Aligning Leadership Development for General Managers with Global Strategy: The Bristol-Myers Squibb Story," *Industrial and Commercial Training* 43, no. 1 (2011), 4–12.

15. Michael Useem, "Four Lessons in Adaptive Leadership," *Harvard Business Review*, November 2010, accessed August 15, 2011, http://hbr.org/2010/11/four-lessons-in-adaptive-leadership/ar/1.

16. Ronald Heifetz, Alexander Grashow, and Marty Linsky, "Leadership in a (Permanent) Crisis," *Harvard Business Review*, July–August 2009, accessed August 20, 2011, http://hbr.org/2009/07/leadership-in-a-permanent-crisis/ar/1.

17. Linda Hill, "Where Will We Find Tomorrow's Leaders?," *Harvard Business Review*, January 2008, accessed September 1, 2011, http://hbr.org/2008/01/where-will-we-find-tomorrows-leaders/ar/1.

18. Peter Cappelli, Harbir Singh, Jitendra V. Singh, and Michael Useem, "Leadership Lessons from India," *Harvard Business Review*, March 2010, accessed July 15, 2011, http://hbr.org/2010/03/leadership-lessons-from-india/ar/1.

19. Dr. Asmus Komm, John McPherson, Magnus Graf Lambsdorff, Dr. Stephen P. Keiner Jr, and Verena Renze-Westendorf, *Return on Leadership: Competencies That Generate Growth* (research report), Egon Zehnder International and McKinsey & Company, 2011.

20. Gary M. Stern, "Company Training Programs: What Are They Really Worth?," *Fortune*, May 27, 2011, accessed July 10, 2011, http://management.fortune.cnn.com/2011/05/27/company-training-programs-what-are-they-really-worth/.

21. Nora Gardner, Devin McGranahan, and William Wolf, "Question for Your HR Chief: Are We Using Our 'People Data' to Create Value?," *McKinsey Quarterly*, March 2011.

22. Stephen B. Kincaid and Diane Gordick, "The Return on Investment of Leadership Development: Differentiating our Discipline, *Consulting Psychology Journal: Practice and Research* 55, no. 1 (winter 2003): 47–57.

23. Edward E. Lawler III, Alec Levenson, and John Boudreau, *HR Metrics and Analytics: Uses and Impacts*, Los Angeles, CA: Center for Effective Organizations, 2004.

24. Lawrence Schein, *The Business Value of Leadership Development*, New York: The Conference Board, 2005.
25. Dave Ulrich and Norm Smallwood, "HR's New ROI: Return on Intangibles," *Human Resource Management* 44, no. 2 (summer 2005): 137–142.
26. Bruce J. Avolio, James B. Avery, and David Quisenberry, "Estimating Return on Leadership Development Investment," *The Leadership Quarterly* 21 (2010): 633–644.
27. Anne Schwartz, "Leadership Development in a Global Environment: Lessons Learned from One of the World's Largest Employers," *Industrial and Commercial Training* 43, no. 1 (2011): 13–16.
28. Adam Bryant, "Google's Quest to Build a Better Boss," *New York Times*, March 12, 2011, accessed June 17, 2011, http://www.nytimes.com/2011/03/13/business/13hire.html?pagewanted=all.
29. Thomas H. Davenport, Jeanne Harris, and Jeremy Shapiro, "Competing on Talent Analytics," *Harvard Business Review*, October 2010, accessed September 1, 2011, http://hbr.org/2010/10/competing-on-talent-analytics/ar/1.
30. Paul W. Farris, Neil T. Bendle, Phillip E. Pfeifer, and David J. Reibstein, *Marketing Metrics: 50+ Metrics Every Executive Should Master*, Upper Saddle River, NJ: Pearson Prentice Hall, 2006.
31. Nancy S. Ahlrichs, *Competing for Talent: Recruitment and Retention Strategies for Becoming an Employer of Choice*, Boston, MA: Nicholas Brealey, 2000.
32. D. Ulrich, ed., *Delivering Results*, Boston, MA: Harvard Business School Press, 1998.
33. Charles T. Horngren, George Foster, Srikant M. Datar, Howard D. Teall, and Maureen Gowing, *Cost Accounting*, 5th ed., Englewood Cliffs, NJ: Prentice-Hall, 1982.
34. H. Saint-Onge, "Shaping Human Resource Management Within the Knowledge-Driven Enterprise," in Dede Bonner, ed., *In Action: Leading Knowledge Management and Learning*, Alexandria, VA: ASTD [American Society for Training & Development], 2002.

Index

A

ABOUT THE AUTHORS

Jack J. Phillips, Ph.D.

Jack J. Phillips is a world-renowned expert on accountability, measurement, and evaluation. Phillips provides consulting services for Fortune 500 companies and major global organizations. The author or editor of more than 50 books, he conducts workshops and presents at conferences throughout the world.

Phillips has received several awards for his books and work. On two occasions, *Meeting News* named him one of the 25 Most Influential People in the Meetings and Events Industry, based on his work on ROI. The Society for Human Resource Management presented him with an award for one of his books and honored a Phillips ROI study with its highest award for creativity. The American Society for Training and Development gave him its highest award, Distinguished Contribution to Workplace Learning and Development, for his work on ROI. His work has been featured in the *Wall Street Journal*, *BusinessWeek*, and *Fortune* magazine. He has been interviewed on several television programs, including CNN.

His expertise in measurement and evaluation is based on more than 27 years of corporate experience in the aerospace, textile, metals, construction materials, and banking industries. Phillips has served as training and development manager at two Fortune 500 firms, as senior human resource officer at two firms, as president of a regional bank, and as management professor at a major state university.

This background led Phillips to develop the ROI Methodology revolutionary process that provides bottom-line figures and accountability for all types of learning, performance improvement, human resources, technology, and public policy programs. Phillips regularly consults with clients in manufacturing, service, and government organizations in over 50 countries in North and South America, Europe, Africa, Australia, and Asia.

Phillips and his wife, Patti P. Phillips, recently served as authors and series editors for the *Measurement and Evaluation Series* published by Pfeiffer (2008), which includes a six-book series on the ROI Methodology and a companion book of 14 best-practice case studies. Other books recently authored by Phillips include *The Green Scorecard: Measuring the ROI in Sustainability Initiatives* (Nicholas Brealey, 2011); *ROI for Technology Projects: Measuring and Delivering Value* (Butterworth-Heinemann, 2008); *Return on Investment in Meetings and Events: Tools and Techniques to Measure the Success of All Types of Meetings and Events* (Butterworth-Heinemann, 2008); *Show Me the Money: How to Determine ROI in People, Projects, and Programs* (Berrett-Koehler, 2007); *The Value of Learning* (Pfeiffer, 2007); *How to Build a Successful Consulting Practice* (McGraw-Hill, 2006); *Investing in Your Company's Human Capital: Strategies to Avoid Spending Too Much or Too Little* (Amacom, 2005); *Proving the Value of HR: How and Why to Measure ROI* (SHRM, 2005); *The Leadership Scorecard* (Elsevier Butterworth-Heinemann, 2004); *Managing Employee Retention* (Elsevier Butterworth-Heinemann, 2003); *Return on Investment in Training and Performance Improvement Programs*, 2nd ed. (Elsevier Butterworth-Heinemann, 2003); *The Project Management Scorecard* (Elsevier Butterworth-Heinemann, 2002); *How to Measure Training Results* (McGraw-Hill, 2002); *The Human Resources Scorecard: Measuring the Return on Investment* (Elsevier Butterworth-Heinemann, 2001); *The Consultant's Scorecard* (McGraw-Hill, 2000); and *Performance Analysis and Consulting* (ASTD, 2000). Phillips served as series editor for ASTD's In Action casebook series, an ambitious publishing project featuring 30 titles. He currently serves as series editor for Elsevier Butterworth-Heinemann's Improving Human Performance series.

Phillips has undergraduate degrees in electrical engineering, physics, and mathematics; a master's degree in Decision Sciences from Georgia State University; and a Ph.D. in Human Resource Management from the University of Alabama. He has served on the boards of several private businesses—including two NASDAQ companies—and several nonprofits and associations, including the American Society for Training and Development and the National Management Association. He is chairman of the ROI Institute, Inc., and can be reached at (205) 678-8101, or by e-mail at jack@roiinstitute.net.

Patti P. Phillips, Ph.D.

Patti P. Phillips is president and CEO of the ROI Institute, Inc., the leading source of ROI competency building, implementation support, networking, and research. A renowned expert in measurement and evaluation, she helps organizations implement the ROI Methodology in countries around the world.

Since 1997, following a 13-year career in the electric utility industry, Phillips has embraced the ROI Methodology by committing herself to ongoing research and practice. To this end, she has implemented ROI in private sector and public sector organizations. She has conducted ROI impact studies on programs such as leadership development, coaching, sales, new-hire orientation, human performance improvement, meetings and events, K–12 educator development, and educators' National Board Certification mentoring.

Phillips teaches others to implement the ROI Methodology through the ROI certification process, as a facilitator for ASTD's ROI and Measuring and Evaluating Learning Workshops, and as professor of practice in the University of Southern Mississippi's Ph.D. in Human Capital Development Program. She serves on numerous doctoral dissertation committees, assisting students as they develop their own research on measurement, evaluation, and ROI.

Phillips speaks on the topic of ROI and accountability at conferences and symposia in countries around the world. She is often heard over the Internet as she presents the ROI Methodology to a wide variety of audiences via webcasts.

Phillips's academic accomplishments include a Ph.D. in International Development and a master's degree in Public and Private Management. She is certified in ROI evaluation and has been awarded the designations of Certified Professional in Learning and Performance and Certified Performance Technologist. She contributes to a variety of journals and has authored a number of books on the subject of accountability and ROI, including *The Bottomline on ROI*, 2nd edition (HRDQ, 2012); *Measuring ROI in Learning and Development: Case Studies from Global Organizations* (ASTD, 2012); *ASTD Handbook of Measuring and Evaluating Training* (ASTD, 2010); *The Green Scorecard: Measuring the ROI in Sustainability Initiatives* (Nicholas Brealey, 2011); *Return on Investment in Meetings and Events: Tools and Techniques to Measure the Success of All Types of Meetings and Events* (Elsevier, 2008); *Show Me the Money: How to Determine ROI in People, Projects, and Programs* (Berrett-Koehler, 2007); *The Value of Learning* (Pfeiffer, 2007); *Return on Investment Basics* (ASTD, 2005); *Proving the Value of HR: How and Why to Measure ROI* (SHRM, 2005); *Make Training Evaluation Work* (ASTD, 2004); *The Bottom Line on ROI* (Center for Effective Performance, 2002), which won the 2003 ISPI Award of Excellence; *ROI at Work* (ASTD, 2005); the ASTD In Action casebooks *Measuring ROI in the Public Sector* (2002), *Retaining Your Best Employees* (2002), and *Measuring Return on Investment* Vol. III (2001); the

ASTD Infoline series, including *Planning and Using Evaluation Data* (2003), *Managing Evaluation Shortcuts* (2001), and *Mastering ROI* (1998); and *The Human Resources Scorecard: Measuring Return on Investment* (Butterworth-Heinemann, 2001). Patti Phillips can be reached at patti@roiinstitute.net.

Rebecca Ray, Ph.D.

Rebecca Ray is senior vice president, human capital at The Conference Board and the leader of the Human Capital Practice. Human capital research at The Conference Board focuses on human capital analytics, labor markets, workforce readiness, strategic workforce planning, talent management, diversity and inclusion, human resources, and employee engagement. In addition to published research, related products and services at The Conference Board include peer-to-peer learning networks, conferences, webcasts, and experiential and other executive events. Ray is also responsible for the Employee Engagement Survey Services line of business, which enhances the research done in the area of engagement. She hosts the monthly Human Capital Watch webcast, which explores current issues, research, and practitioner successes for the members of The Conference Board.

Ray was previously senior vice president, global talent management and development for MasterCard Worldwide, where she was responsible for organizational learning, training, management and leadership, development, employee engagement, performance management, executive assessment, coaching, organizational development, and succession planning. She also has held executive roles at Comcast Communications, American Skandia, Prudential Securities, and Merrill Lynch. She taught at Oxford and New York Universities and led a consulting practice for many years, offering leadership assessment and development services to Fortune 500 companies and top-tier professional services firms. Ray was named "Chief Learning Officer of the Year" by *Chief Learning Officer* magazine and one of the "Top 100 People in Leadership Development" by Warren Bennis's *Leadership Excellence* magazine. She serves on the advisory boards for New York University's Program in Higher Education/Business Education at The Steinhardt School of Education, and the University of Pennsylvania's Executive Program in Work-Based Learning Leadership. Ray is the author of numerous articles and books, as well as several plays, and she holds a doctorate from New York University.